IMAGES
of America

MIDDLETOWN

THE STEEL CITY

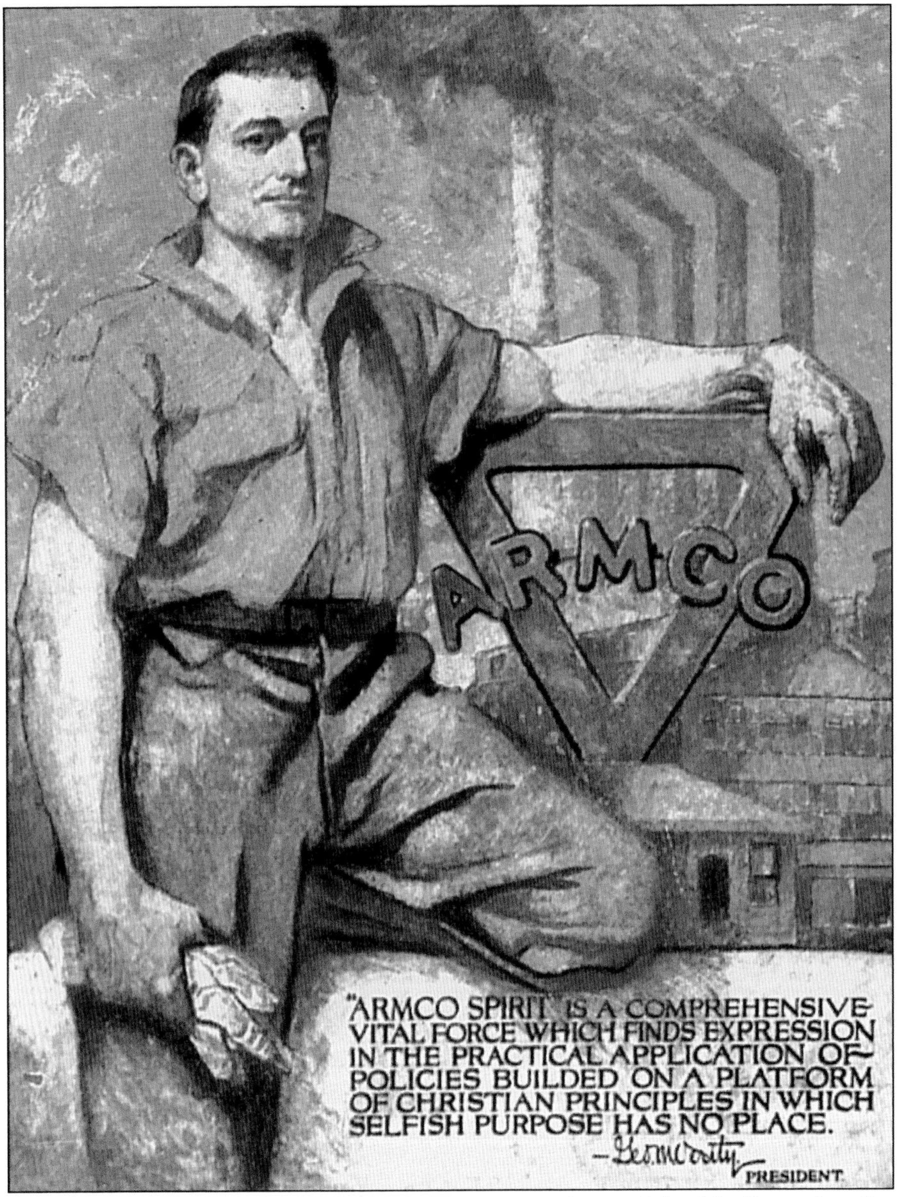

Armco Spirit, a painting by Raymond Perry, expresses that indefinable "something" about old Armco. On a huge canvas, the artist's brush created a strong figure of the quintessential happy, self-reliant steel worker. He was, in reality, a composite of 12 men, each from a different department at Armco, and each caught in a photograph from which Perry took certain features. In the background stands the giant steel mill with smoke rising from its stacks.

Not only was the original canvas displayed at the general offices, but copies appeared on company publications during much of the century as well. Armco President, George M. Verity, commissioned the painting, which was unveiled January 9, 1920.

Even today, after one hundred years, this photo still represents steel making in Middletown. Armco began building its plant in 1900, and on the morning of February 7, 1901, came that first order—"Tap the heat." The steel industry in Middletown was born.

IMAGES
of America

MIDDLETOWN

THE STEEL CITY

Roger L. Miller and George C. Crout

ARCADIA
PUBLISHING

ISBN 978-0-7385-0729-3

Published by Arcadia Publishing
Charleston, South Carolina

Printed in the United States of America

Library of Congress Catalog Card Number: 00-104291

For all general information contact Arcadia Publishing at:
Telephone 773-549-7002
Fax 773-549-7190
E-Mail sales@arcadiapublishing.com
For customer service and orders:
Toll-Free 1-888-313-2665

Visit us on the Internet at www.arcadiapublishing.com

Contents

ACKNOWLEDGMENTS

No one could ever list all the people whose photographs found their way into this book. Since many never labeled their work with a name or studio, they will forever remain unknown. From over one thousand pictures the authors have selected those that best tell the story of Middletown's industrial growth during the twentieth century, especially that of the local steel industry. To Thomas C. Portsmouth, Armco's long-time professional photographer (1914–1950), and his assistant, Bob Stark, goes the credit for many fine shots of the steel company's progress. Other industrial photos have come from the professional studios of Tobias, Reeder, Kramer, Murray, and Watson. The work of restoring old pictures and preparing them for publication was that of Scott Tobias of Middletown's oldest studio, founded by his great-grandfather over one hundred years ago.

Of special interest are the aerial photos included here, for they are from the files of William P. Mayfield, the nation's pioneer aerial photographer. As he hailed from Dayton, just north of Middletown, local industries, including Armco, used the services of his studio for much of their work. Today, such pictures are considered art masterpieces.

Much of the material copied by the camera came from photographs and books collected by long-time local historian Wilfred D. Vorhis, an Armco official employed from 1911 to 1954. Retiree Vorhis, as well as many other Armco/AK Steel retirees, have supplied many treasured photographs that have made this book possible. This material will be placed in the custody of the local library. The organizations who have cooperated in the compilation of this book include the Middletown Public Library, the *Middletown Journal*, Middletown Historical Society, Middletown News-Agency, Armco Steel Corporation, and AK Steel Corporation, as well as other industries in the city.

The following Middletonians, both of the past and the present, have graciously permitted the use of their photographs: Jack Mokry, Howard Borneman, Cliff W. Van Gilder, Luther Pratt, Bert Ruoff, Steve Countryman, J.L. Glass, Bernard and Gloria Annenberg, William Alford, Ben McIntire, Lynn Reese, Herbert Fall, Merle Rhodes, Marilyn Moran, Dick Miller, Brenda and Carl Lakes, and Robin Richardson.

A very special note of appreciation is due Mrs. Roger "Penny" Miller for her help, assistance, and support in preparing this manuscript for publication.

(Note: More information about Middletown local history, Armco, and AK Steel can be accessed on the Internet at www.middletown.com or www.middle-america.org.)

Introduction

Middletown, the Steel City, located in the Mid-Miami River valley of southwestern Ohio, is within six hundred miles of two-thirds of the United States population. Interstate 75 runs through its eastern section, while State Routes 4, 73, and 122 wind their way through the town. Middletown's location in the midst of these resources created a natural market for steel, especially in a region that was to become known for automobile and appliance manufacturing.

In 1900, George M. Verity, founder of the American Rolling Mill Company (soon known as Armco), started looking for a site for a new, integrated steel plant. He noted the city's excellent location, and observed that it was served by five major rail lines and a canal. With this transportation readily available, he could move the raw materials to his plant as well as ship out finished products.

Verity's steel company grew into the largest employer in Middletown and Butler County. Success came from its specialization in filling orders that other companies wouldn't accept. This led, in 1910, to the development by Armco of the first separate research department in the industry. Research resulted in many improvements in electrical steel, ingot iron, and rust-resisting coatings. It also resulted in the development of the first continuous rolling mill in 1924, engineered by John B. Tytus Jr., and considered to be one of the ten greatest industrial inventions of the twentieth century.

When the trade publication *New Steel* listed the eleven leading steel executives of the century, Armco and AK Steel had two of them—George M. Verity, the founder, and Thomas Graham, who streamlined the plant by improving its productivity and enabling the company to survive in the new era of world trade.

This book recounts one hundred years of steel making in Middletown, and the cooperative relationship between the city and the company. While at its peak, Armco employed about half of the workers in the city. Other industries also played an important role, and all enjoyed a cooperative relationship within the Industrial Council formed by local industries. With Armco's leadership, Middletown earned the sobriquets "City With a Soul," and "Peaceful Valley." Accordingly, Armco will share the pages of this book with the other industries that made Middletown such an outstanding community. As proof, in 1958 it received the national award of an "All-America City."

This book is a tribute to an industrialist who was interested in more than making steel. He improved working conditions for the steel worker through reforms of medical benefits, housing, education, and recreation. His revolutionary ideas regarding a better workplace helped to create the National Safety Council, the eight-hour day, and equal pay for equal work. These policies spread not only throughout the steel industry, but to other, unrelated sectors of commerce as well.

INTO A NEW MILLENNIUM

George M. Verity incorporated his small company on December 27, 1899, entering into an agreement with the Industrial Commission of Middletown to locate his plant in that city along the Miami Erie Canal. He envisioned taking iron, coke, and limestone to make basic steel, which he would then turn into a finished product. Prior to that, many small mills attended to only part of the process. One mill would melt the iron, for example, while another would roll steel into sheets, galvanize the sheets, or make the finished product (such as steel roofing). Verity wanted to put all operations together in one plant. The first heat was tapped from the open hearth furnace on February 7, 1901.

Middletown was economically dominated by Armco for most of the twentieth century. But in the 1980s, the steel industry began to falter both locally and nationally due to subsidized foreign imports. Armco's attempt at diversification, to compensate for the ever-fluctuating steel market, led to an expansion into unfamiliar fields that was not overwhelmingly successful. This, in turn, led to corporate restructuring, downsizing, and eventually to a new company that was formed from Armco's Eastern Steel Division. Basic steel plants were located in Middletown, Ohio, and Ashland, Kentucky. The new company became known officially as the AK Steel Corporation, and on September 29, 1999, it purchased what remained of the original Armco, resulting in a merger.

During the past century, great technological changes and advances took place in the steel industry. These changes enabled far fewer employees to produce more steel, which resulted in a loss of jobs throughout the industry. The steel industry and other related fields, which at mid-century had produced 50 percent of local jobs, provided employment to less than 30 percent of the working population by the year 2000. Manufacturing dropped to second place, and the service sector became the town's major employer. However, as the millennium began, steel was still the biggest single employer in Middletown and in the county.

Yet the nature of local industry had changed, as once home-owned companies were purchased and merged into large national and international conglomerates. Local control was lost, in addition to many who were once a part of the old management group. While confident optimism had greeted the arrival of the twentieth century, skepticism and anxiety were expressed as the latest millennium was celebrated. Yet all know that Middletown will survive and prosper far into the future.

One

Middletown and Armco

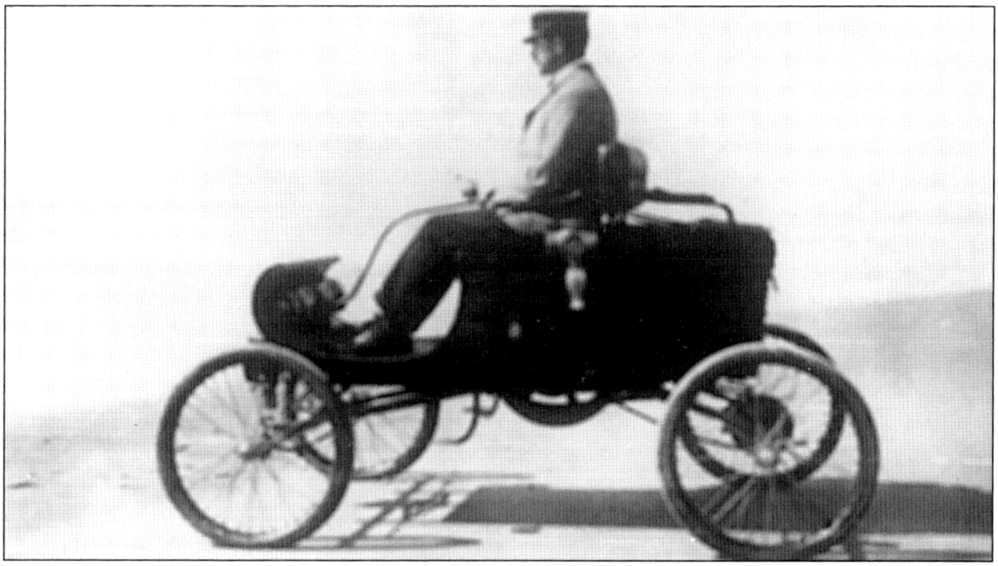

By 1902, George M. Verity had worked so hard to set up his new mill and move into a new home that he was near nervous exhaustion. His doctor advised him to seek more recreation, so he decided to take up what was considered a new sport—"automobiling." He purchased a one-cylinder, curved-dash Oldsmobile, and surprised the town by driving it down fashionable South Main Street by himself. The only other car in town, purchased a few months earlier by tobacco tycoon, Paul J. Sorg, was driven by a chauffeur.

The 37-year-old president of the new American Rolling Mill Company was now a citizen of a new town, head of a new industry, and driving a new automobile. Somehow, with the new century ahead it all seemed symbolic. Mr. Verity, as everyone called him, often offered a ride to pedestrians along the street as a way of getting acquainted with neighbors. But this remarkable man would take Middletown on the ride of its life, and his mill and his ideas would transform an old river and canal town into a modern city. During the coming century, the population would skyrocket from a mere 9,215 to well over 50,000 people, due in a large part to Verity's steel mill—Armco.

By the end of the century, when the industry's trade publication, *New Steel*, picked its outstanding executives of the past one hundred years, George Matthew Verity was high on the list. The above picture was taken from the original in Verity's personal scrapbook.

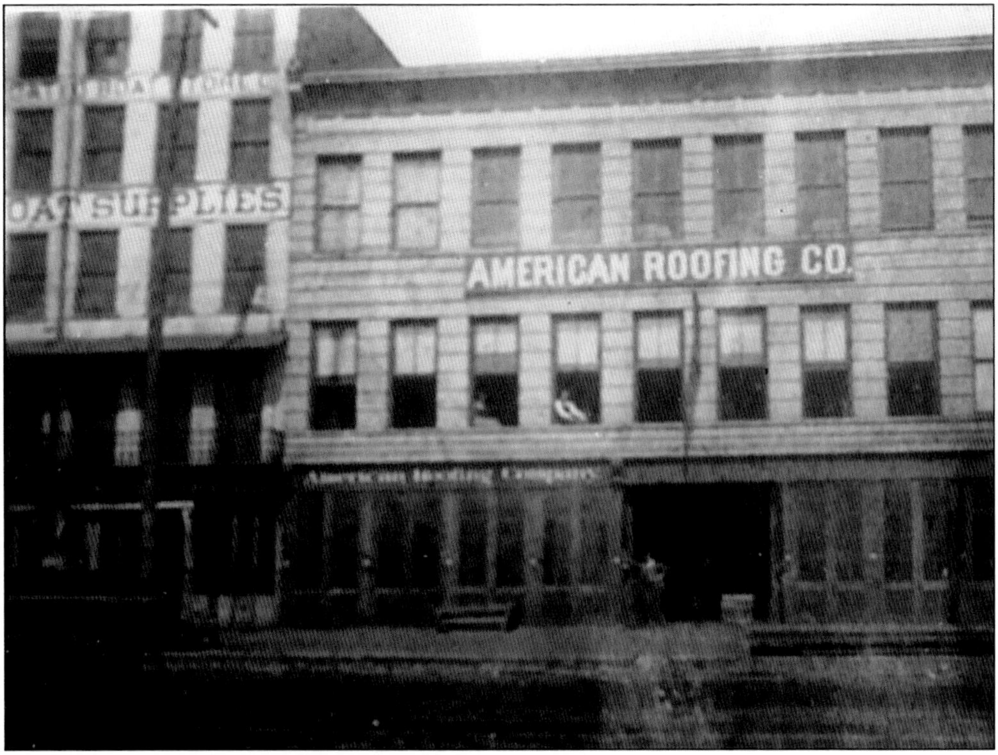

The coming of Armco to Middletown wasn't just random chance. In 1899, while looking ahead to the next century, local business leaders such as E.H. McKnight saw the need for new industry. They had heard that a Cincinnati manufacturer, The American Steel Roofing Company, was looking for a site on which to erect an integrated steel mill.

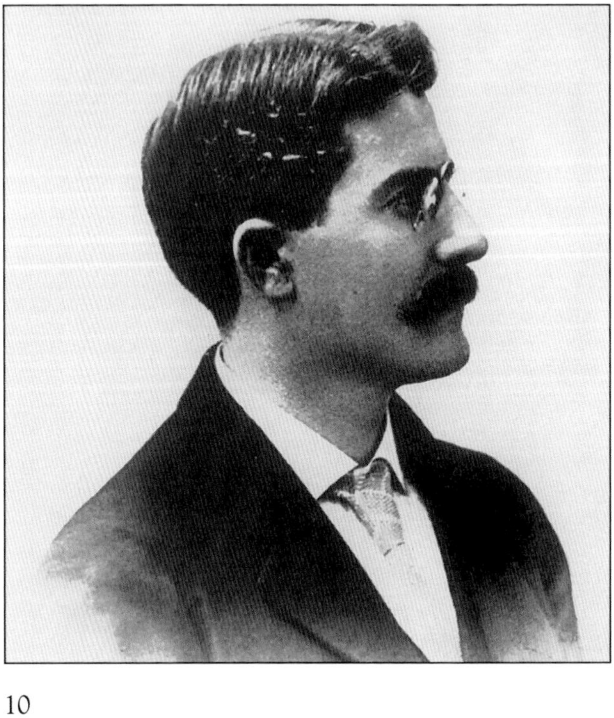

Verity became manager, and then partner in the American Steel Roofing Company along Cincinnati's public landing. He realized that in order to make money in such a business the company would have to roll its own sheets, which he planned to do. During their first meeting, the Middletown representatives learned that Verity had almost decided to locate his company in Zanesville, Ohio, which had made him an attractive offer.

When Verity promised to consider Middletown, the local Industrial Commission set a date for him to visit the city. They met for lunch at the U.S. Hotel, and Verity was introduced to the local bankers, who were greatly impressed by him.

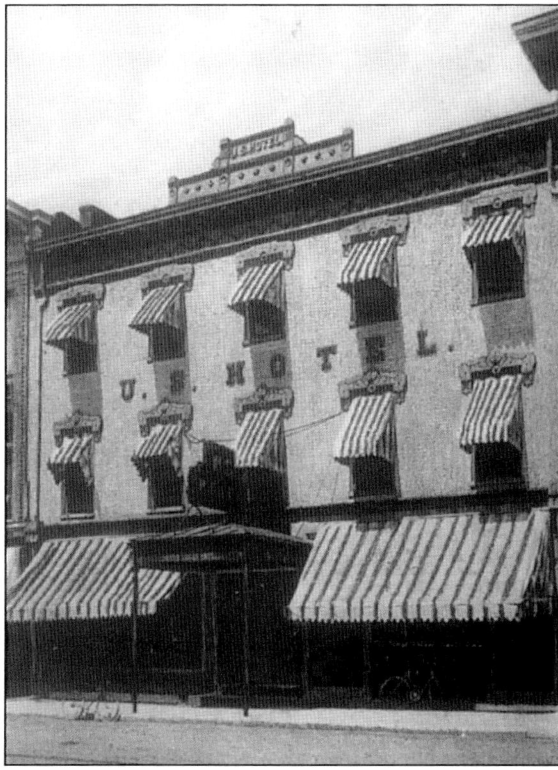

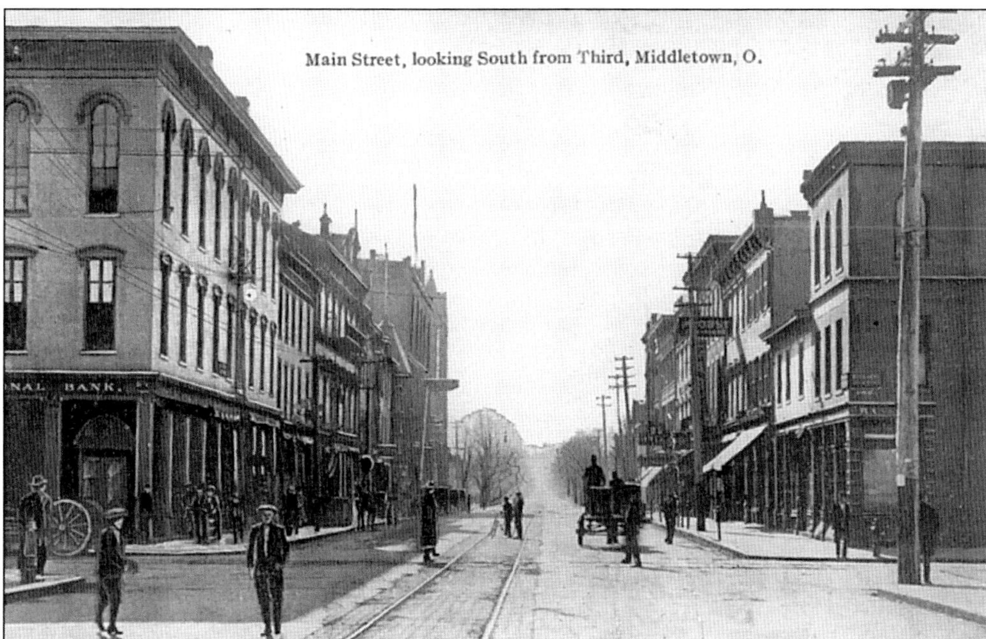

After a good meal, E.H. McKnight and the two other Commission members climbed into a waiting carriage, to visit the site being offered to Verity for his steel mill. They headed north on Main Street, which had just been paved with sheet asphalt (very impressive for a small town), to Third Street (Central Avenue) and the business center.

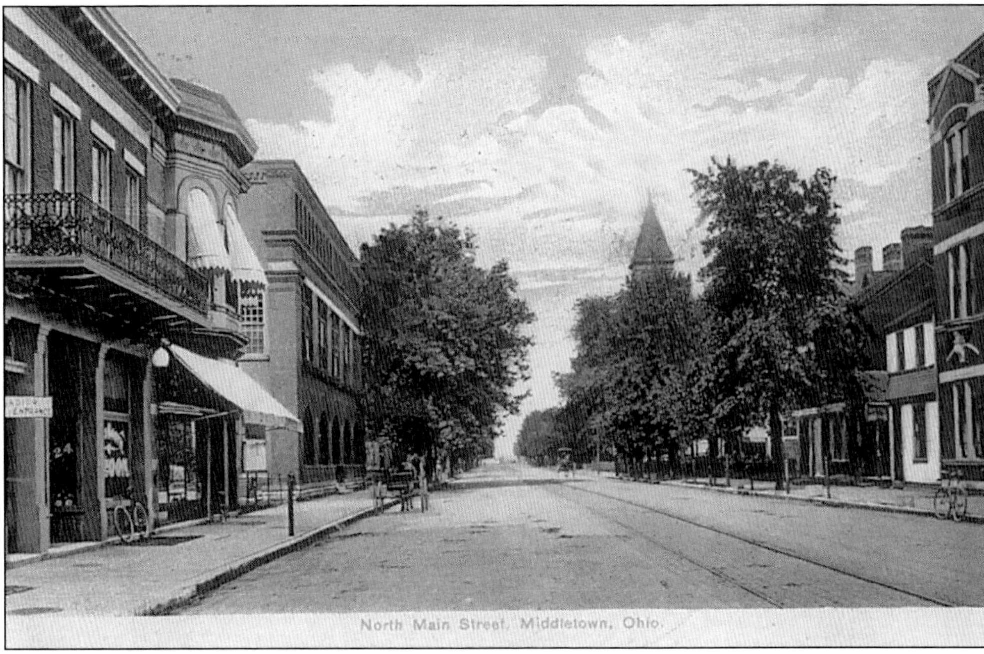

As the horses stopped at the intersection, Verity took a quick look up North Main Street and observed the well-kept stores, the Tytus Paper plant at the end of the block, and the attractive, new North School across the street.

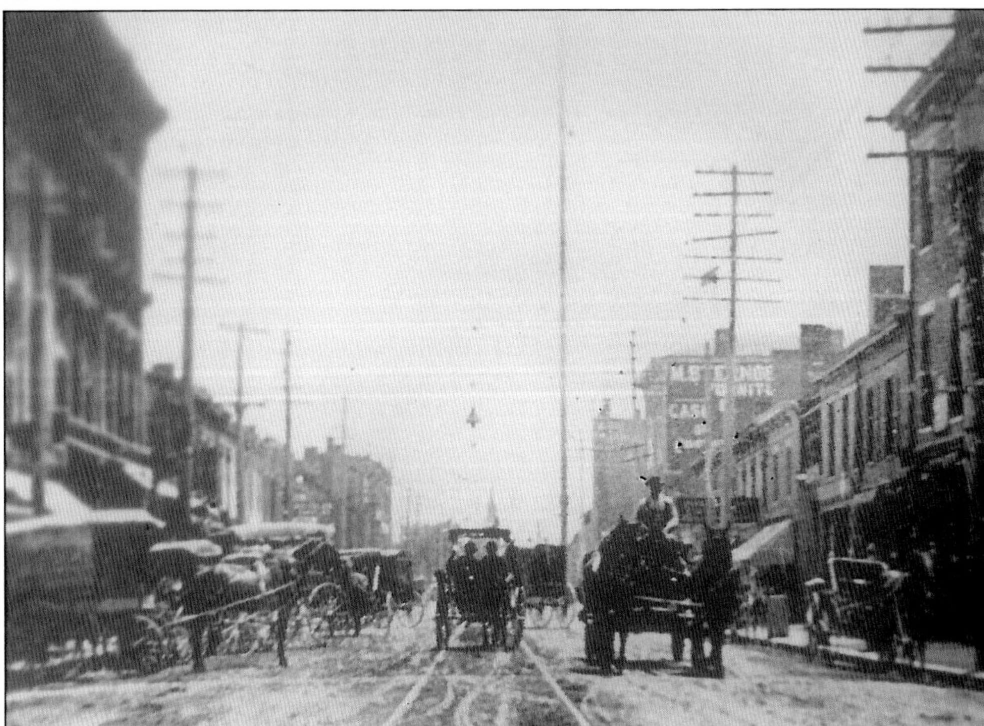

At Third Street the carriage turned the corner, and the horses clattered along the new brick pavement. Verity noted this sign of progress along with the new businesses along the street.

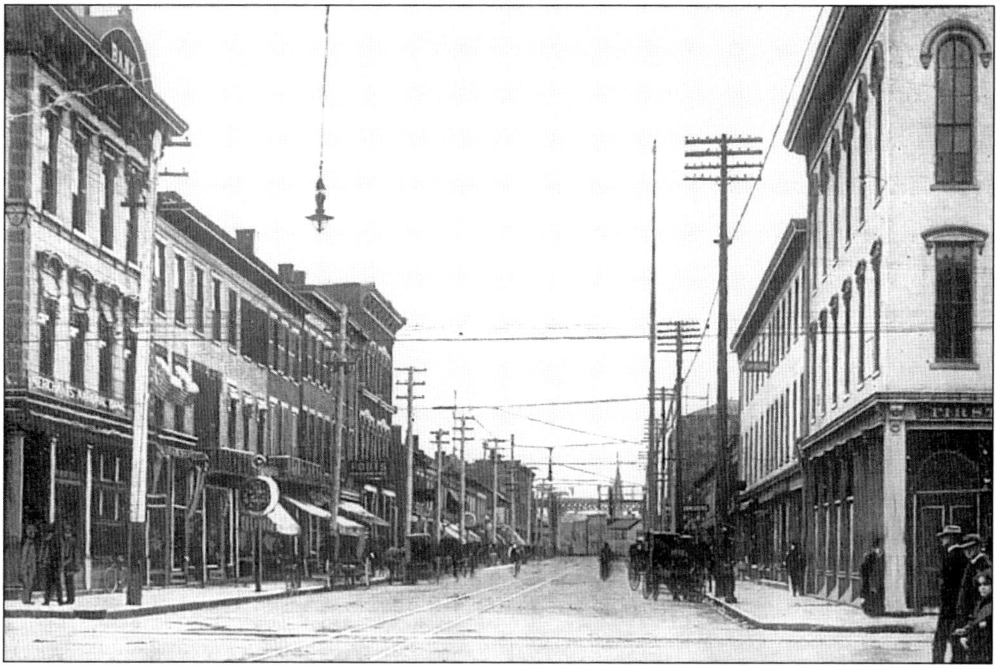

On Third Street, past Broad Street, was the lift bridge over the canal. Verity noticed that the town was growing east at a fast pace, and that new business buildings were under construction.

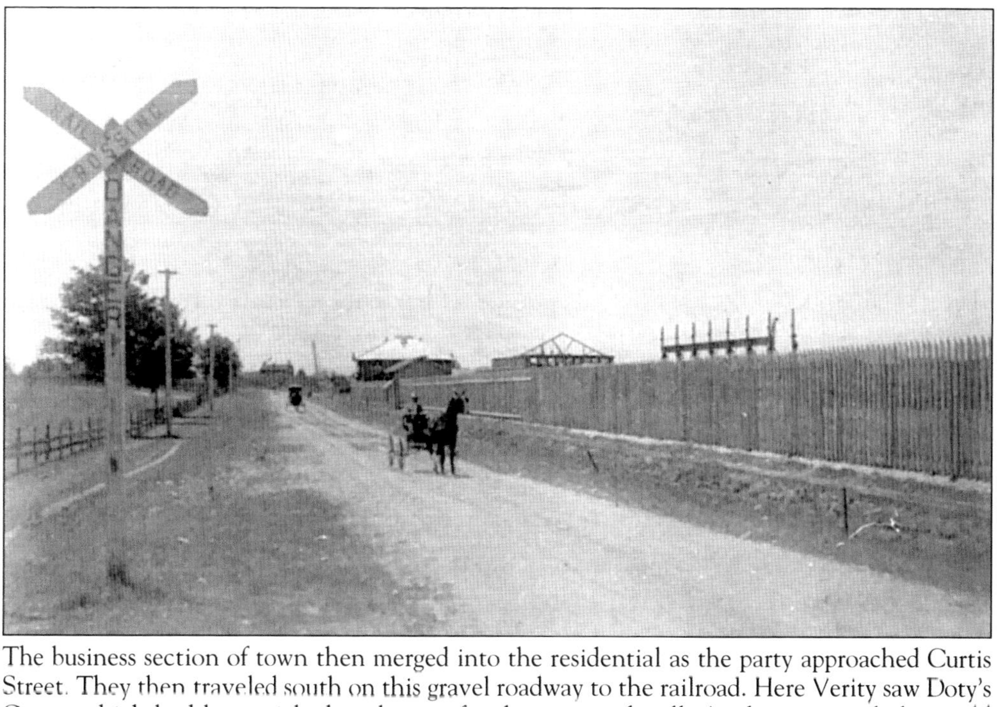

The business section of town then merged into the residential as the party approached Curtis Street. They then traveled south on this gravel roadway to the railroad. Here Verity saw Doty's Grove, which had been picked as the site for the proposed mill. At that time only he could envision a steel mill rising there.

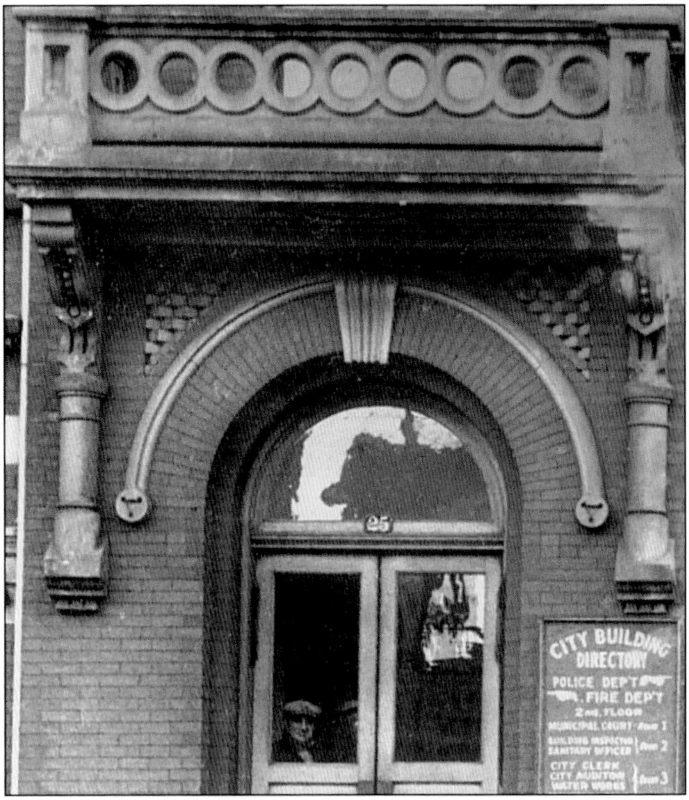

On a separate trip to the city, Verity visited the City Building to meet with local leaders. It was an ornate structure erected in 1880. One side was reserved for the police department and jail. On the second floor were city offices and the Mayor's Courtroom.

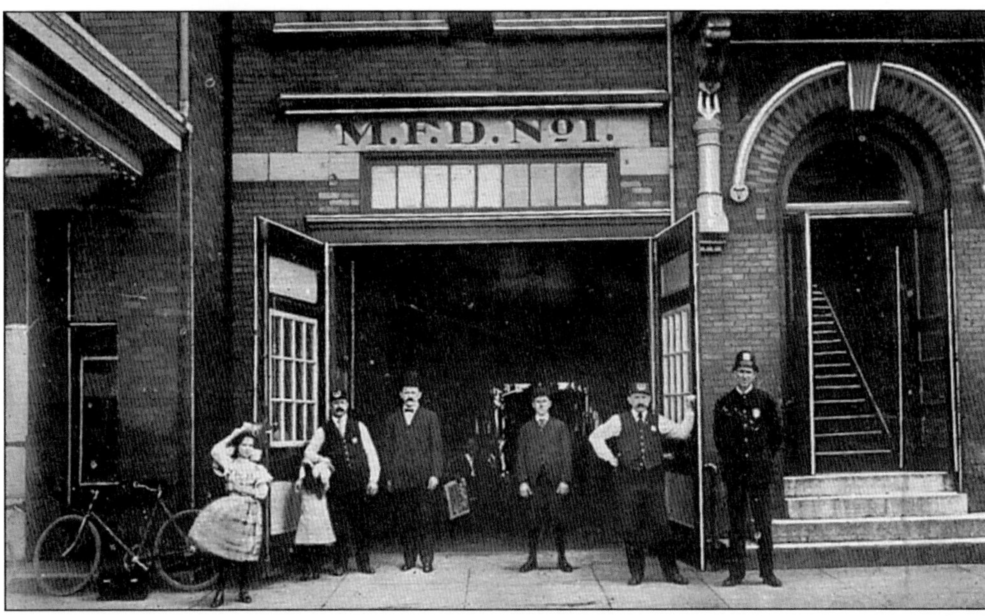

The north half of the building was reserved for the fire department and its equipment, which was of great interest to Verity, for he realized that running a steel mill might require its services from time to time. He found the equipment adequate, the horses well-kept, and reasoned that the station wasn't too far from the mill site.

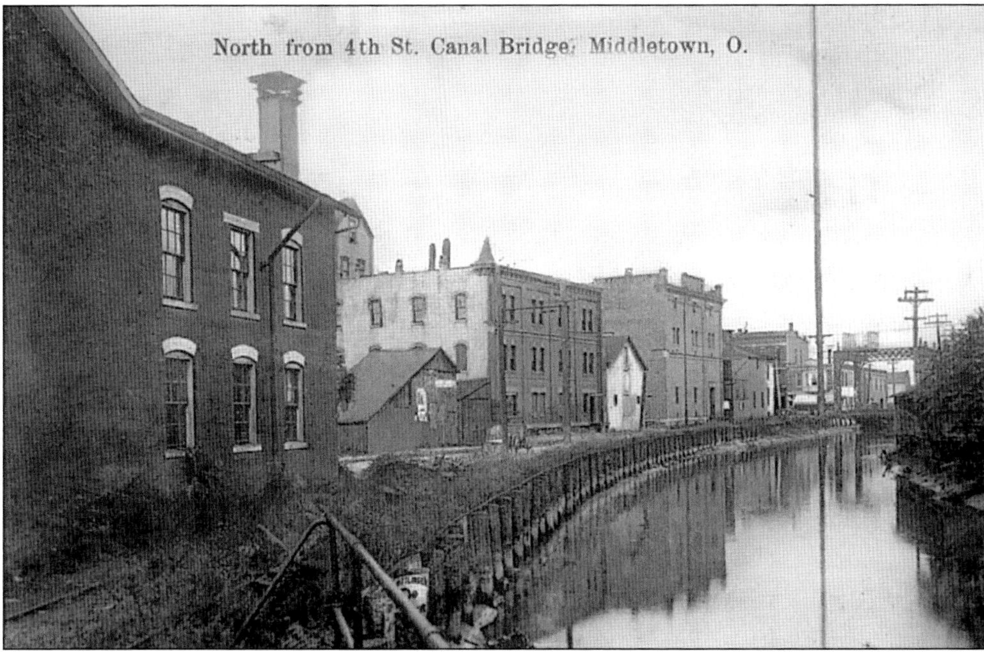

The steel executive asked the city fathers the most questions about the Miami-Erie canal. They assured him that they had the word of the governor of Ohio that it would become a barge canal, like the Erie Canal in New York State. (Looking north from the Fourth Street bridge, note the Sebald Brewery.)

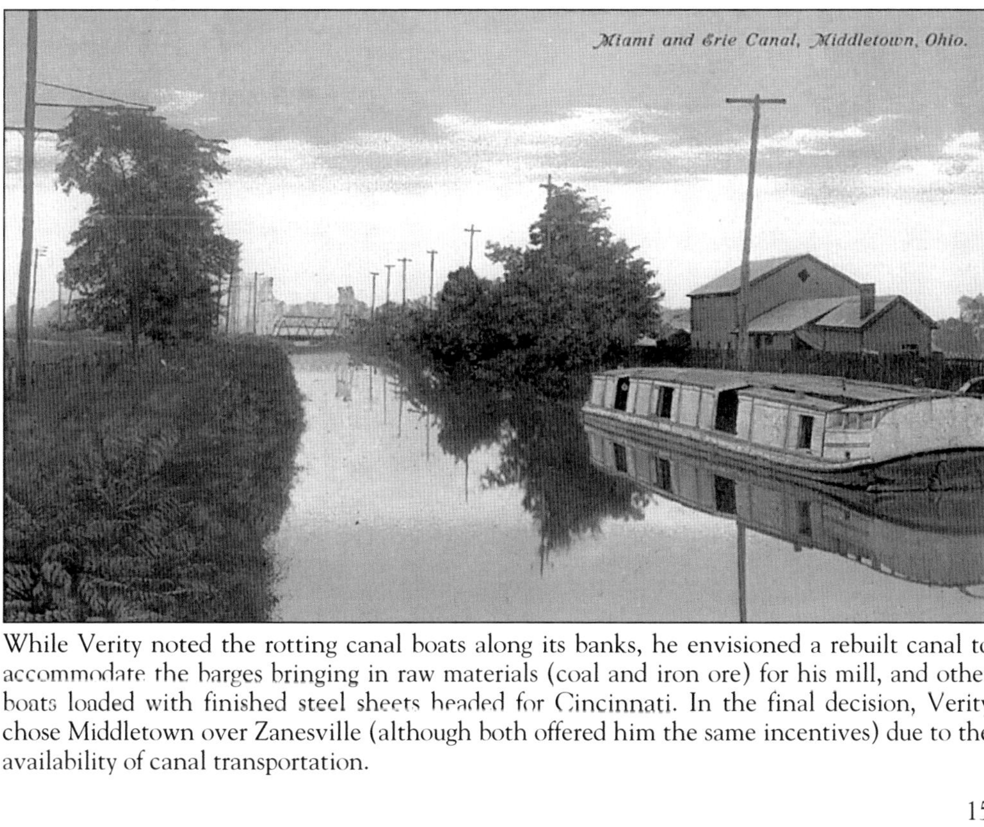

While Verity noted the rotting canal boats along its banks, he envisioned a rebuilt canal to accommodate the barges bringing in raw materials (coal and iron ore) for his mill, and other boats loaded with finished steel sheets headed for Cincinnati. In the final decision, Verity chose Middletown over Zanesville (although both offered him the same incentives) due to the availability of canal transportation.

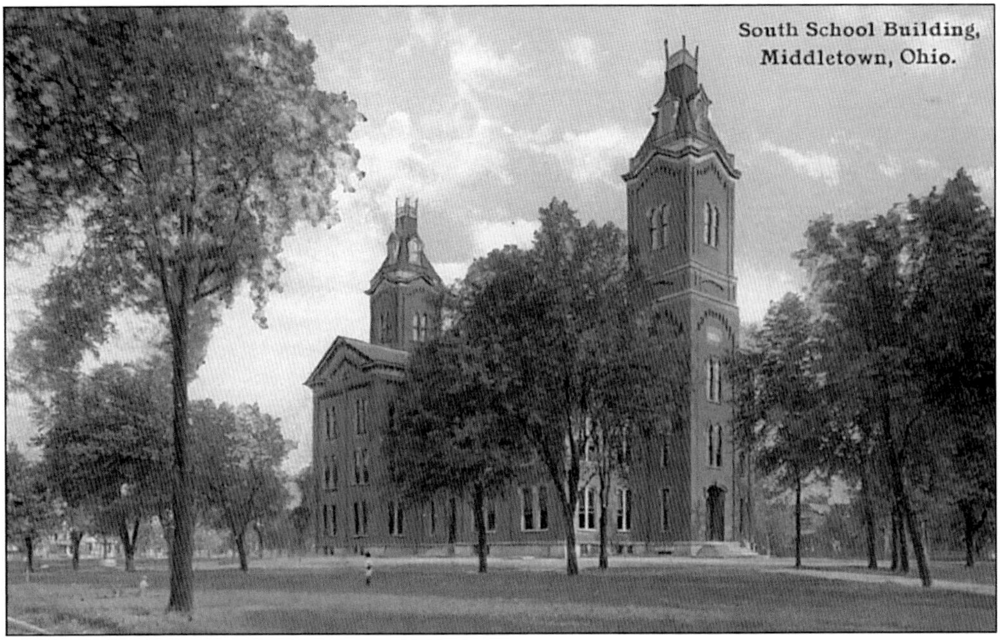

Verity also visited the South School building on South Main Street. He had a personal reason for visiting the building as he had three children—Calvin, Leah, and Sara—who would be enrolled there. He was not impressed by the large classes and the meagerly-equipped building. As a result, Verity was a member of the school board by 1905.

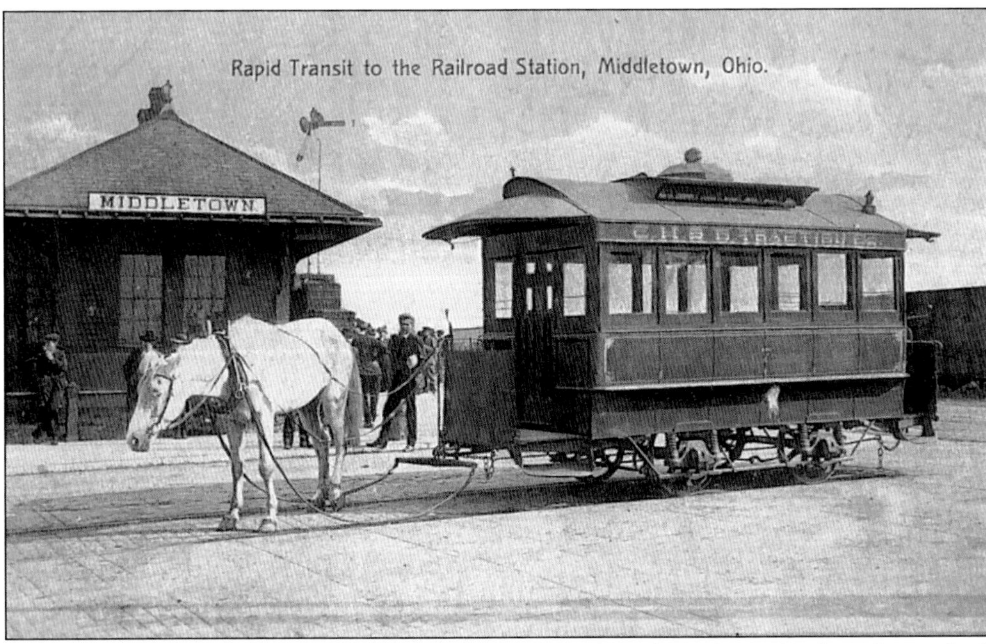

Verity was also unimpressed by the old Middletown and Madison Street Railway line, which began in 1879 and was now much outdated. Often pulled by a mule or two, depending on the load, it was always late. However, the new electric traction line, which started operating on South Main Street in 1897, could bring buyers who had business at the mill to the city.

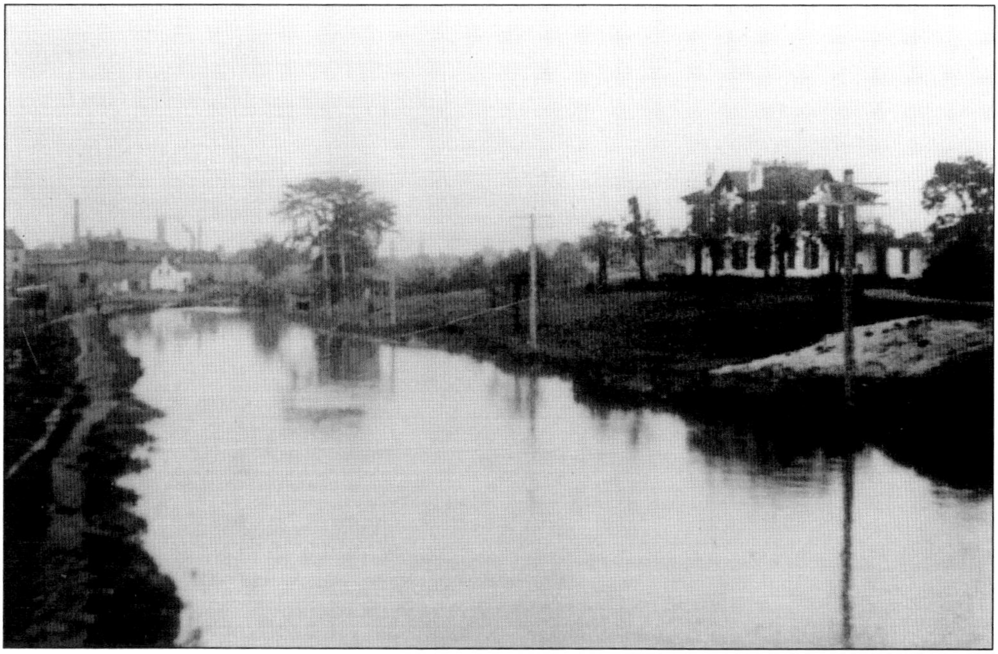

On December 29, 1899, Verity and his attorney met with city officials, including city solicitor Benjamin F. Harwitz. At 2:00 a.m. on December 30, 1899, a contract was signed to bring Verity and his steel plant to Middletown. On January 8, 1900, the city council passed an ordinance issuing bonds to buy Doty's Grove, with the stipulation that the aged Doty descendant in residence be permitted occupancy until death.

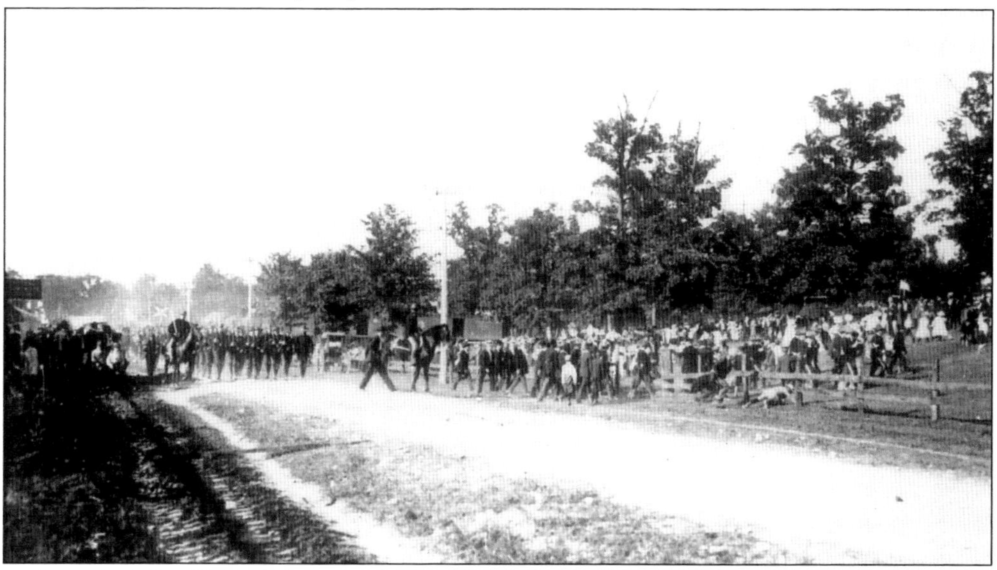

On July 12, 1900, Wilfred D. Vorhis, then a high school student, wrote the following in his diary: "This afternoon a bunch of us, all high school boys and girls, and probably half of Middletown marched down Curtis Avenue behind the band and the local unit of the National Guard, to witness the laying of the cornerstone for the new steel plant of the American Rolling Mill Company." Vorhis later graduated, attended business college, and spent 39 years as an Armco official. He also became a town historian.

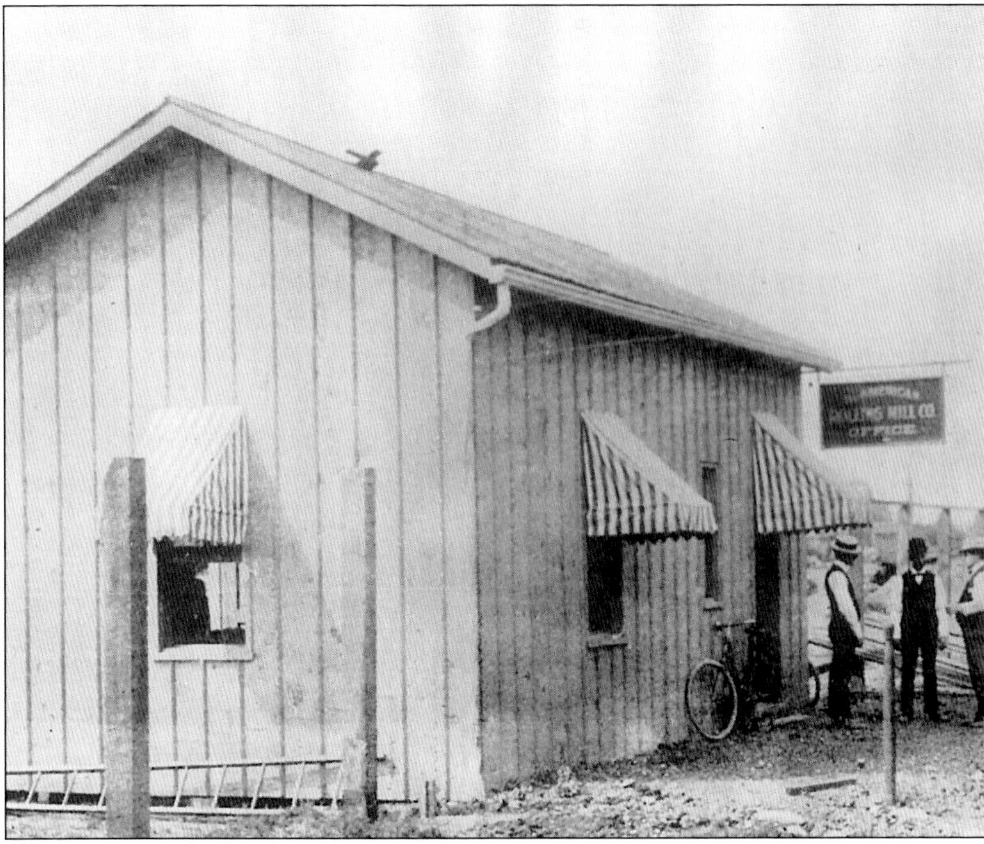

During the construction of the plant, Verity supervised the work from this temporary office building on Curtis Avenue, using a bicycle to make inspections.

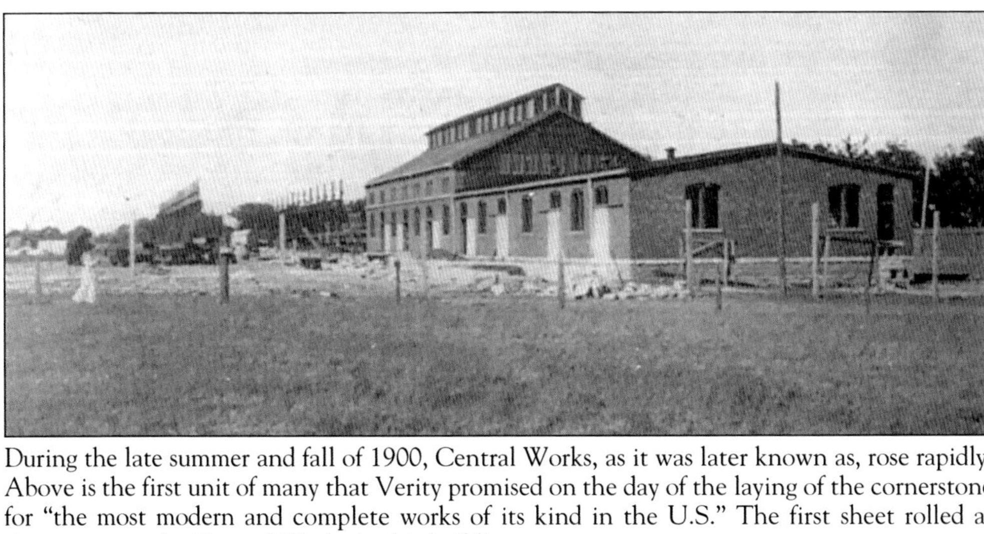

During the late summer and fall of 1900, Central Works, as it was later known as, rose rapidly. Above is the first unit of many that Verity promised on the day of the laying of the cornerstone for "the most modern and complete works of its kind in the U.S." The first sheet rolled at Armco was at the Central Works in this building.

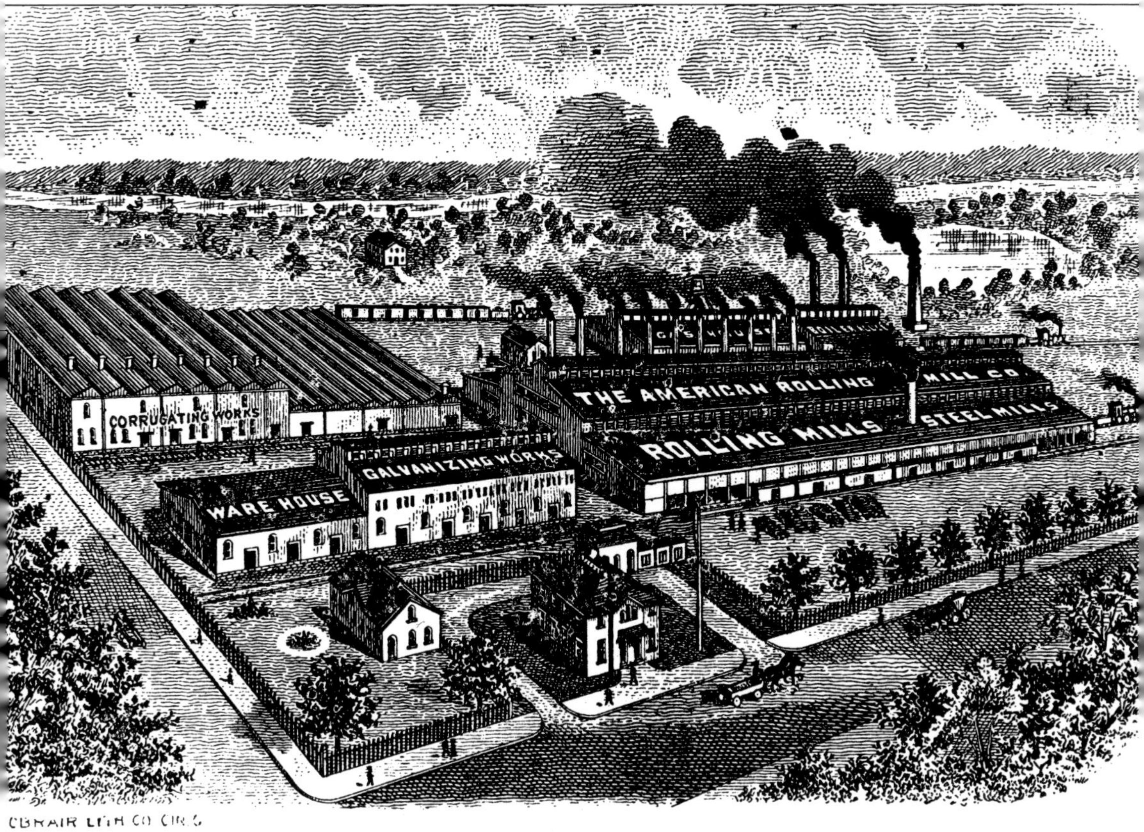

MAIN OFFICE, MILLS & FACTORY, MIDDLETOWN, O.
BRANCH OFFICE & WARE HOUSE, CINCINNATI, O.

On January 1, 1901, Editor John Q. Baker of the *Daily Signal* reported that "within a short time [the wheels would] begin to turn" at the big, new plant of the American Rolling Mill Company, with five hundred men on the job. On that date he noted that the buildings "were all completed and the machinery was being put in place." He ran the above lithographic print of the architect's original sketches. (Note in the background the Miami-Erie Canal, and the old Doty homestead.)

The plant was, in fact, unique. It was the first in the world where pig iron and scrap were converted at one site into a finished product for consumer use. One of these products was corrugated steel roofing, ready for application. An open hearth furnace, a bar mill, and sheet mills with their heating furnaces, as well as galvanizing and factory departments would eventually be seen on the site.

The first five years were difficult due to the problems inherent in setting up such an innovative plant, and finding a niche in the market amid the established steel giants. But by the end of those years, Armco employed seven hundred men and had generated sales of over $1 million a year.

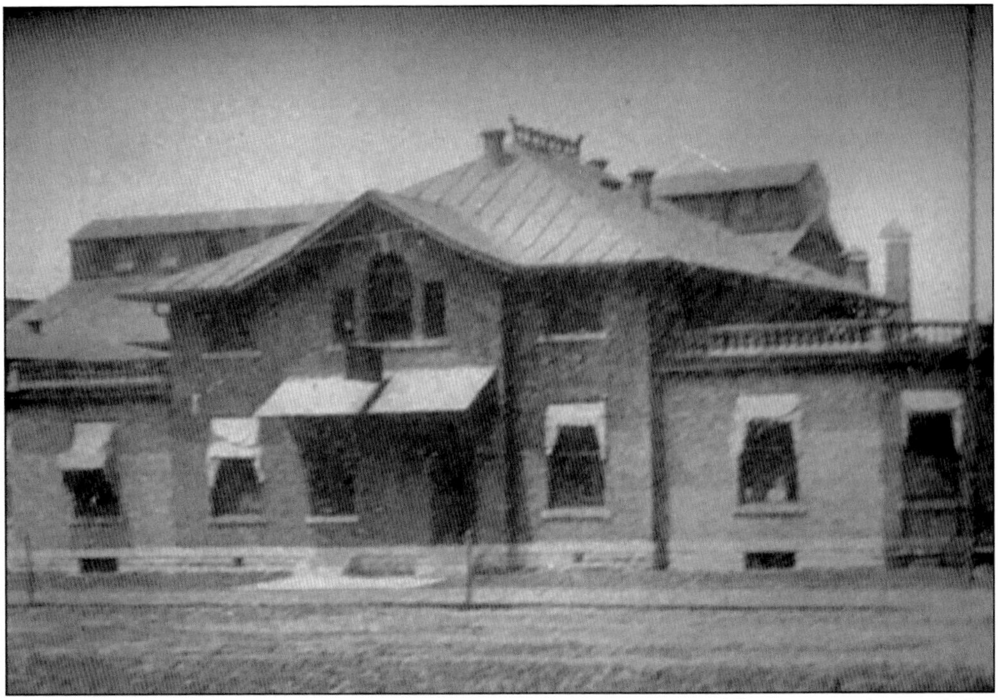

Here is the first general office building. On January 4, 1901, the *Middletown Signal* carried this notice: "The American Rolling Mill Company moved its office force here from Cincinnati yesterday. The mill will start up during the present month."

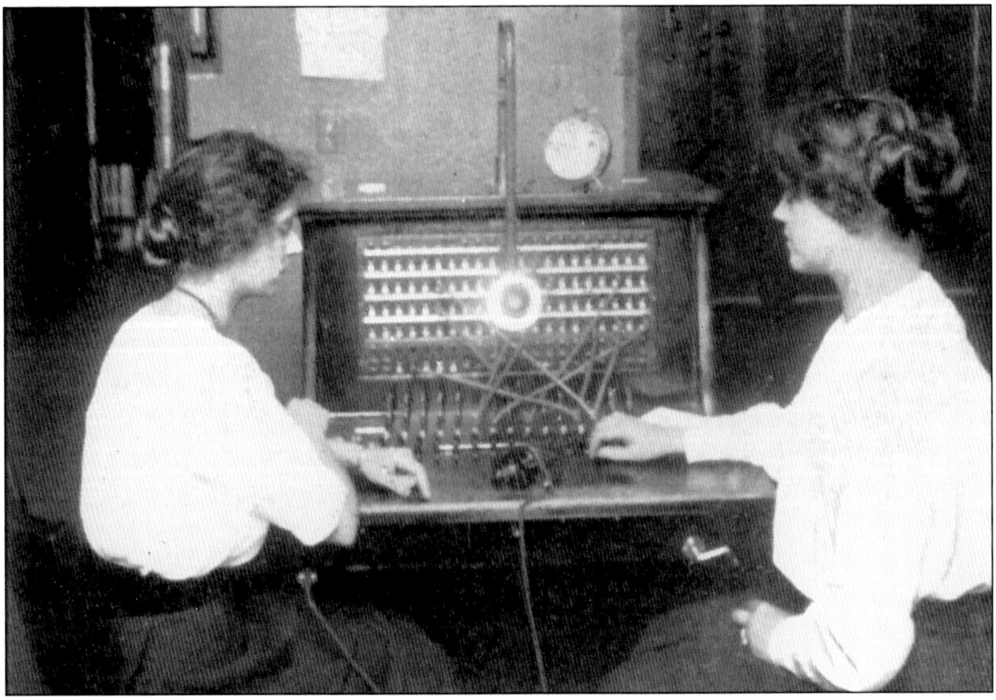

A look inside the office would show this switchboard where Misses Florence Boxwell and Blanche Gilmore made the connections cheerfully and efficiently.

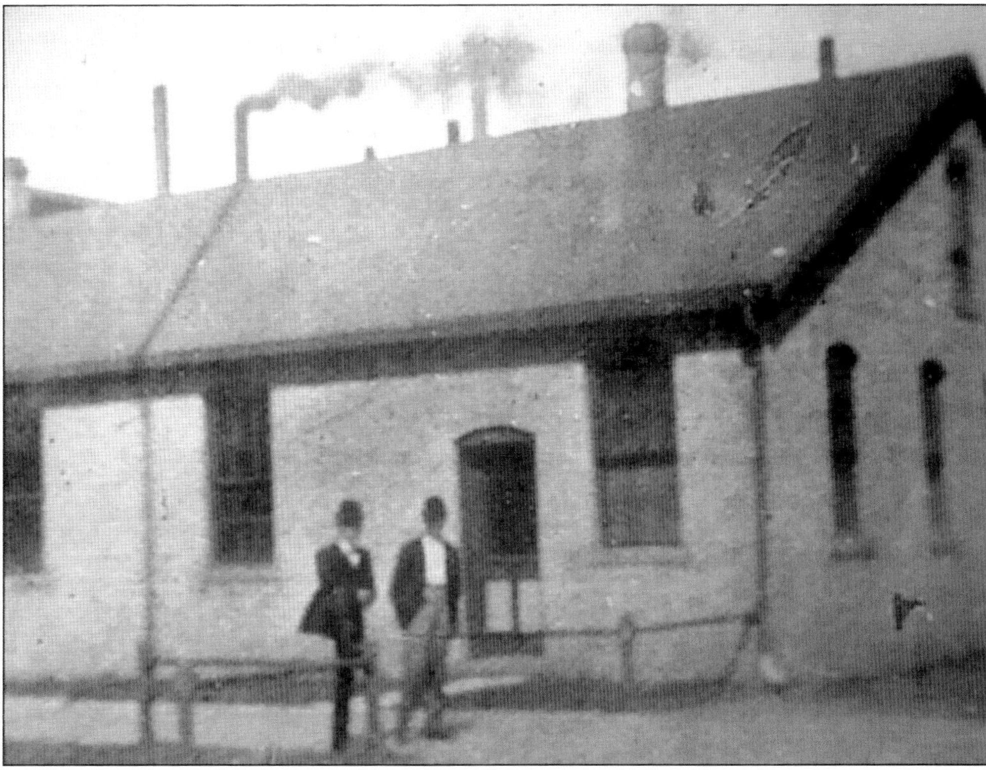

From the very beginning (1901), Armco has been dedicated to research. The small building already pictured, which served as an office during construction, was remodeled and equipped for a chemical laboratory. As research expanded in 1904, the above structure, 40 by 60 feet, was erected for that purpose.

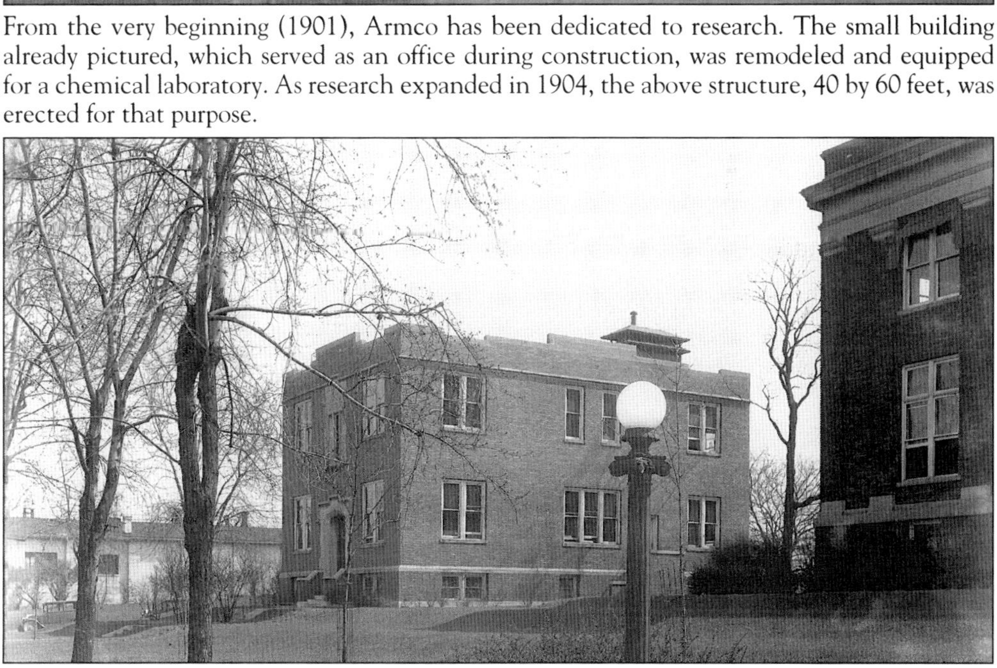

In 1909 this three-story, fireproof, brick building was erected across the street from the company's office. This became the first such structure devoted entirely to research in the steel industry. It was destroyed by a gas explosion in 1935 (fortunately, no one was injured), leading to the erection of the present research center dedicated on November 5, 1937.

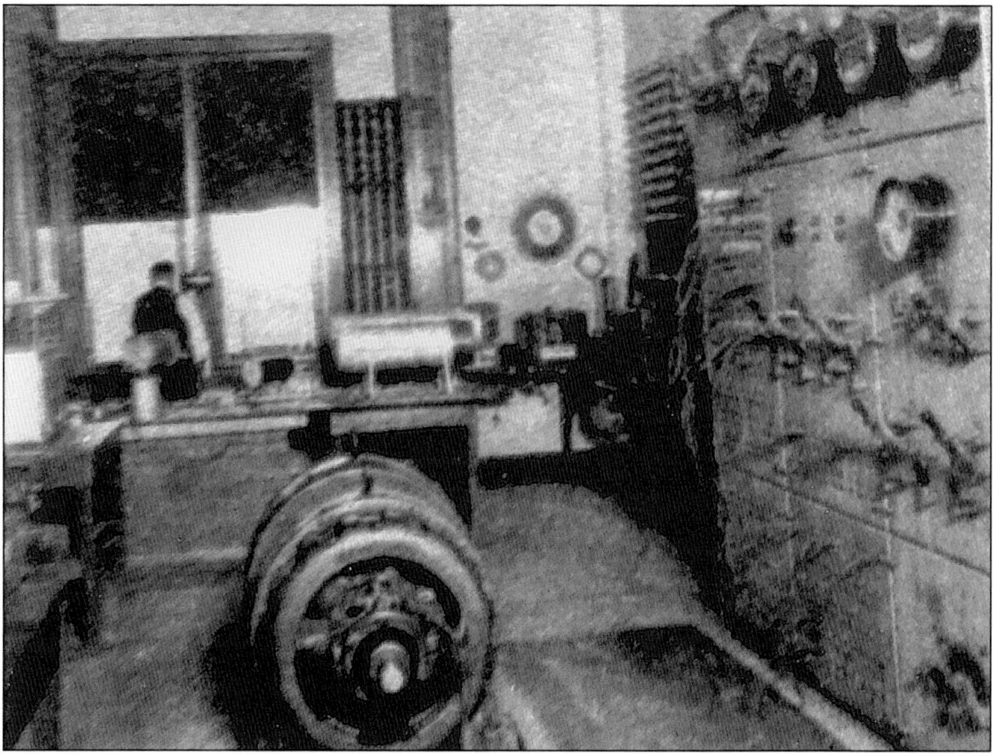

This photo was taken inside the research building shown above. It is the electrical laboratory in 1920. Research was responsible for Armco quality control, as well as experimenting with techniques for improving the manufacturing process.

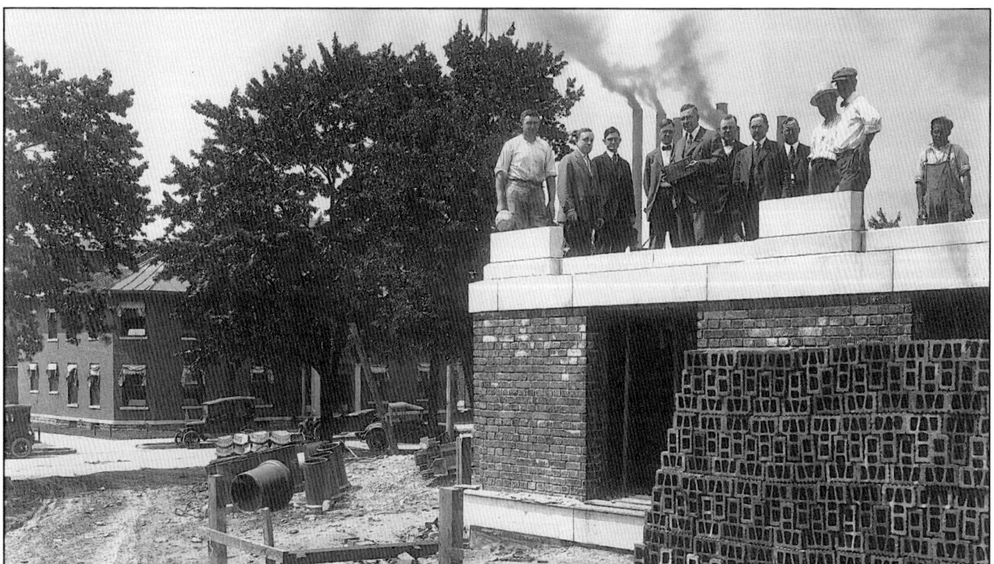

This photograph is of the laying of the cornerstone of the new general office building on July 11, 1916. The men pictured include representative workers, as well as Armco officials W.J. Beck, Charles R. Hook, W.D. Vorhis, N.W. Collard, S.R. Rectanus, R.B. Carnahan, and C.W. Davis.

Two

ONE HUNDRED YEARS OF STEEL MAKING

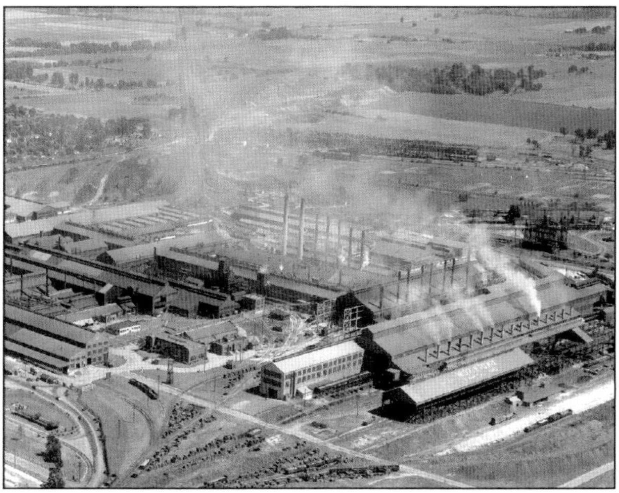

On February 7, 1901, the first heat of steel was tapped at Open Hearth Furnace Number One at the new plant of the American Rolling Mill Company on Curtis Street. From Mr. Verity's leather-bound personal diary came this entry under that date: "Run first heat in open hearth furnace at 2:04 a.m. Made about 60 percent perfect ingots..." While many technological changes would take place in various places throughout the century, Middletown remained the Steel City. Included in this chapter are some of the highlights of steel making at Armco, along with the dedicated workers who made it the nation's premier steel plant during the past century.

At first, Middletown seemed a poor location for the steel industry. The basic raw materials—iron ore, coal, and limestone—were far removed. Although George M. Verity had initially planned to use canal transportation, this did not happen, and the area was served by an excellent railroad net, which was able to bring raw materials in and ship the finished steel sheets out. The city's central location in regard to markets for steel was a great asset, as it was situated at a point where the needed materials could converge.

It was also an area full of available and skilled labor, consisting of men used to hard work on farms where, as youth, they had developed their mechanical abilities. Additionally, Armco's advanced and fair labor policies made for a loyal work force. Through research, Armco developed its special niche in the steel industry.

Above is a prized photo from the Mayfield collection of the Middletown Works at the middle of the twentieth century, including a view of the open hearth furnace complex. At that time, Armco covered approximately 2,800 acres, including 30 miles of roads and some 130 miles of railroad tracks.

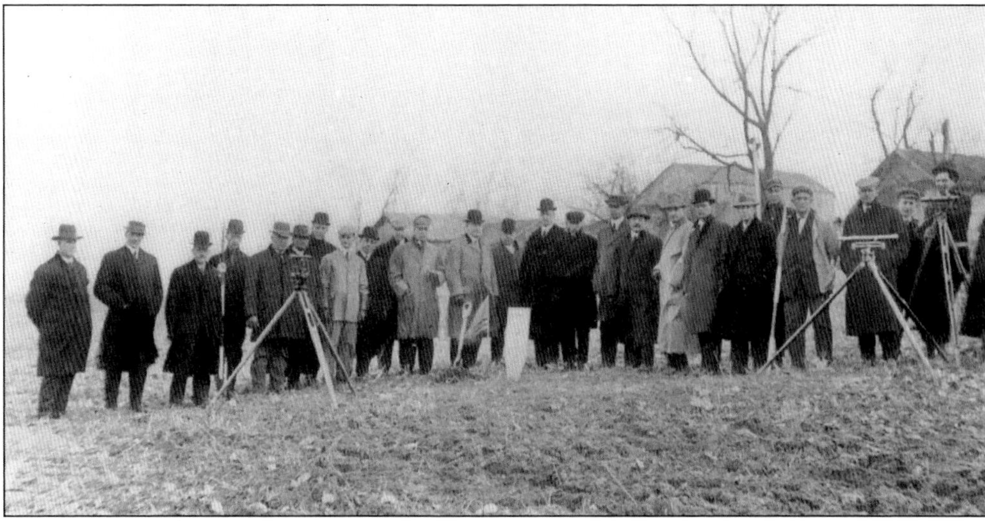

The groundbreaking for Armco's new East Works took place on March 7, 1910. It would take Armco into the big mill operation. This mill rose in what had been a farmer's cornfield.

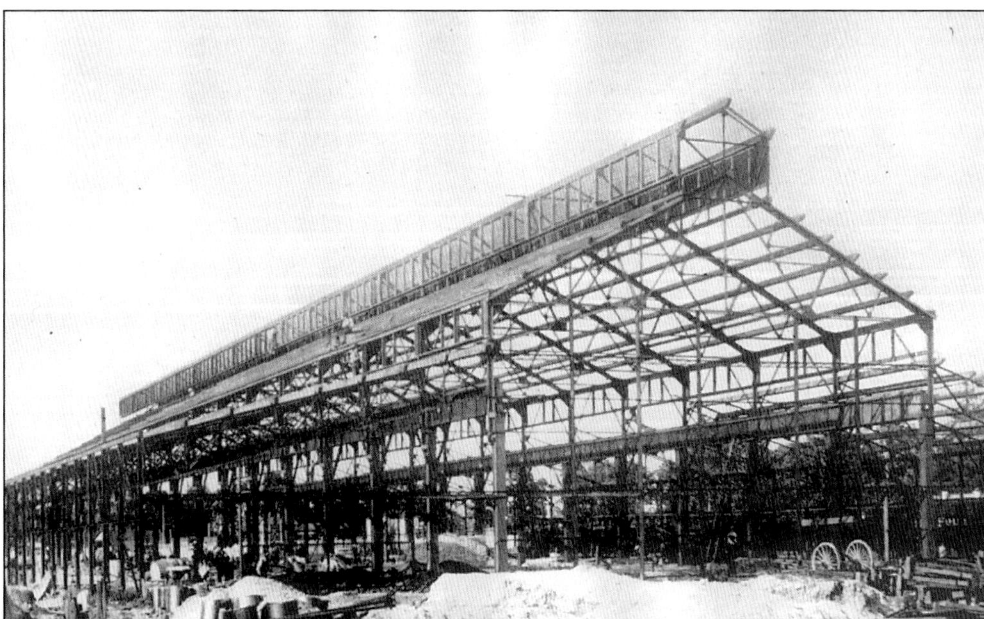

This is steel work going up on what was one of the first buildings at the Middletown Works, which began as East Works.

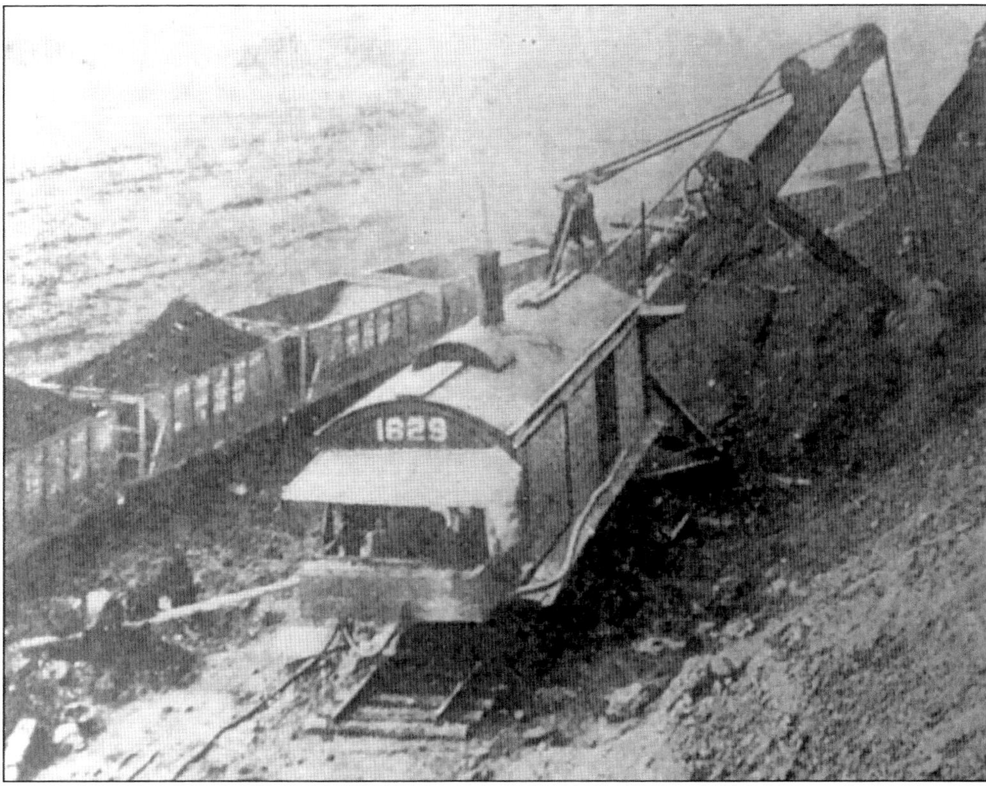

Armco's source of iron ore was the high-quality ore found in the Mesabi Range of the Lake Superior District. Pictured here is the Frantz Ore Mine, as the ore is mined with steam shovels and loaded onto railroad cars.

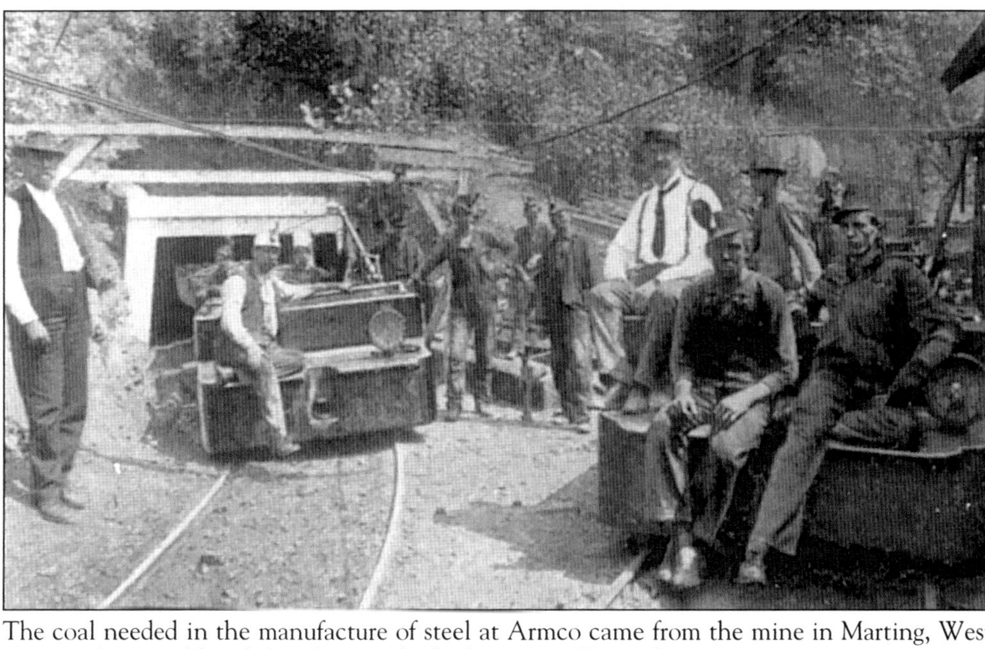

The coal needed in the manufacture of steel at Armco came from the mine in Marting, West Virginia (pictured here), but Armco also had mines in Kentucky.

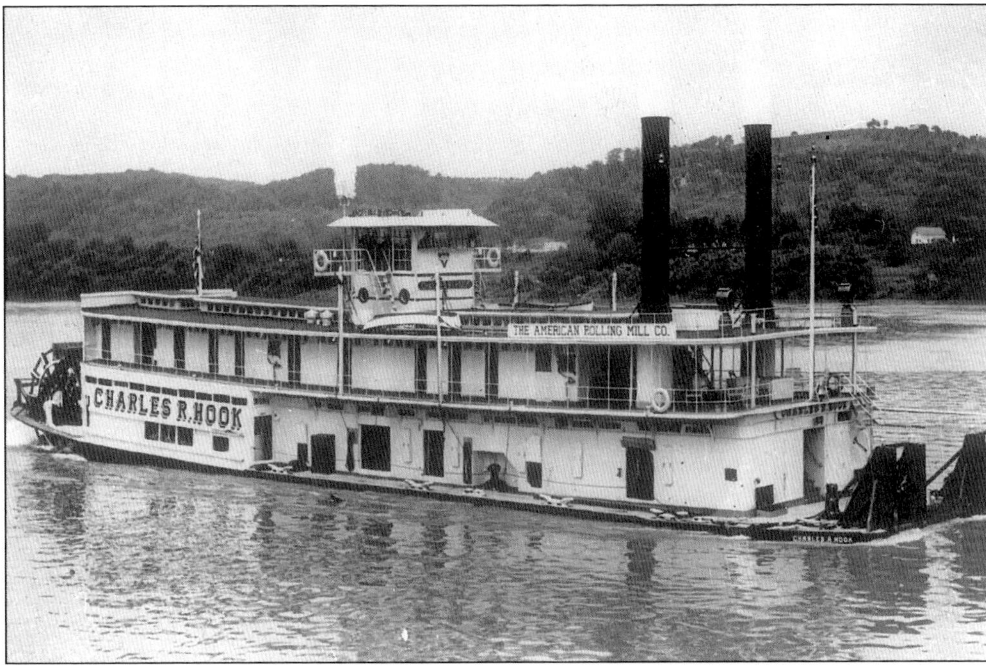

Armco made use of water transportation, as barges were cheaper than railroads. Boats brought coal to Cincinnati from mines in West Virginia and Kentucky. Longtime Armco employee C.W. Van Gilder, who contributed these photographs, recalled that his first job with the company was in 1941 as a member of a 17-man crew serving on the tugboat *Charles R. Hook*.

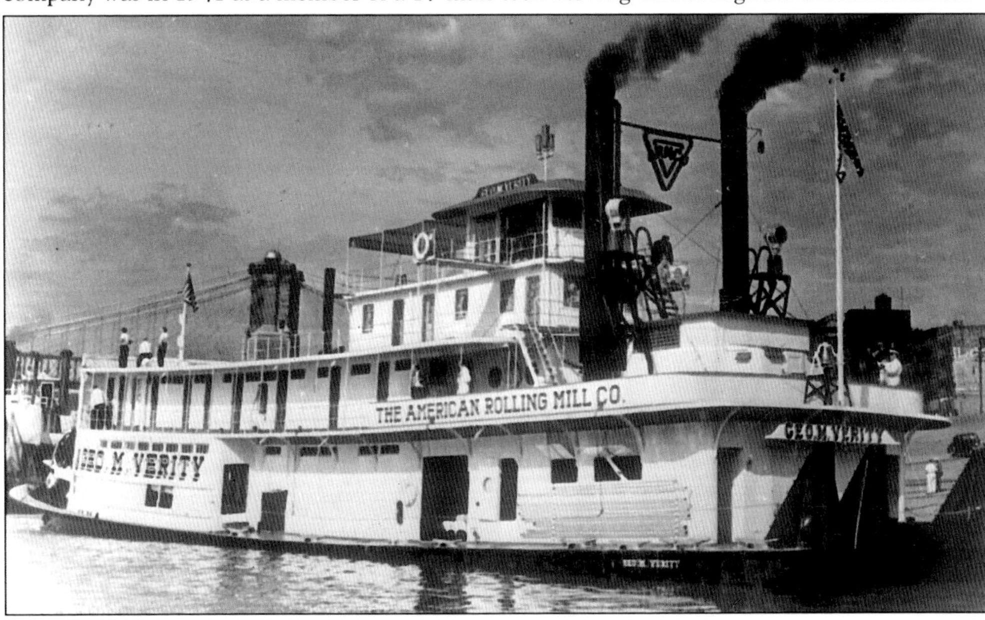

Armco operated the *George M. Verity* and the *Weber W. Sebald* on the Ohio and Kanawha Rivers. Armco also had interests in a company with a fleet on Lake Erie, that delivered iron ore from the Lake Superior District to ports in Toledo and Cleveland, where it was re-shipped by rail to Middletown. Incidentally, during World War II, a 10,000-ton *Liberty Ship* was christened to honor George M. Verity on September 17, 1944.

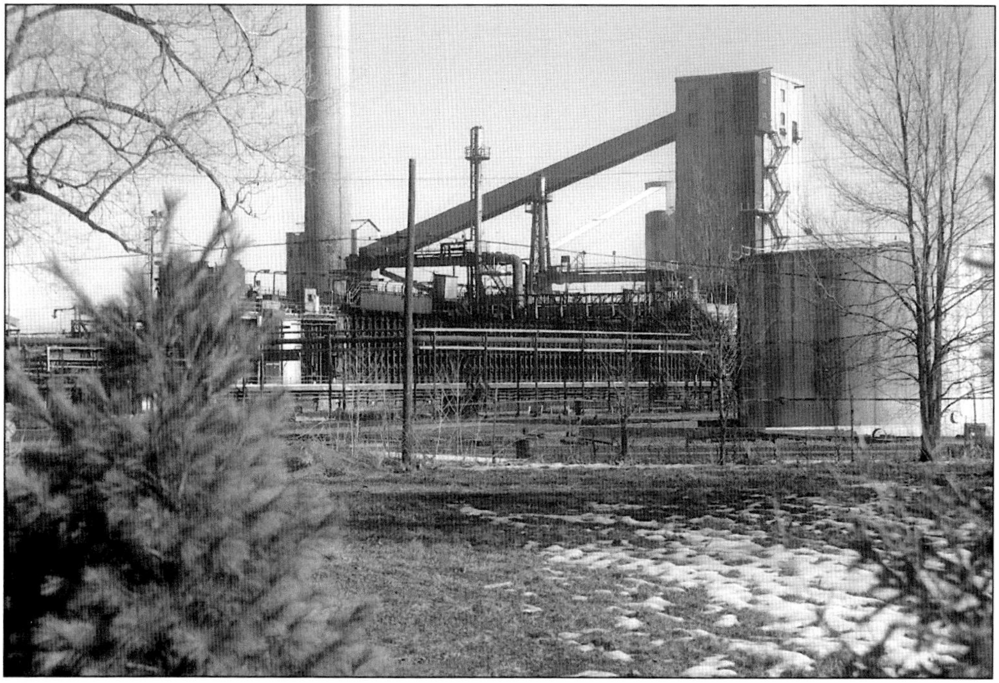

The iron-making process all begins at the coke oven complex as seen here from Ottawa Street. Armco first bought its coke from Hamilton, Ohio. However, to augment this supply, the Willputte Coke Ovens were built in Middletown. In 1977, the Still Coke Ovens were put into production as the Willputte Battery was improved. The Still ovens are no longer in use, and have been torn down.

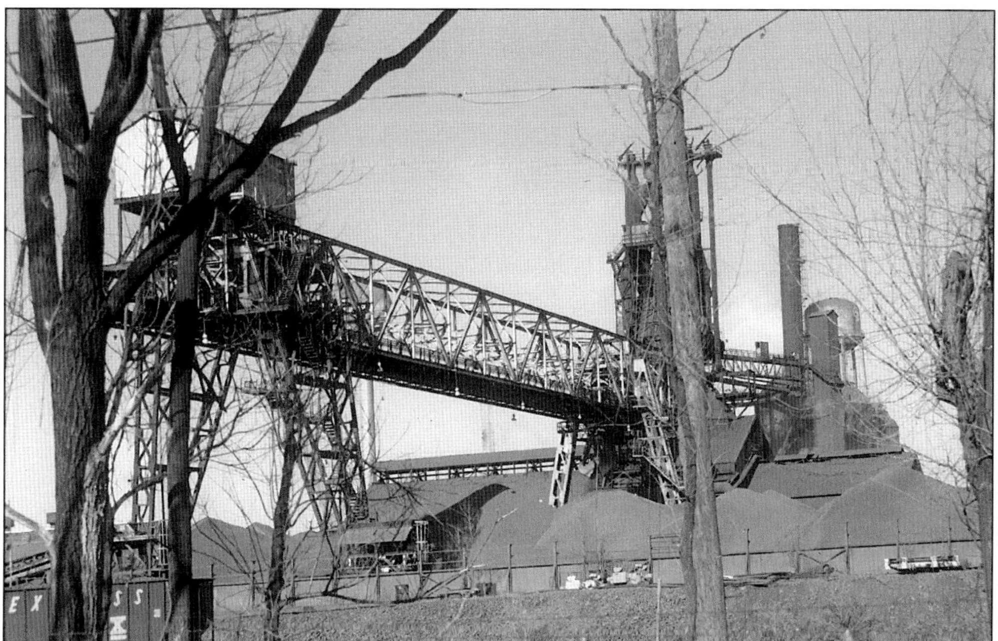

Photographed from outside the fence, with the blast furnace partially hidden by the telephone pole, is a recent view of the furnace with iron ore awaiting processing.

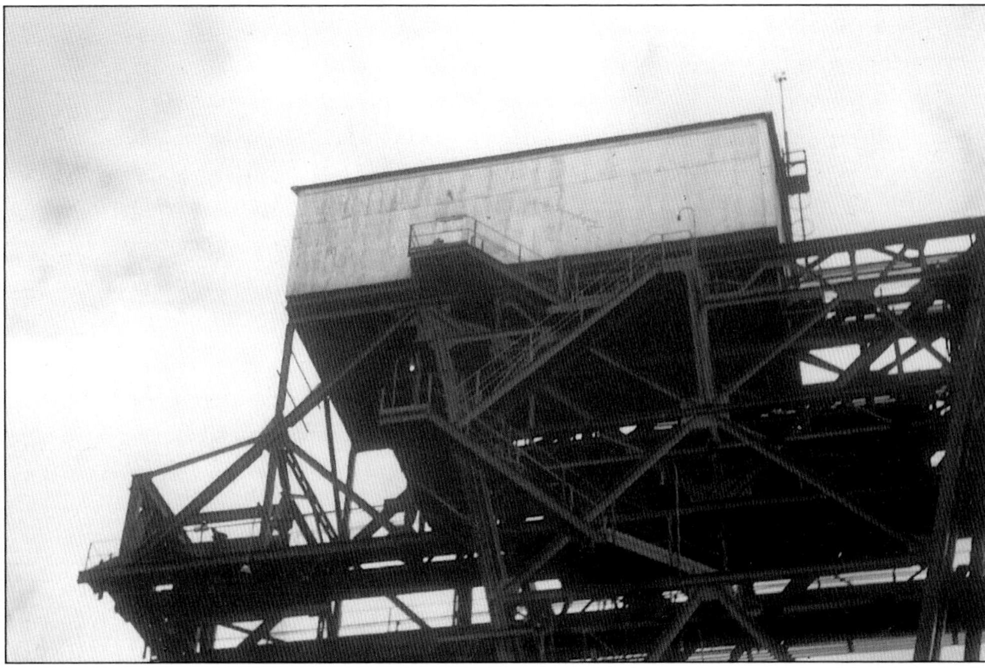

From this ore bridge at East Works, Jack Mokry took the following pictures. The ore bridge is a room high in the air which contains the necessary equipment to convey the iron ore to the blast furnace.

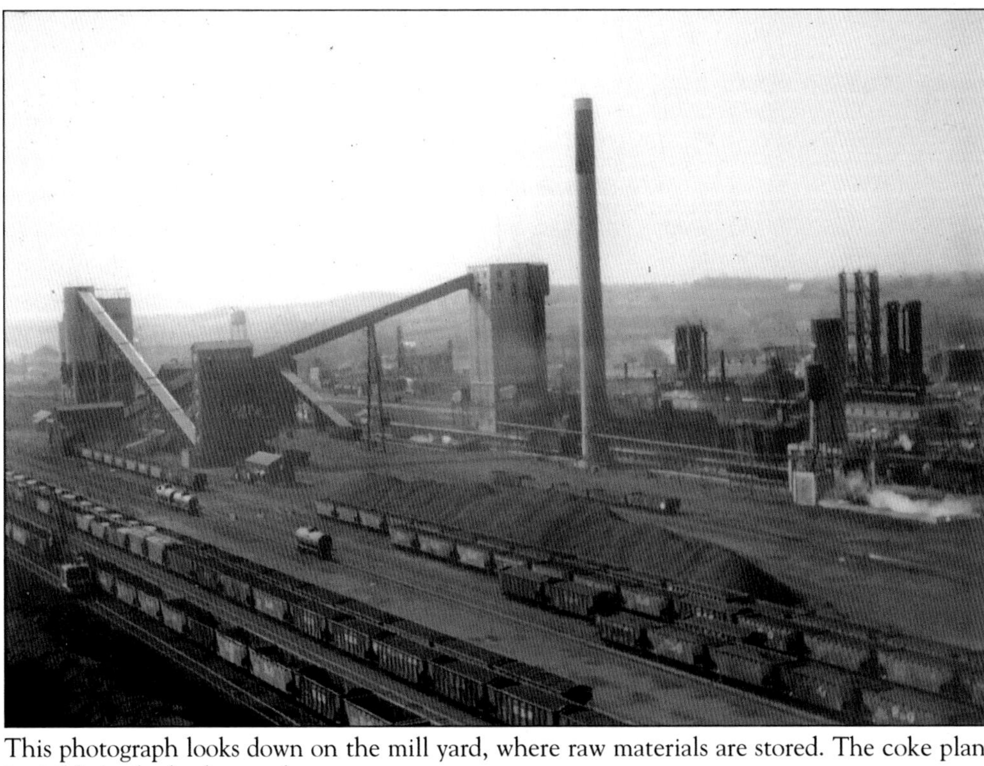

This photograph looks down on the mill yard, where raw materials are stored. The coke plant is visible in the background.

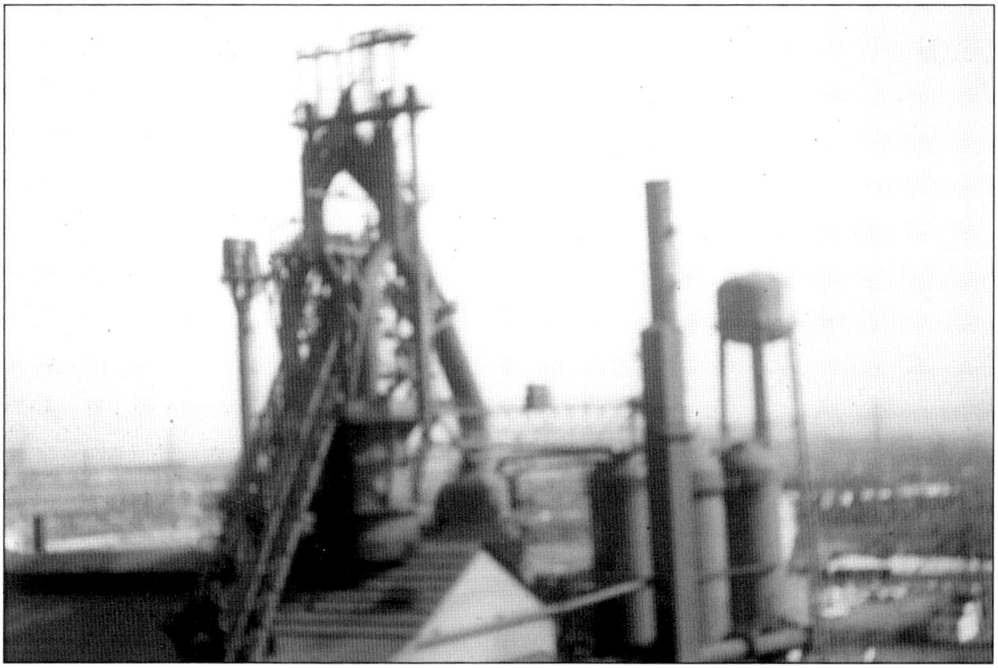

This is a photo of the top of the blast furnace taken from the ore bridge. The blast furnace takes basic raw materials (iron ore, limestone, and coke), and produces molten iron, which in earlier days was carried to the open hearth furnaces for processing into steel.

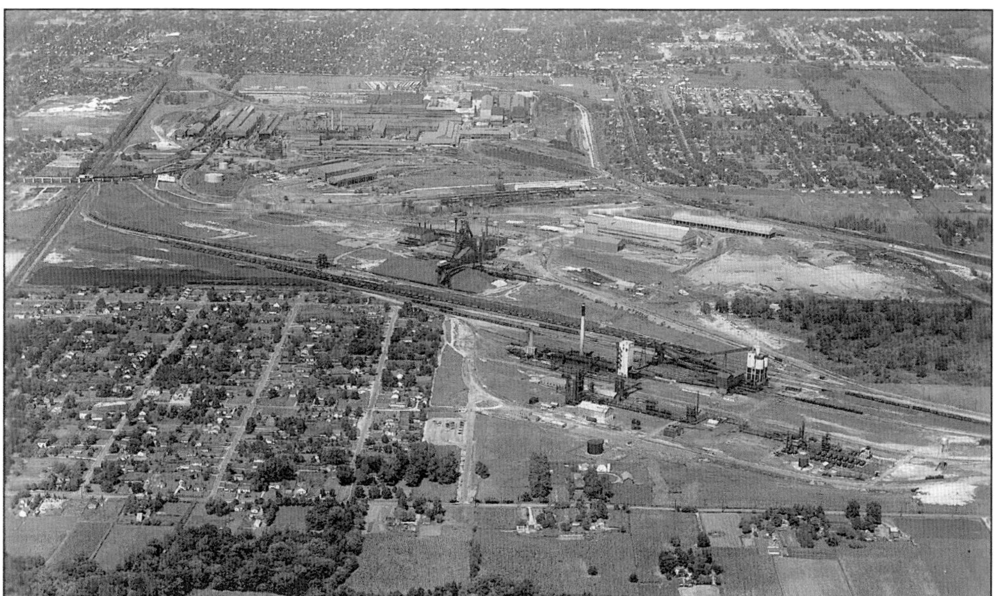

This blast furnace (in the center of the photo), when built in 1953 to augment the two blast furnaces at New Miami (Hamilton), was the pride of Armco. It was built on what had been a three-hundred-acre cornfield. The result was that Armco increased production of the Middletown Division by 15 percent, and added five hundred people to the payroll. In 1997, AK Steel updated its computer system at a cost of $10 million.

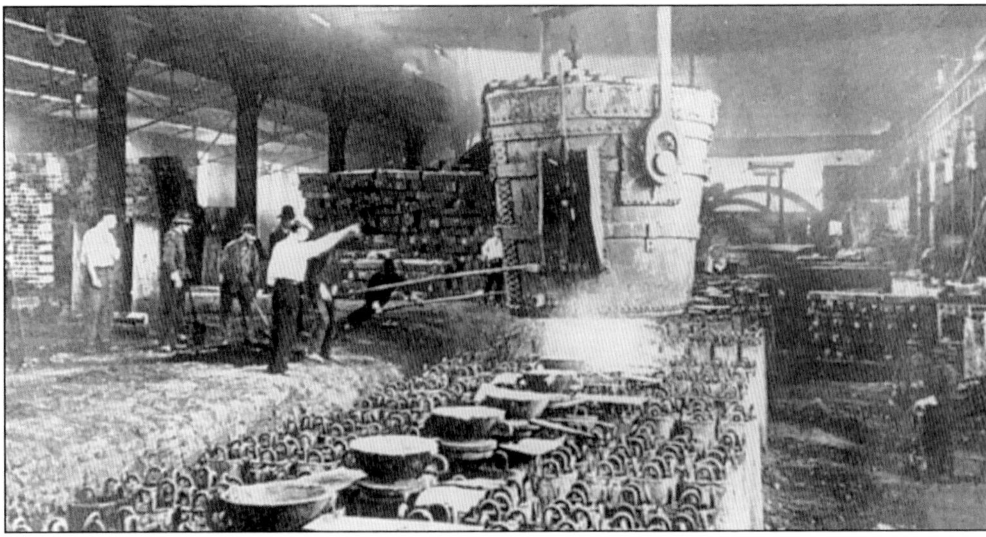

Many difficulties were encountered in rolling ingot iron into sheets. An Armco crew was the first to discover the critical temperatures at which it could be rolled, and those best for making a pack of perfect sheets. Armco patented the process and turned out the purest iron in the world. Pictured here is the pouring of that first ingot iron heat in 1908. The men in white shirts, from left to right, are as follows: Calvin Verity, Earl Emerson, Bus Ahlbrandt, and Charles Hook (by the ladle).

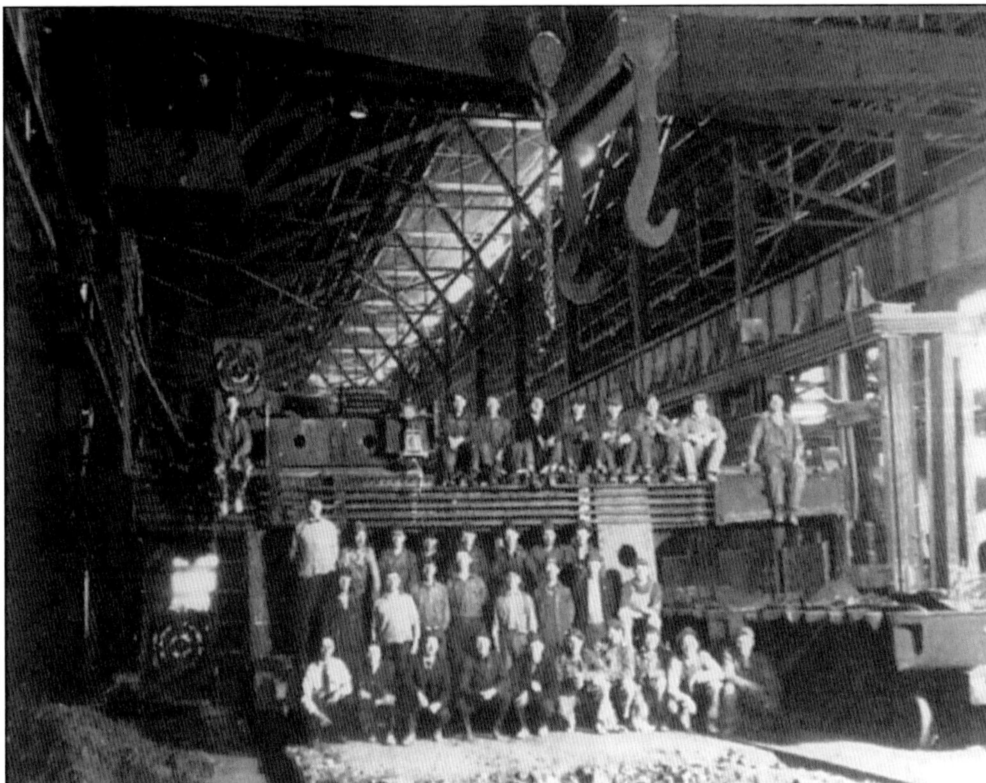

This is an open hearth pit crew in 1921. The man in charge of the crane cab was Jesse Selby.

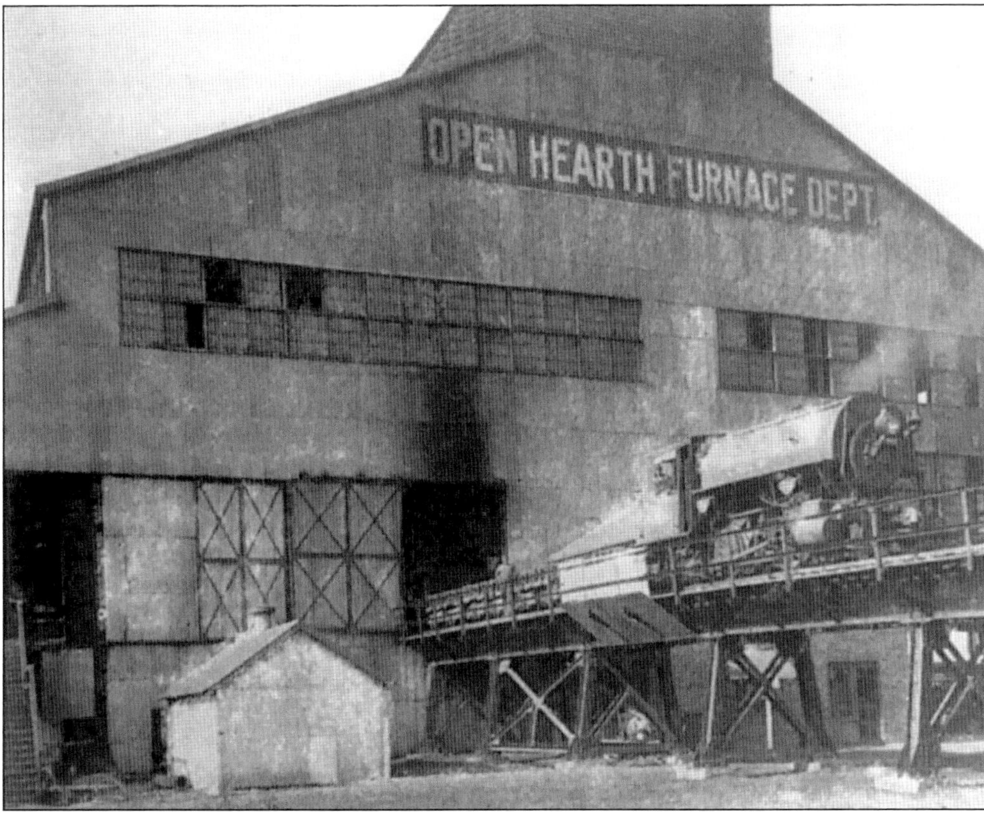

The materials came to the floor of the open hearth (East Works Number One) by means of charging buggies. All materials had been weighed to ensure the correct proportions.

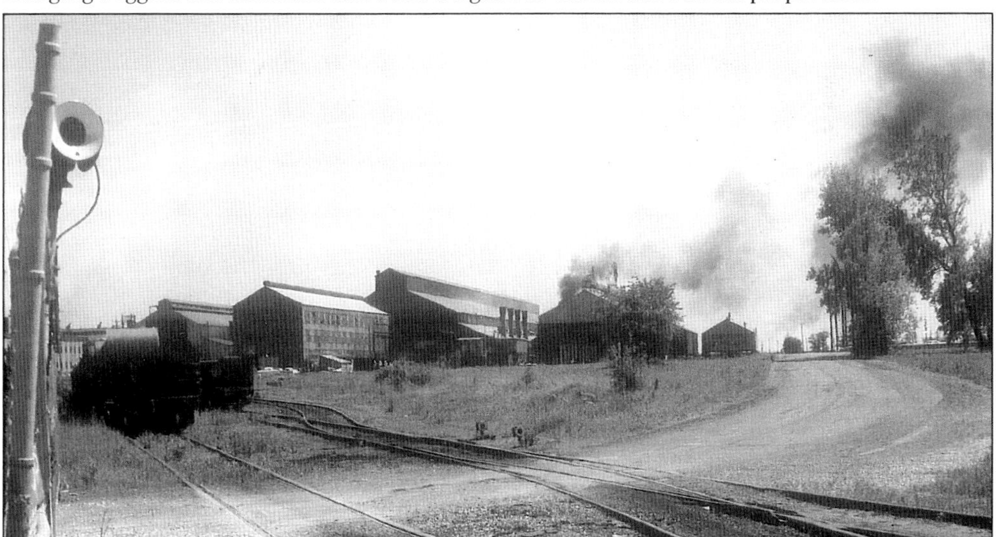

The Number One (eight furnace shop) Open Hearth at Armco East Works was shut down on June 21, 1969, after 58 years of operation. It had produced 34 million tons of steel. Many of its workers were transferred to the new Basic Oxygen Furnace (BOF), its replacement. The last heat was tapped at Number Two Open Hearth on November 3, 1984.

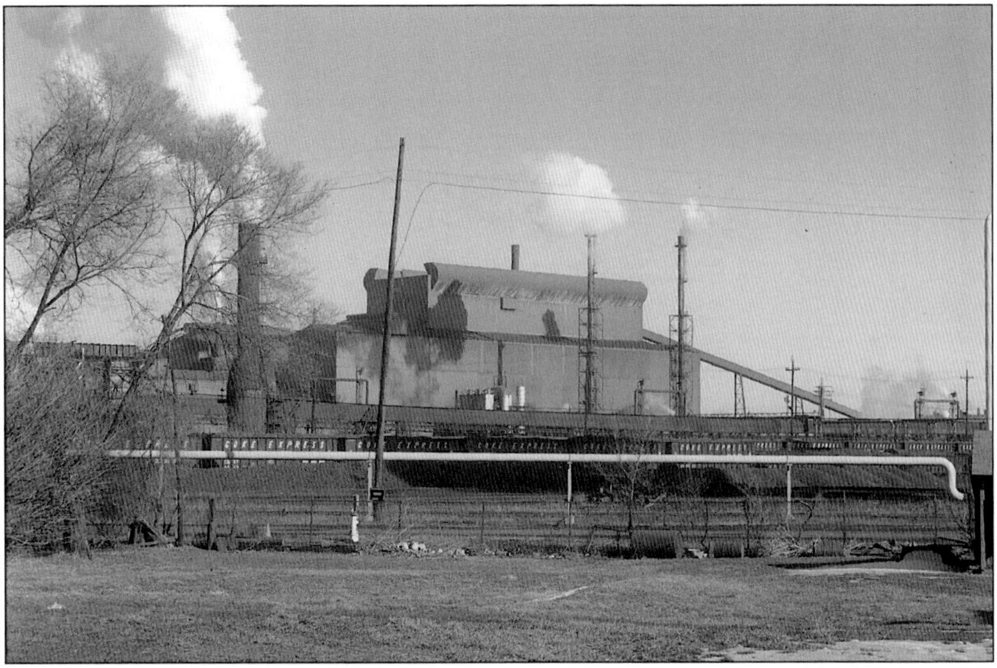

This is the BOF complex at AK Steel as viewed from Ottawa Street. Iron ore and coke, along with limestone, are blended in the blast furnace to produce pig iron. This then goes to the BOF.

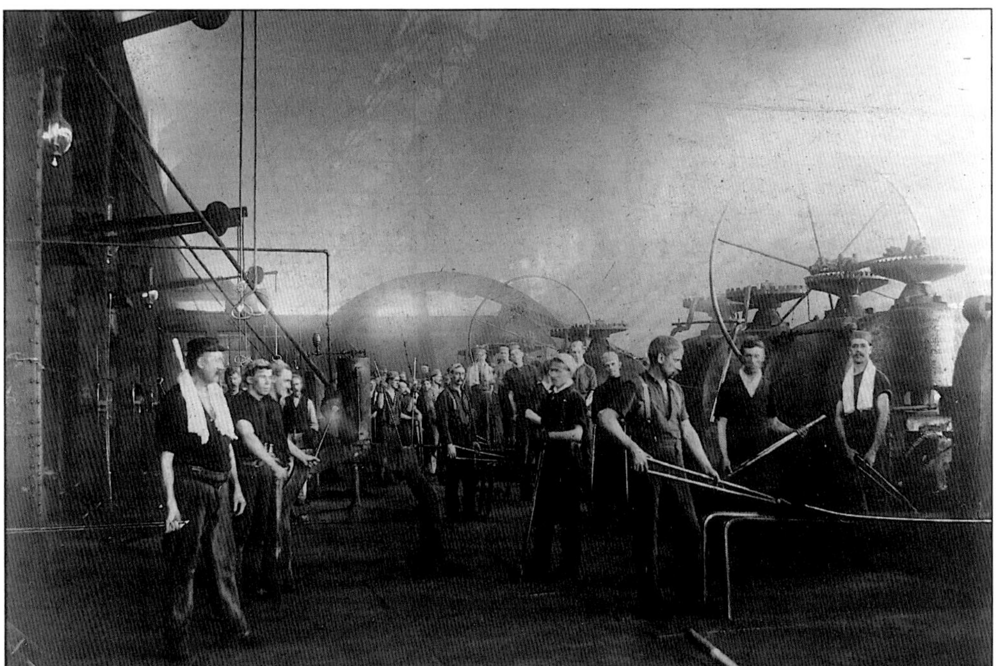

The earliest photographs inside the mill on Curtis Street were taken in 1906. Here is one of a sheet mill crew at work before the days of the continuous mill.

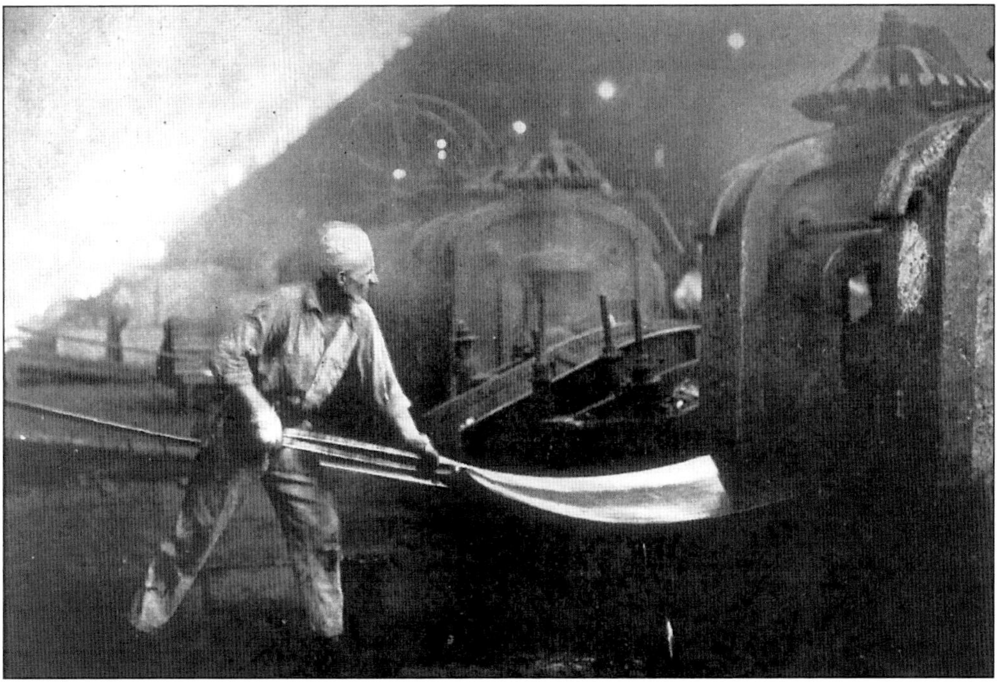

This is a photograph of a catcher on an old hand-operated sheet mill.

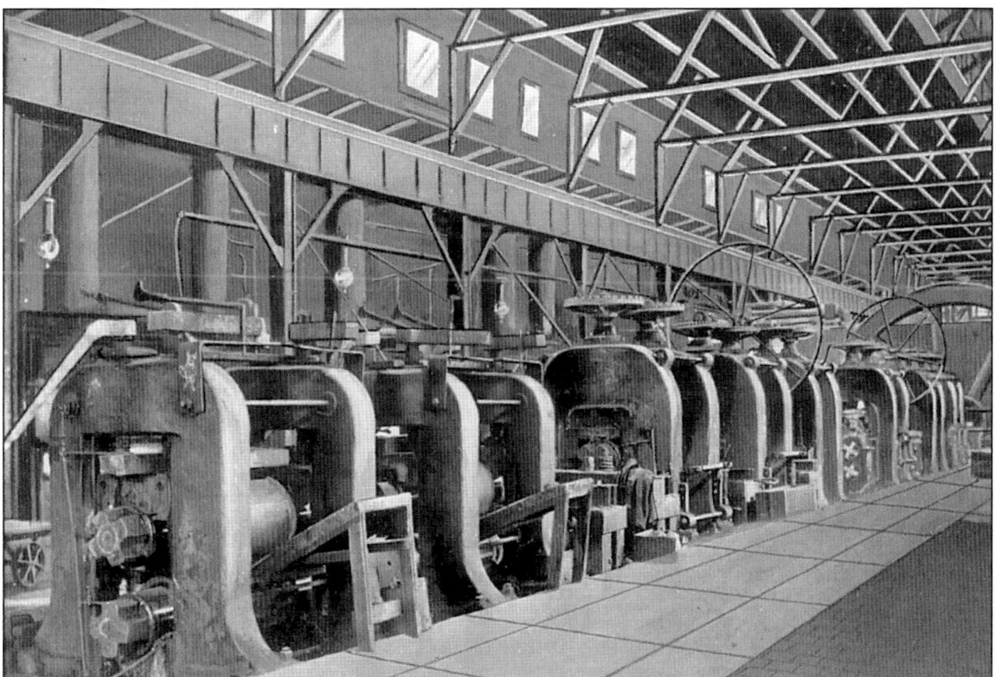

Work at the old hand-operated sheet mill has been described as the hardest and most grueling labor of mankind. J.B. Tytus, inventor of the continuous mill that replaced the sheet mill, when confronted by a critic who accused the new mill of being "a monster taking men's jobs," replied, "Did you ever try your hand at the kind of work it eliminated?"

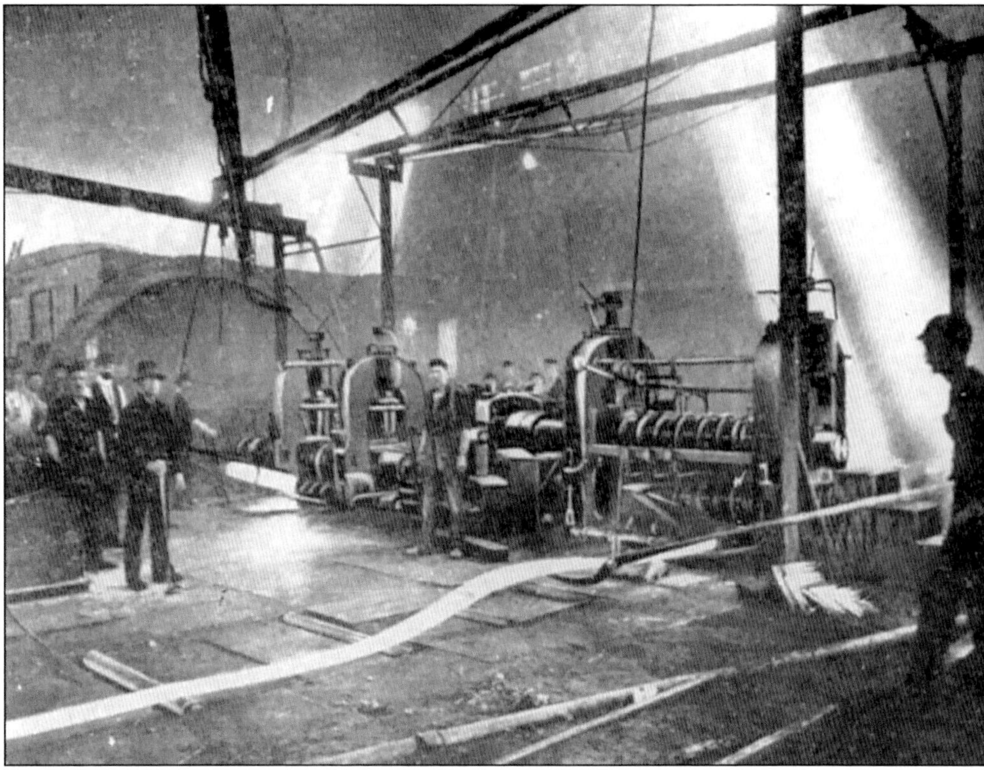

This is the old method of handling ingots in the bar mill.

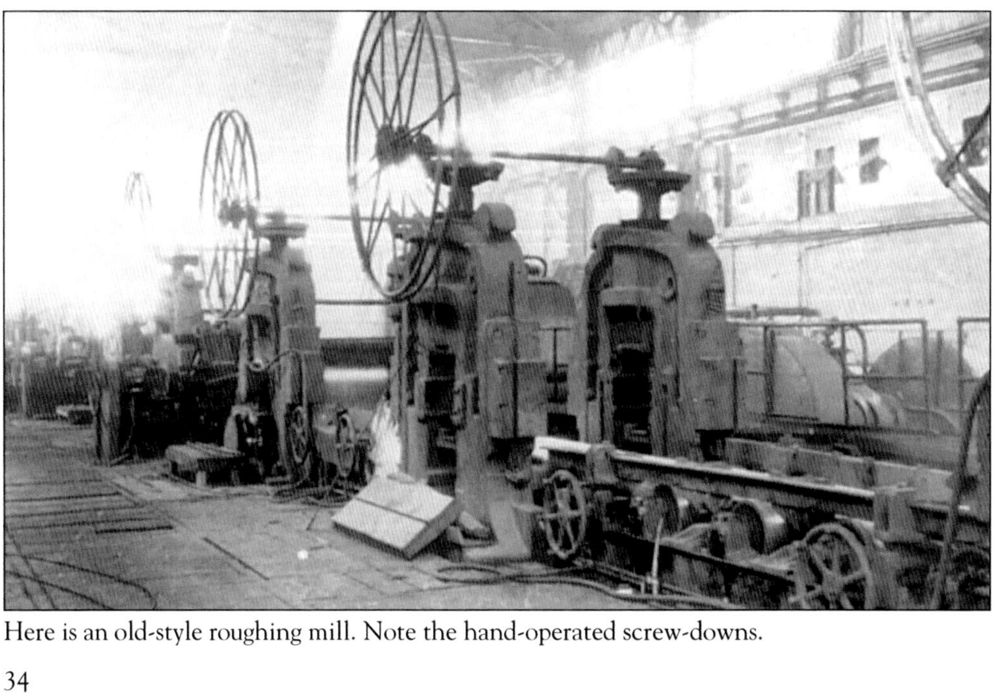

Here is an old-style roughing mill. Note the hand-operated screw-downs.

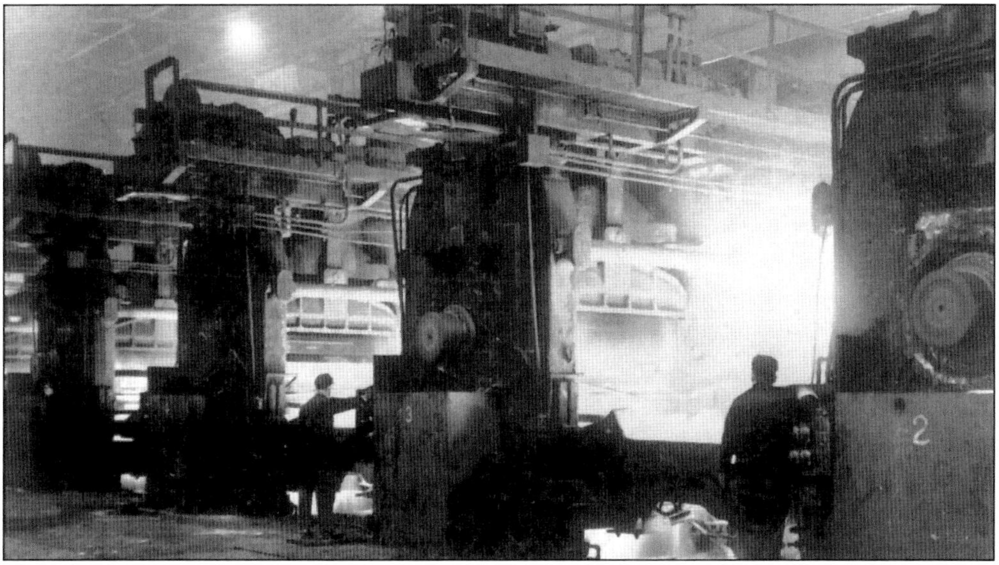

In this hot strip finishing mill, a 12,000-pound ingot was stretched into a rolled coil of metal a quarter mile long.

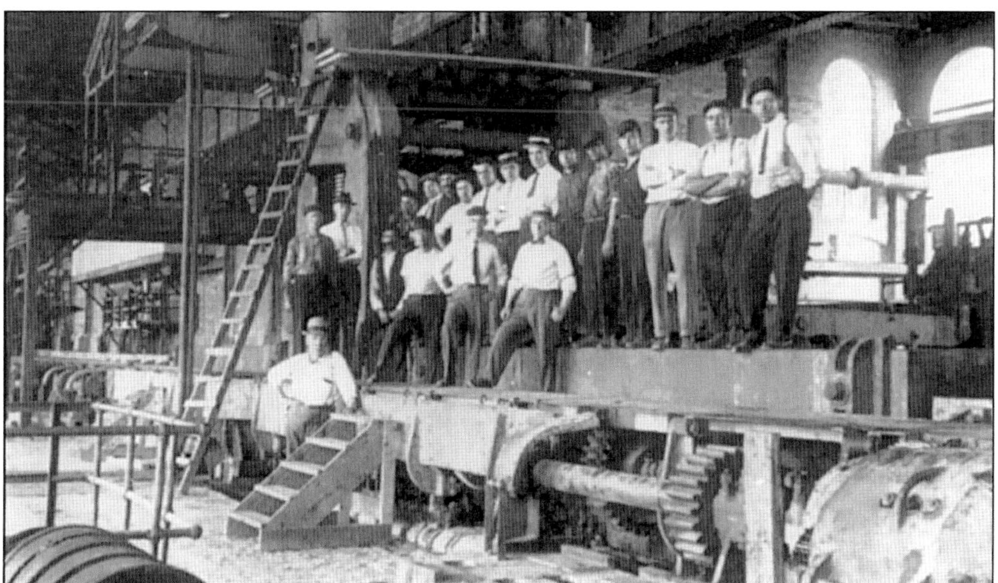

Armco was ready to roll its first ingot in this slab mill at East Works in Middletown in September, 1911.

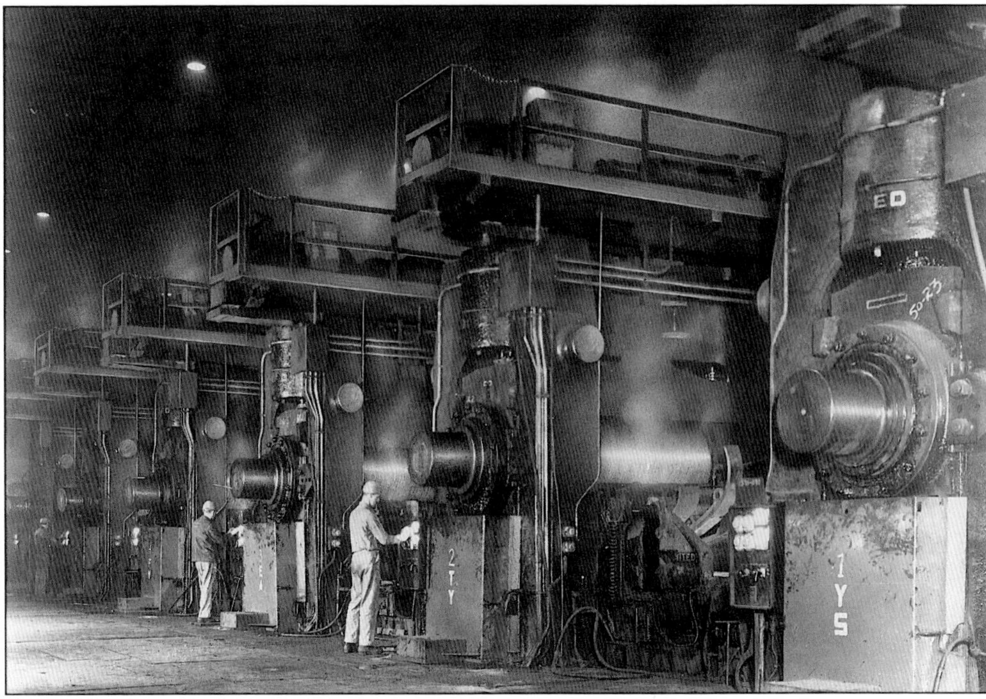

The continuous method of rolling steel begins with a hot ingot at the soaking pits. This ingot is then flattened at the slab mill. The slab is reheated before traveling through the continuous roughing and finishing mills, where it is reduced in thickness and becomes a long strip of steel that is coiled up at the end of the process.

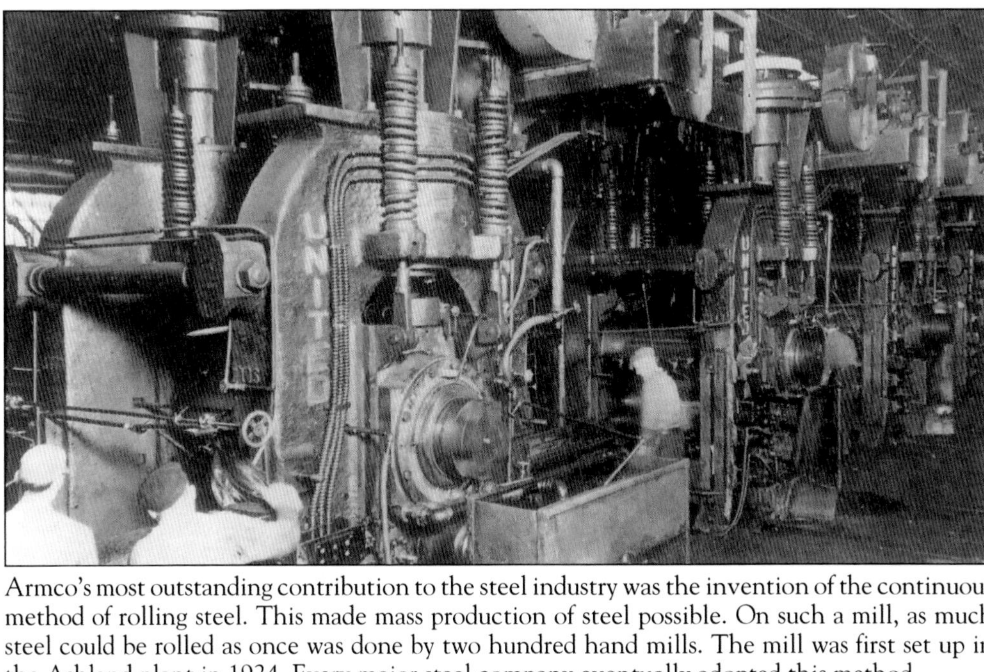

Armco's most outstanding contribution to the steel industry was the invention of the continuous method of rolling steel. This made mass production of steel possible. On such a mill, as much steel could be rolled as once was done by two hundred hand mills. The mill was first set up in the Ashland plant in 1924. Every major steel company eventually adopted this method.

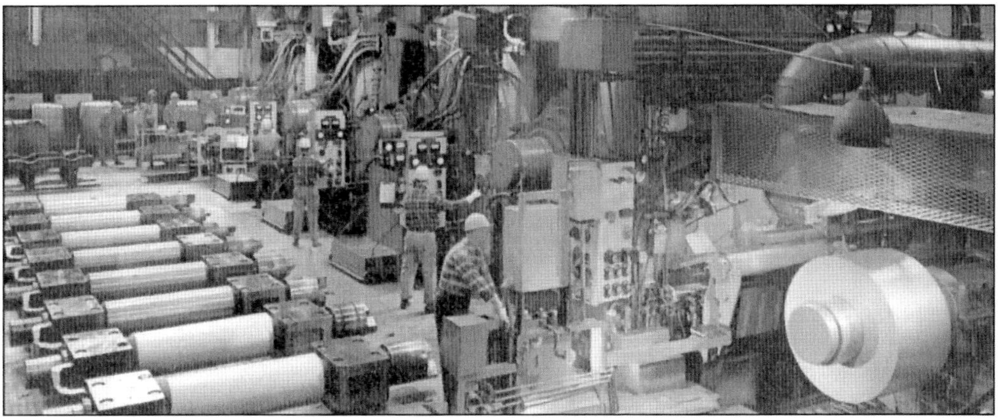

Hot-rolled steel is pickled (cleaned) and then rolled on one of two cold strip mills. After passing through the rolls, the strip is wound into coils. Operators at each of the four stands of this mill control the amount of roll pressure and tension necessary to produce steel that has a bright, smooth surface. The two mills were later replaced by one newer mill.

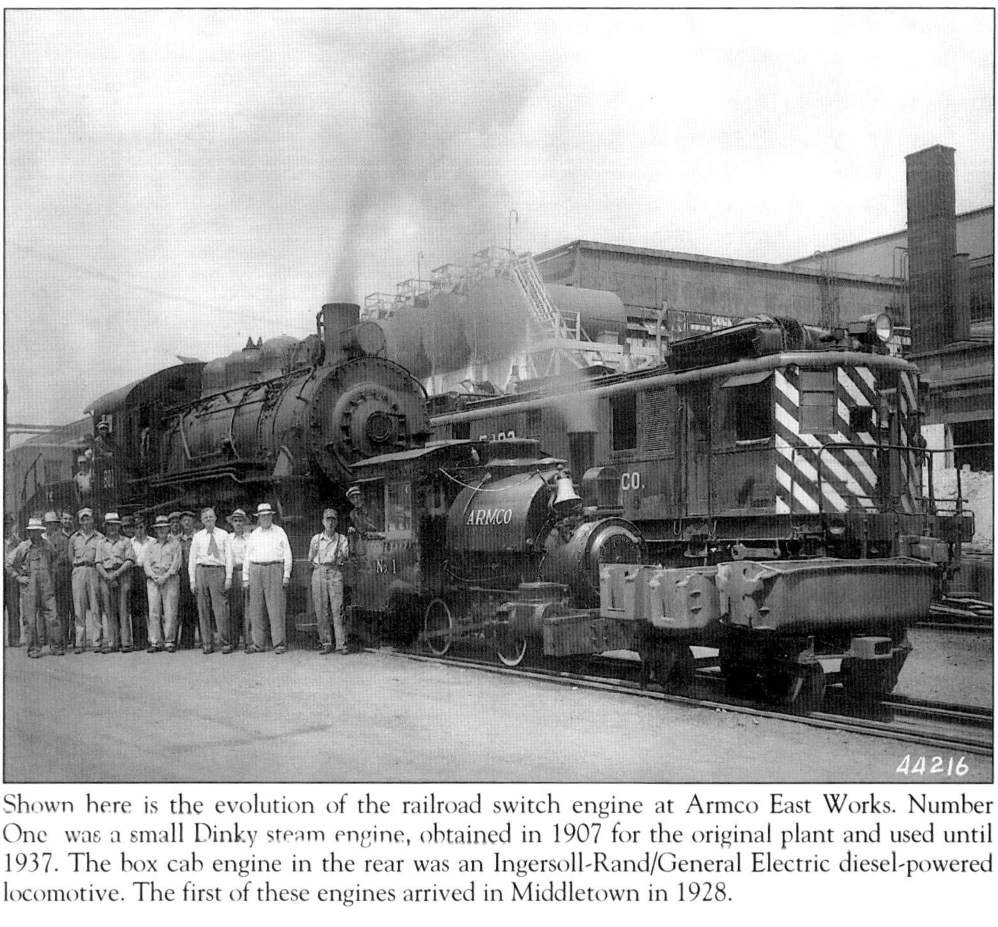

Shown here is the evolution of the railroad switch engine at Armco East Works. Number One was a small Dinky steam engine, obtained in 1907 for the original plant and used until 1937. The box cab engine in the rear was an Ingersoll-Rand/General Electric diesel-powered locomotive. The first of these engines arrived in Middletown in 1928.

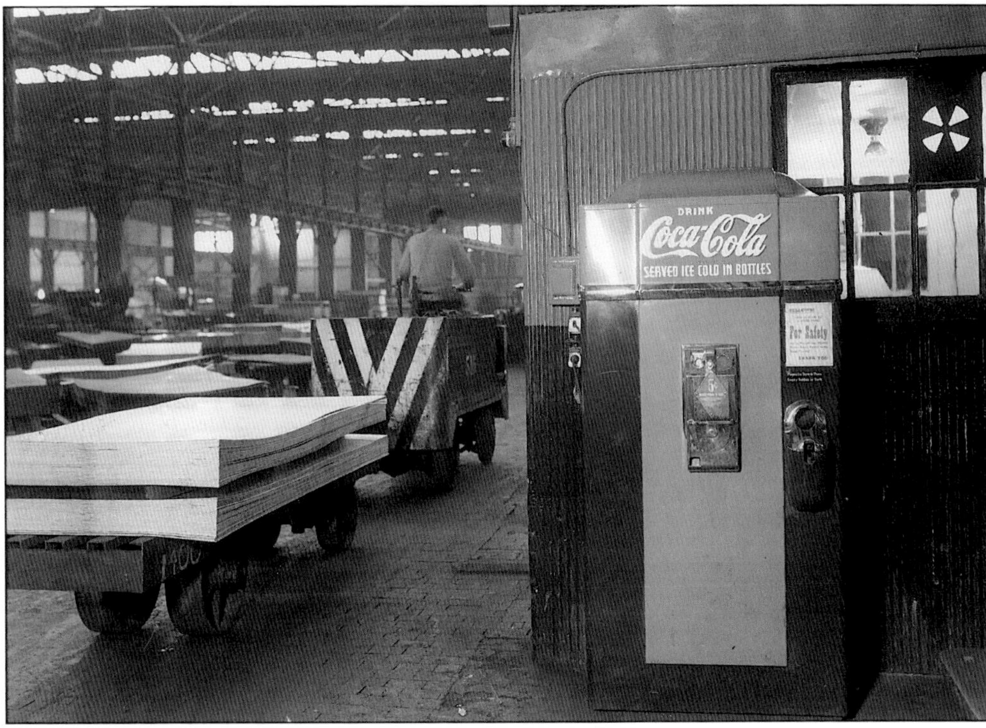

This is a photo taken in the 1950s at the west processing department. This group was responsible for annealing, temper rolling, and finishing steel sheets and coils. Shown is a small office and recreational area.

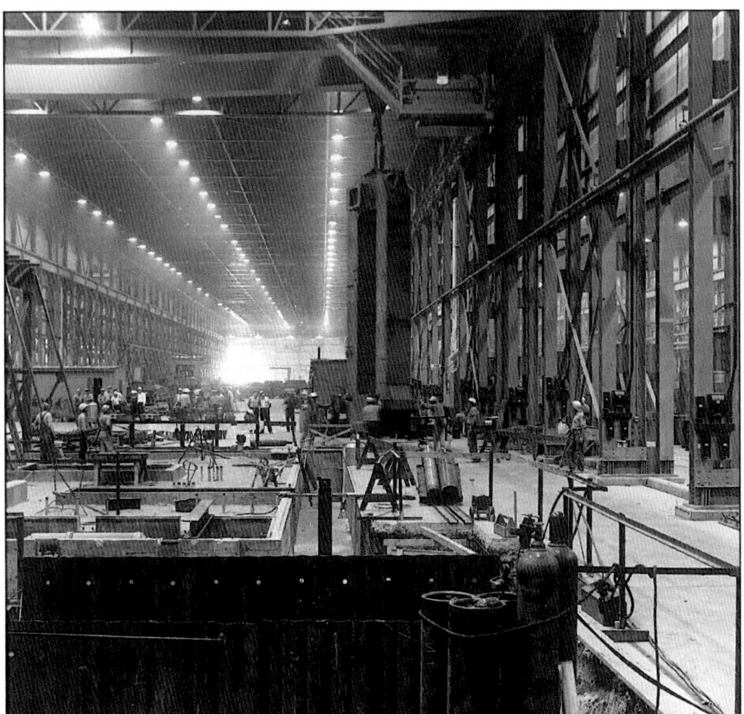

Immediately after annealing, both sheets and coils were passed through the temper mill, giving the steel the desired stiffness needed as well as improving its surface and flattening the sheet. Today the process is restricted to coils. Temper Mill Number Six, under construction in 1965, rolled its first coil in 1966.

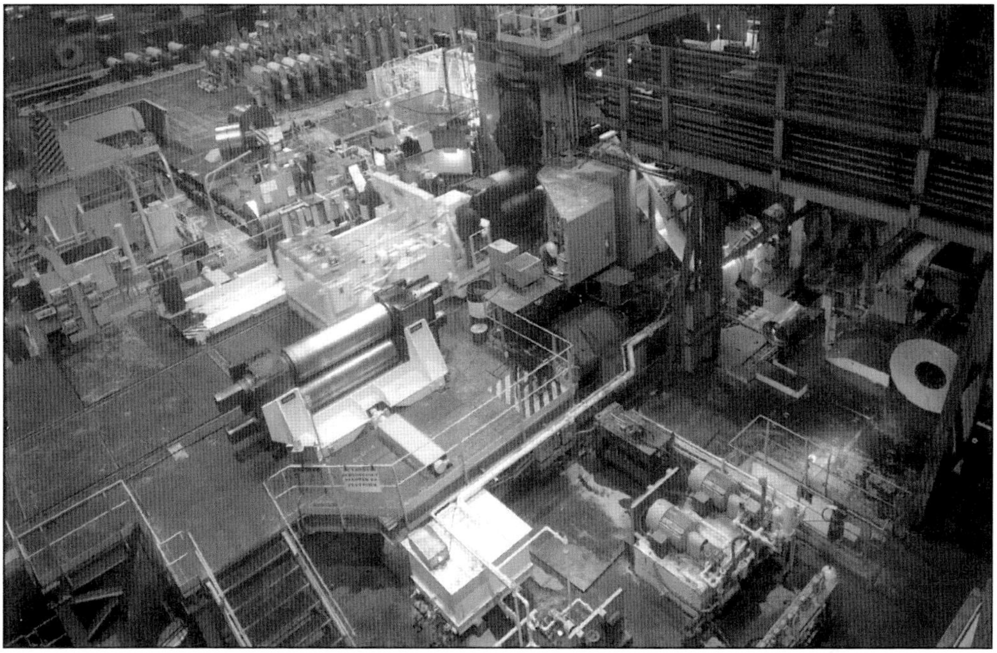

Here is Coil Temper Mill Number Six after the installation of a semi-automatic roll changer. This photo shows the rolls in the process of being changed.

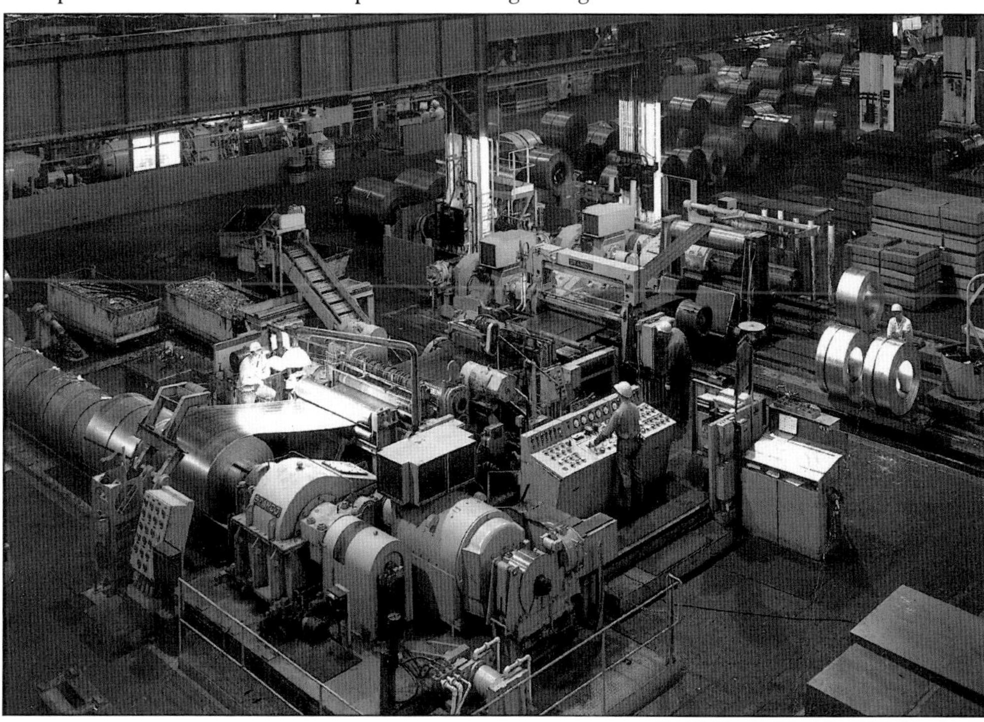

This is a 1950s Slitter Shear line in the east processing department. "Slittering," which made smaller width coils out of wide ones, involved unwinding the coil and then side-shearing before rewinding. When the unit became obsolete it was shut down, and the work was turned over to outside specialty processors.

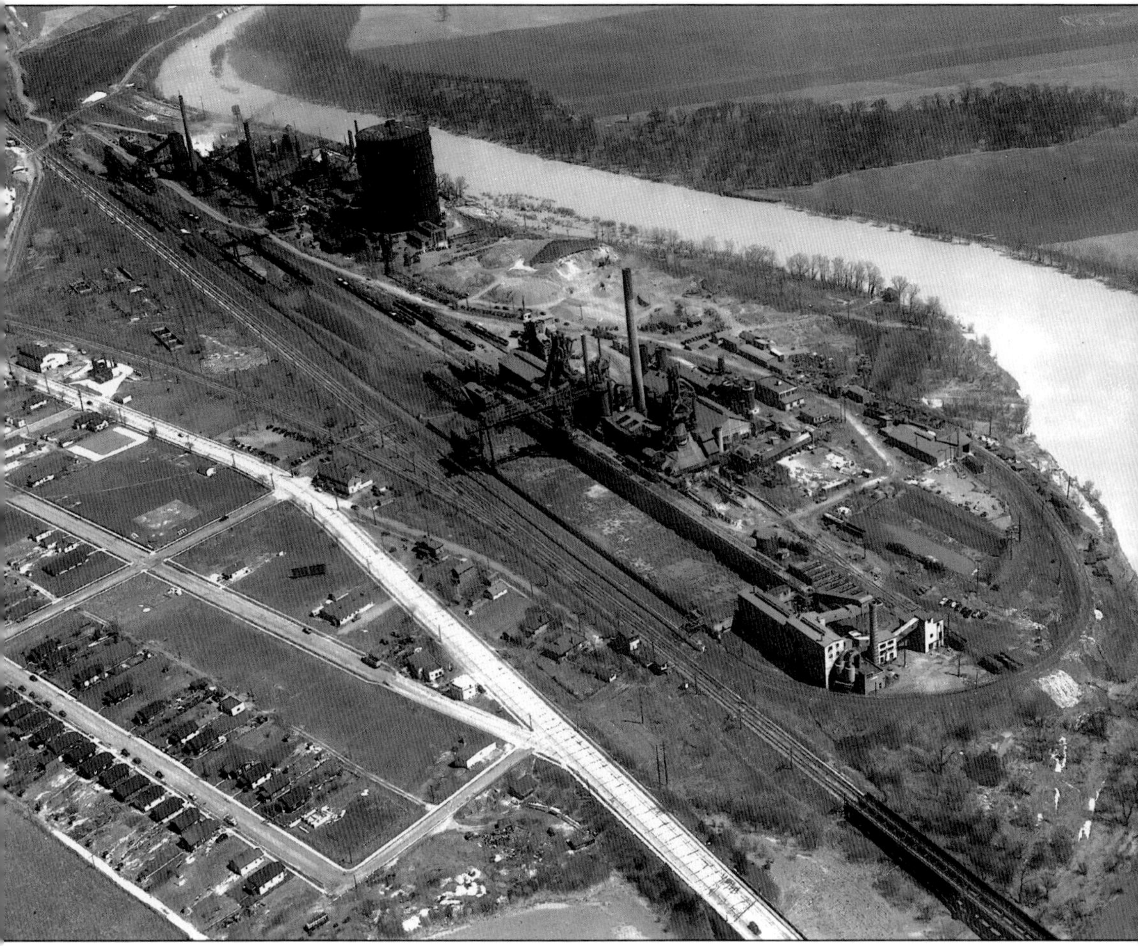

The Hamilton plant, located in New Miami, consisted of two blast furnaces and one hundred ten coke ovens in four batteries. It had been purchased in partnership with Koppers Coke Company in 1927. Eventually it came under Armco ownership, and was operated as such until July of 1988. By July of 1989, it had been leveled to the ground. In 1982, Armco acquired new coke-making facilities at Ashland, and installed Dravo-Still batteries at Middletown. (Mayfield collection, 1957.)

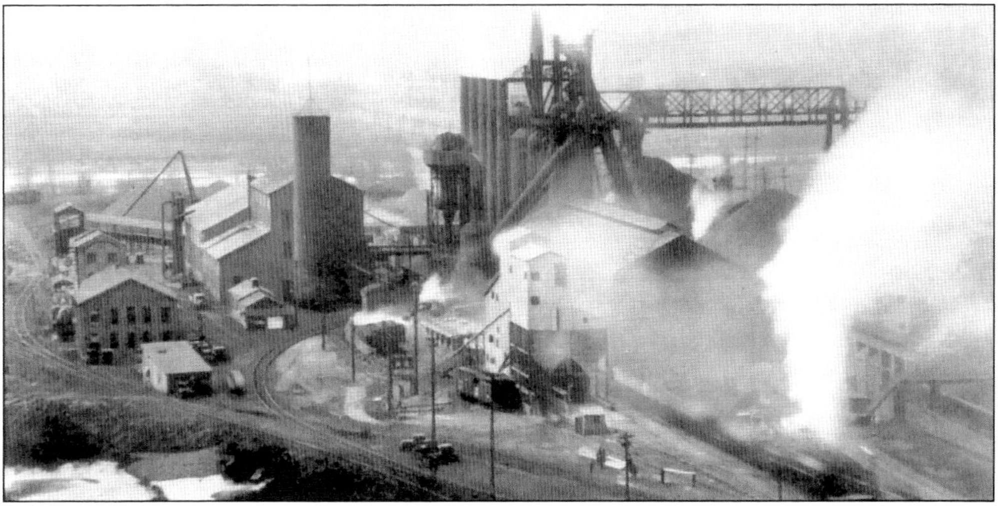

The two Armco blast furnaces in Hamilton (New Miami) made the pig iron that fed the open hearths in Middletown, which was about 12 miles away.

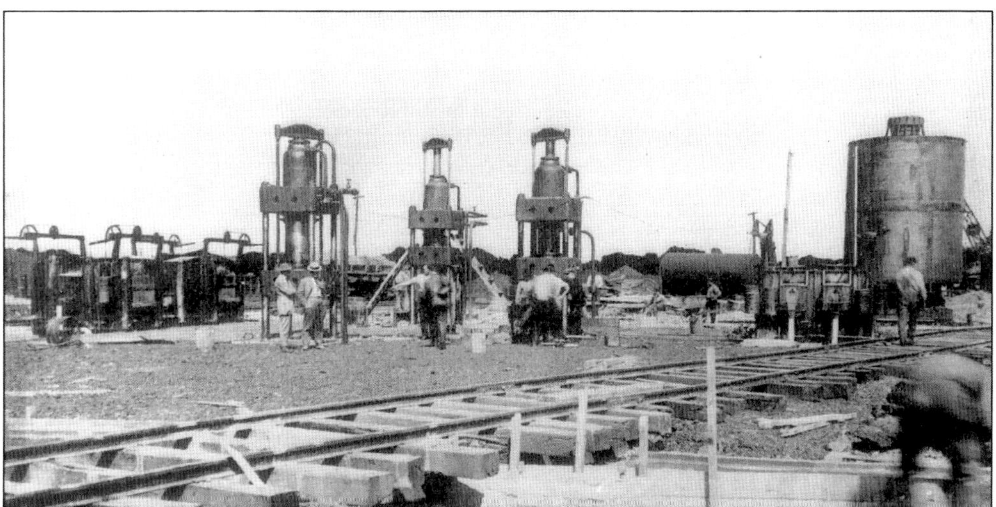

During World War I, the demand for Armco products was so great that shell casings were made out-of-doors, even as the roof was being built overhead.

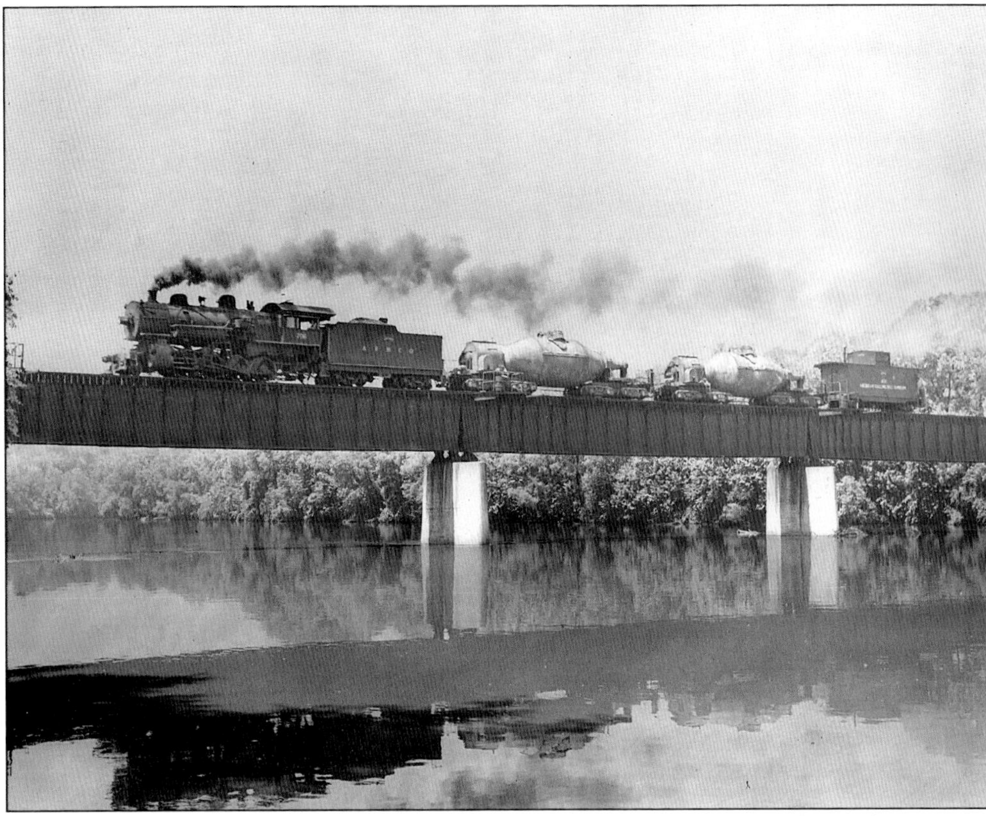

Hot, molten iron was taken from the blast furnace at Hamilton and poured into thermos cars in order to transport it the 12 miles to Middletown, over what was called "the old Pumpkin Vine line." At Middletown, the iron was charged into the open hearth furnaces. In this view, the locomotive pulls the cars across the specially-reinforced railroad bridge over the Great Miami River.

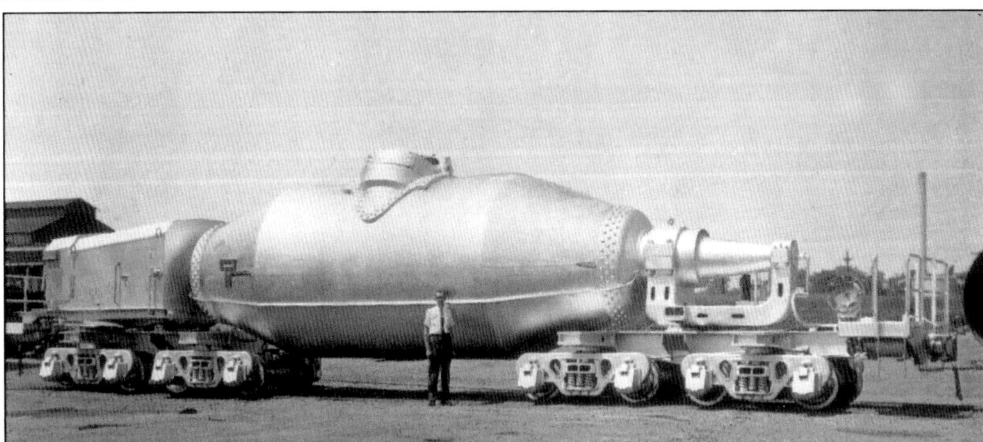

The 60-foot-long ladle cars, often called "thermos cars," had 16 wheels and carried loads of up to 200 tons. They were capable of withstanding temperatures of 2,800 degrees. The cars made their first trip in 1928, their last in 1994. They are now used only between AK Steel's Blast Furnace and its Basic Oxygen Furnace.

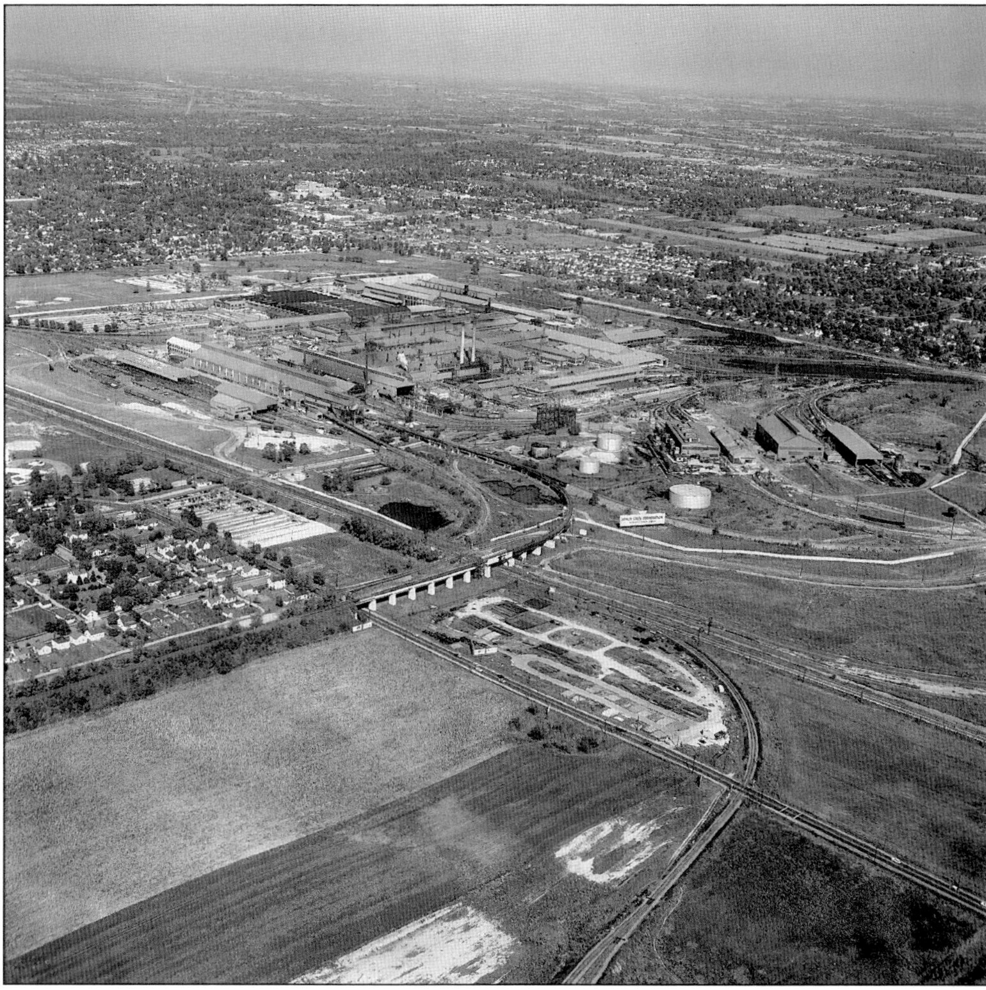

Armco Steel was a major contractor in the development of the atomic bomb. It constructed the 406,550-pound magnet used in the cyclotron that was required for basic research in the bomb's development. Armco cast cyclotron cores from ingot iron that weighed 30 to 200 tons each. W.E. Dannecker was the head of the project, and A.L. Young was the superintendent of the huge 12-pit foundry, where as much as 420,000 pounds of hot iron could be poured into one casting. Here is an aerial view of the complex where cyclotrons were cast. (Mayfield collection, 1942.)

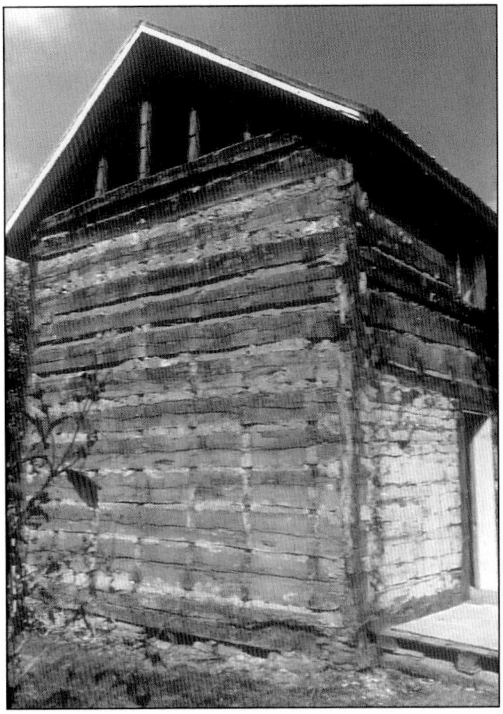

In 1953, Armco discovered that this log house stood on property they had acquired along Jackson Lane for their future expansion. In 1964, while preparing the site for the new plant, it was disassembled and moved to another location, and construction of Project Six Hundred began. This project was so named because its cost was initially estimated at $600 million, but the final tally exceeded $1 billion.

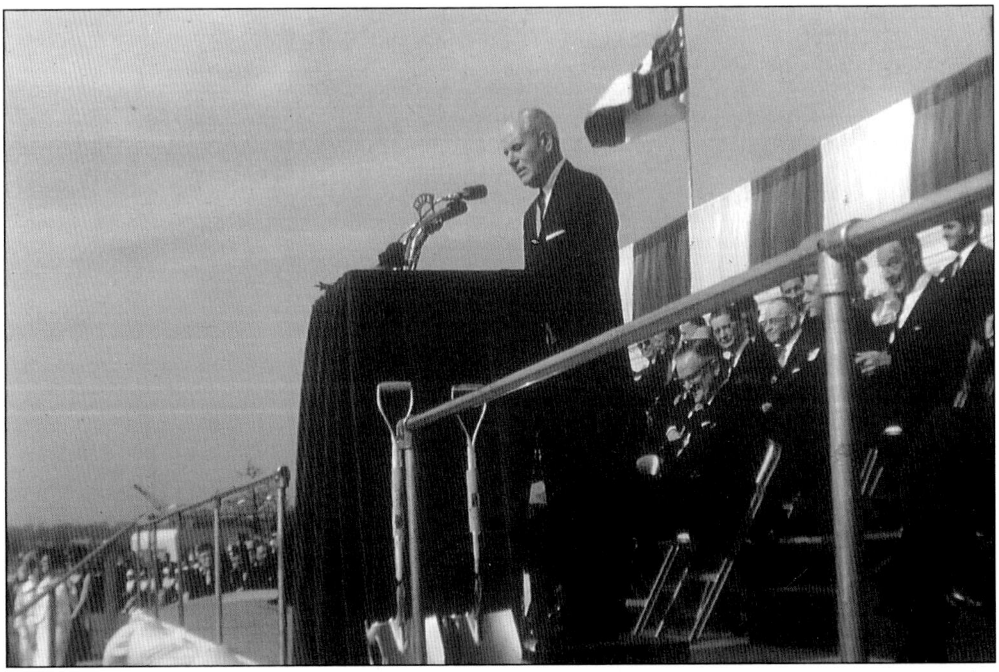

On April 16, 1964, Armco President Logan T. Johnson announced plans for an expansion at the Middletown Works. On April 22, 1965, he spoke at the groundbreaking ceremonies that began Project Six Hundred—the biggest and most expensive construction project ever undertaken at Middletown or Armco. Even Ohio Governor James Rhodes was in attendance and manned a ceremonial shovel. Here, Johnson is welcoming the crowd gathered for that historic occasion.

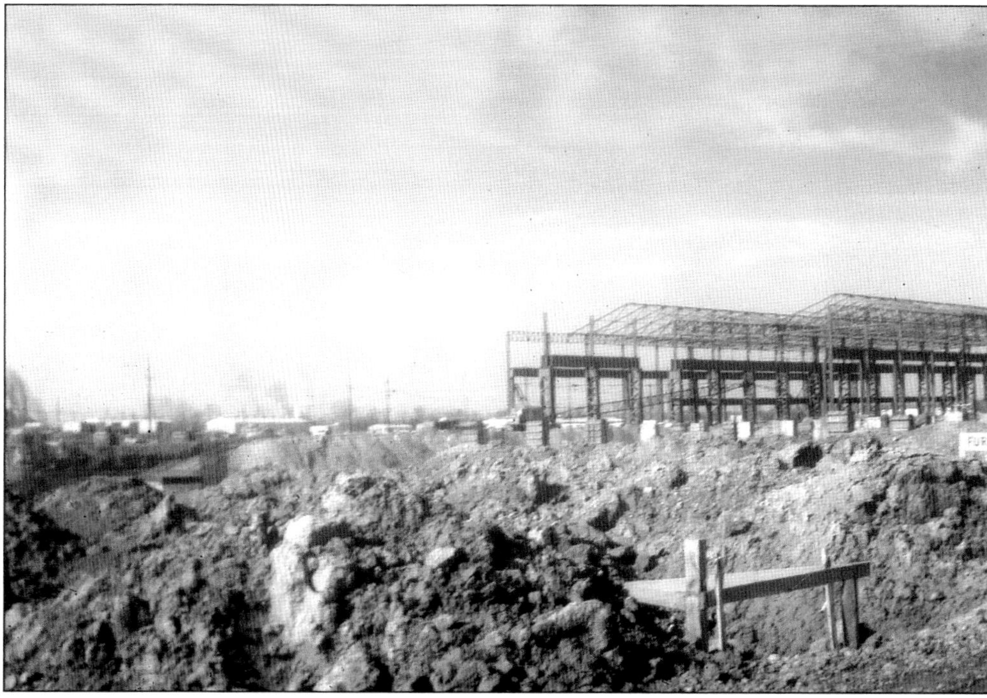

On the day of the groundbreaking, courtesy buses took guests on a tour of the grounds where sites were marked with the projects to be constructed. Visitors were told that Project Six Hundred would take more than 72,000 tons of steel—enough to build the Golden Gate Bridge—and 440,000 cubic yards of concrete—enough to build a four-lane highway to Columbus, Ohio. About 3,500 construction workers were needed.

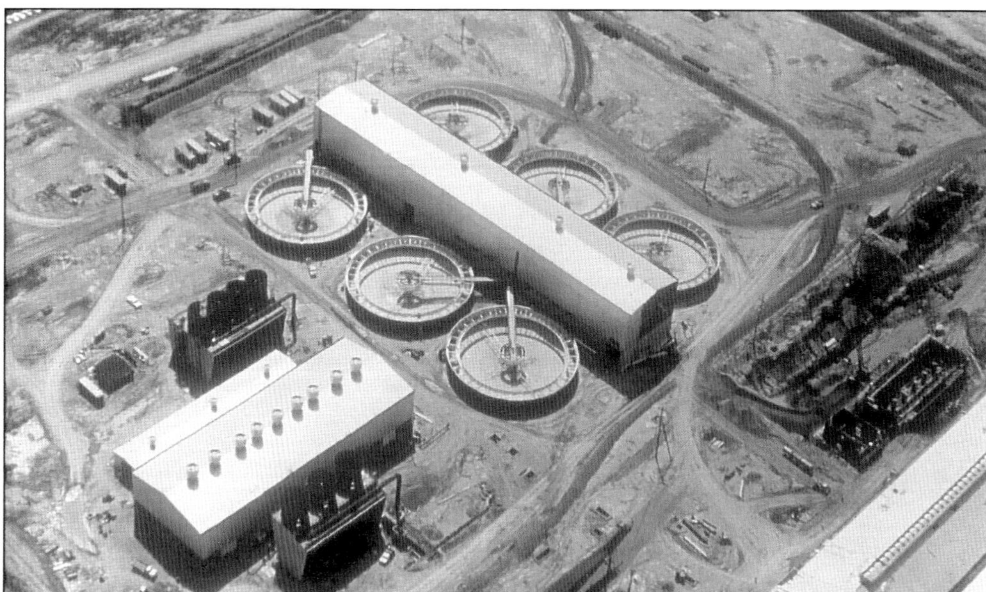

Among the features of Project Six Hundred was a pump house with six giant clarification units. Each basin held 1,700,000 gallons of water. Waste water was cleaned prior to its re-usage inside the pump house. This was enough water to supply the city of Cincinnati, Ohio.

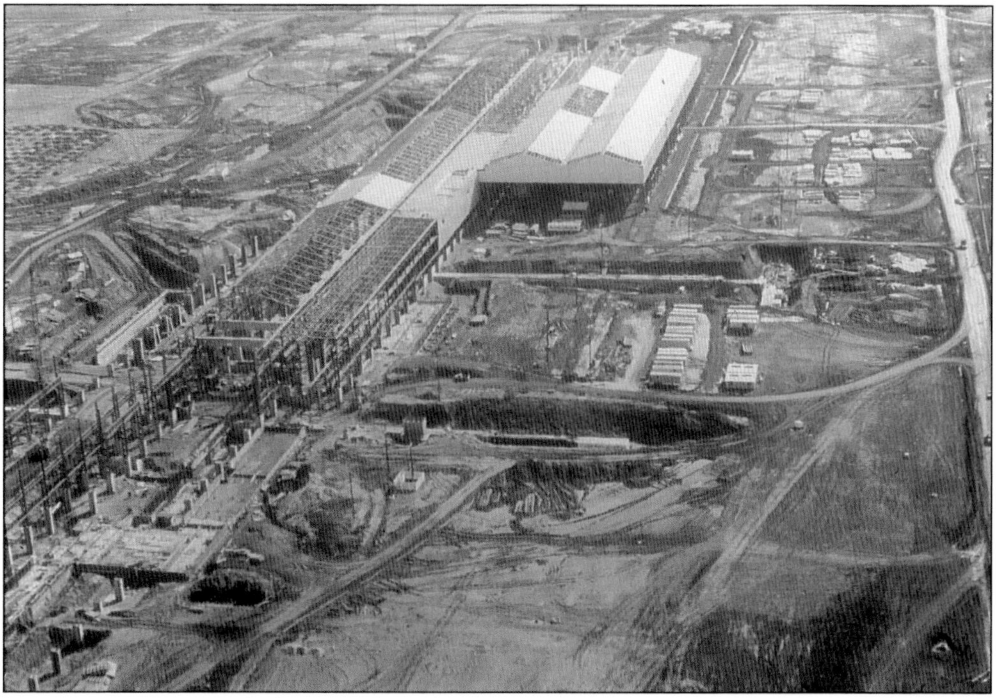

Here is an aerial view looking southward, as Project Six Hundred was under construction in March of 1966. During this project, Armco reached its peak local employment record of 8,000.

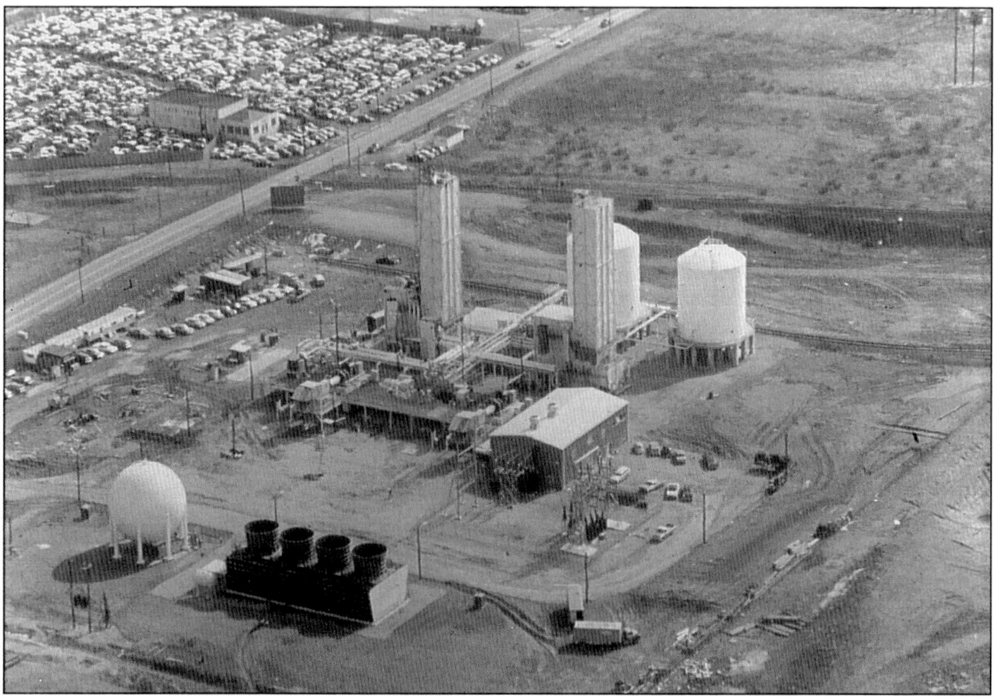

Project Six Hundred included the building of support service units for the new Armco Plant, including this oxygen plant on Yankee Road. Its capacity was more than 800 tons of oxygen per day.

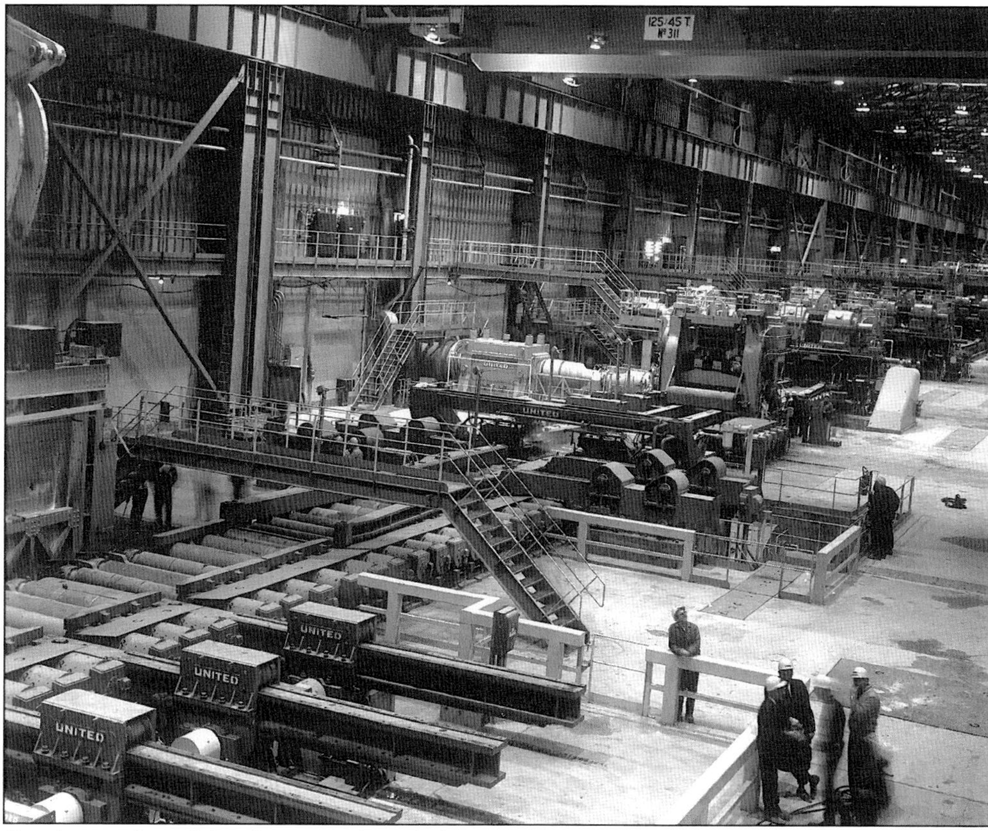

On August 31, 1968, this 86-inch-wide hot strip mill in the Project Six Hundred complex officially replaced the old East Works mill that had been in operation for 40 years.

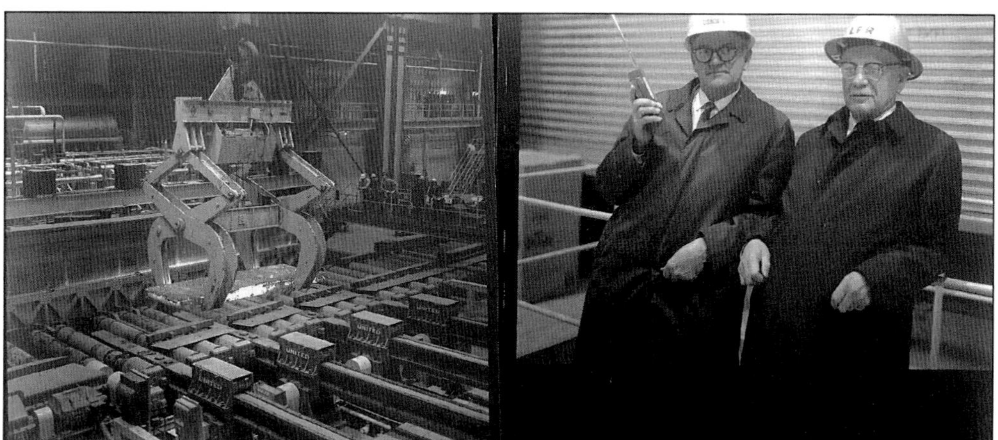

Engineers watched that first slab as it began its experimental journey to make certain that the new equipment was operating as designed. The photographer's camera followed the slab through the new mill that night. (Courtesy of the Vorhis Collection.)

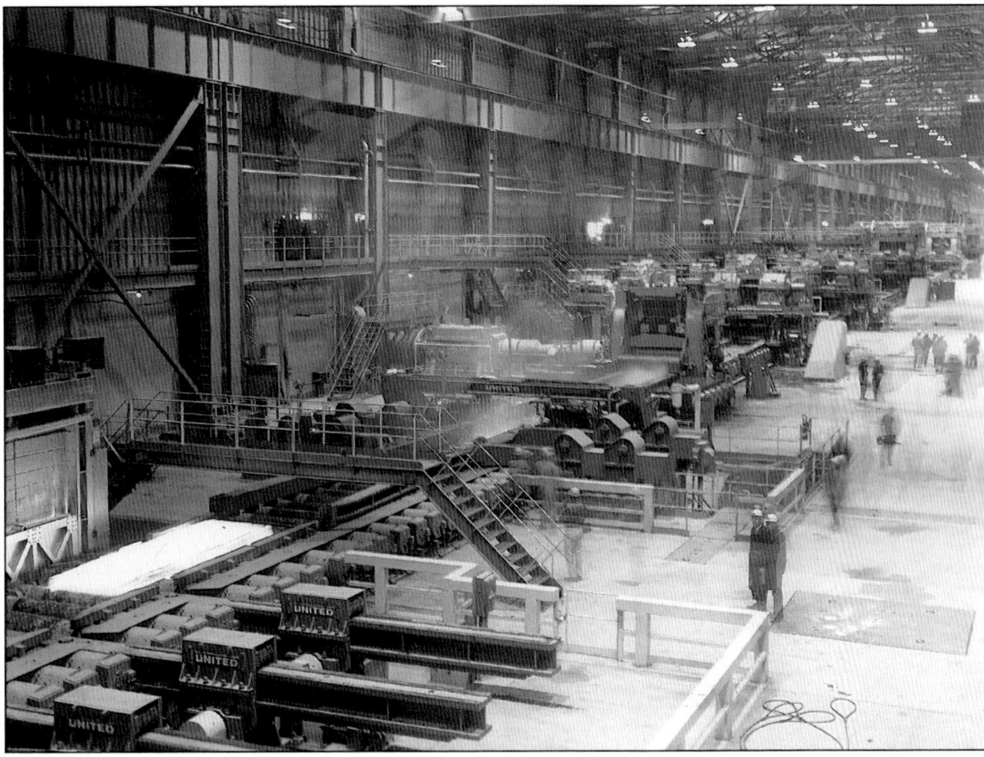

A glowing slab begins its travels. Such slabs average 9.5 inches thick, and are 30 feet long.

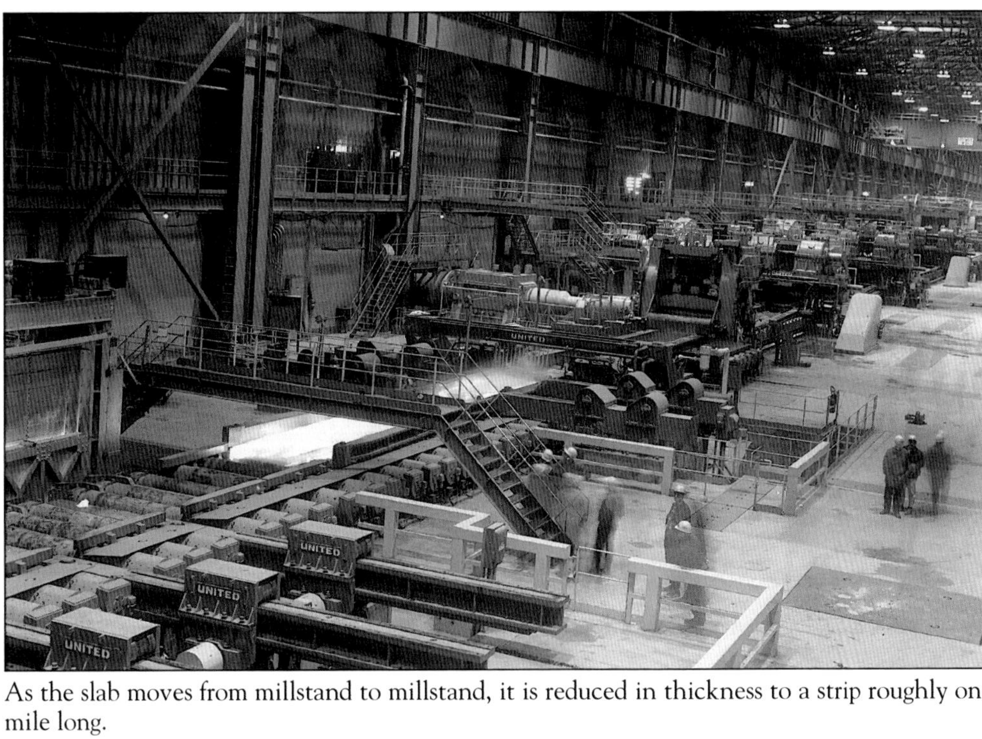

As the slab moves from millstand to millstand, it is reduced in thickness to a strip roughly one mile long.

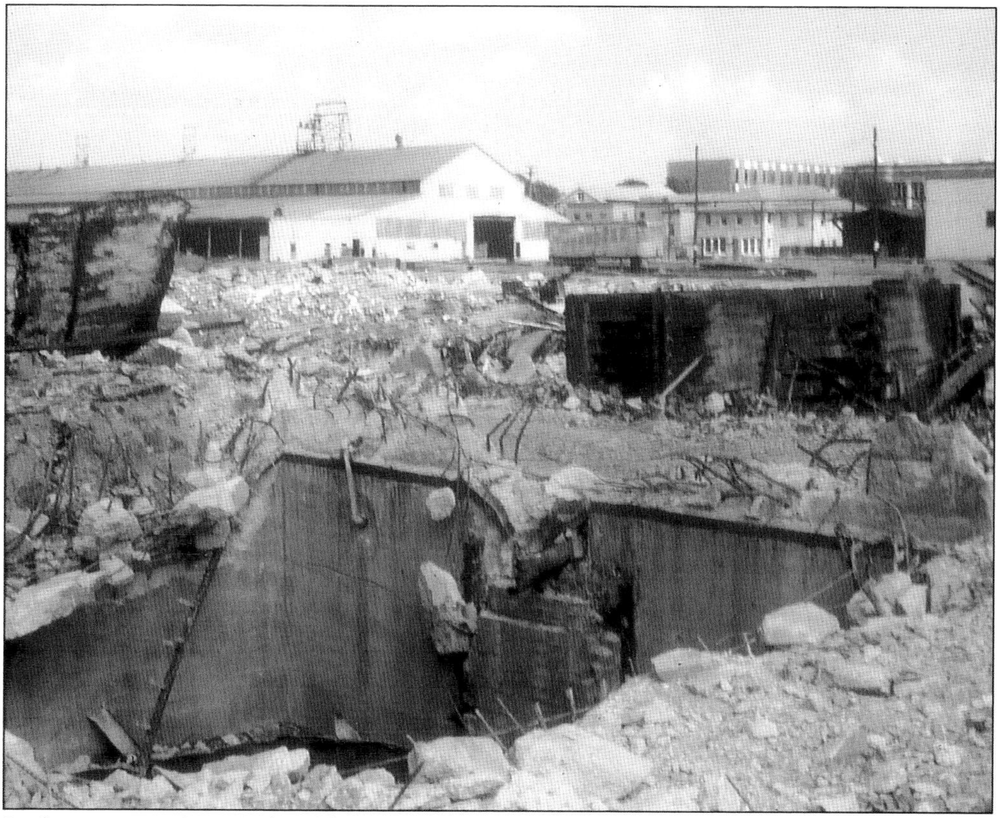

In the summer of 1975, the old Central Works (later Fabricating) was demolished. The scene was one of utter desolation. The company planned to use the land for expansion of the general office complex.

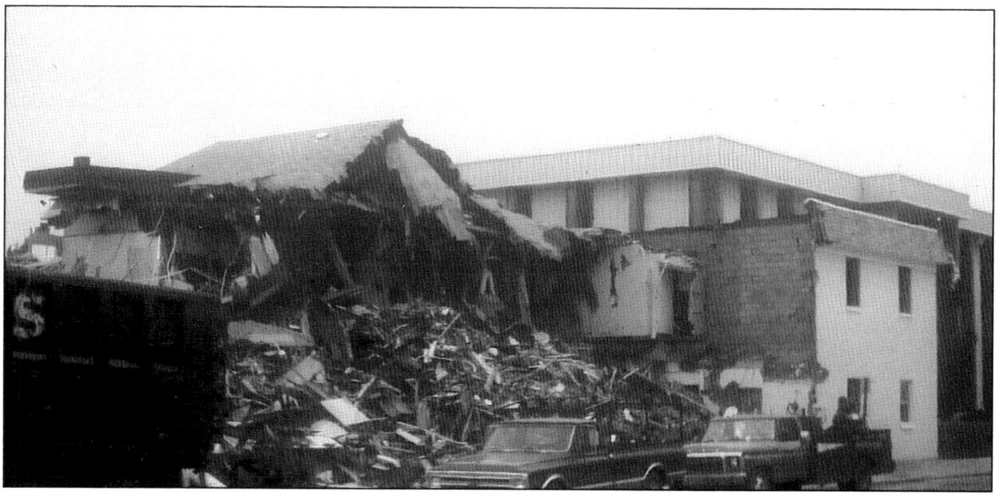

The last original Armco building left standing on the west side of Curtis Street was the old general office building. After the new one had been constructed, it was used for other purposes. It was demolished the last week of July, 1983. An adjacent structure, not seen in this photo, was known as the saw-tooth building, and it came down in April of 1977. The building in the far right of the photo still stands today and was not a part of the original complex.

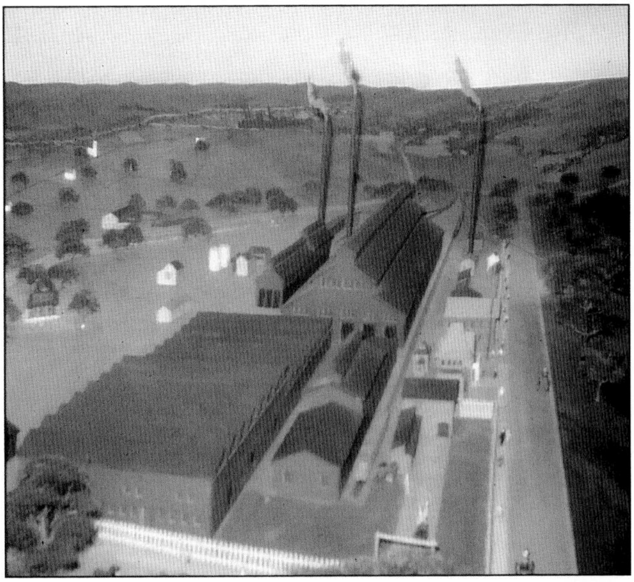

Today the old Central Works is only a memory, preserved by an artist in this drawing.

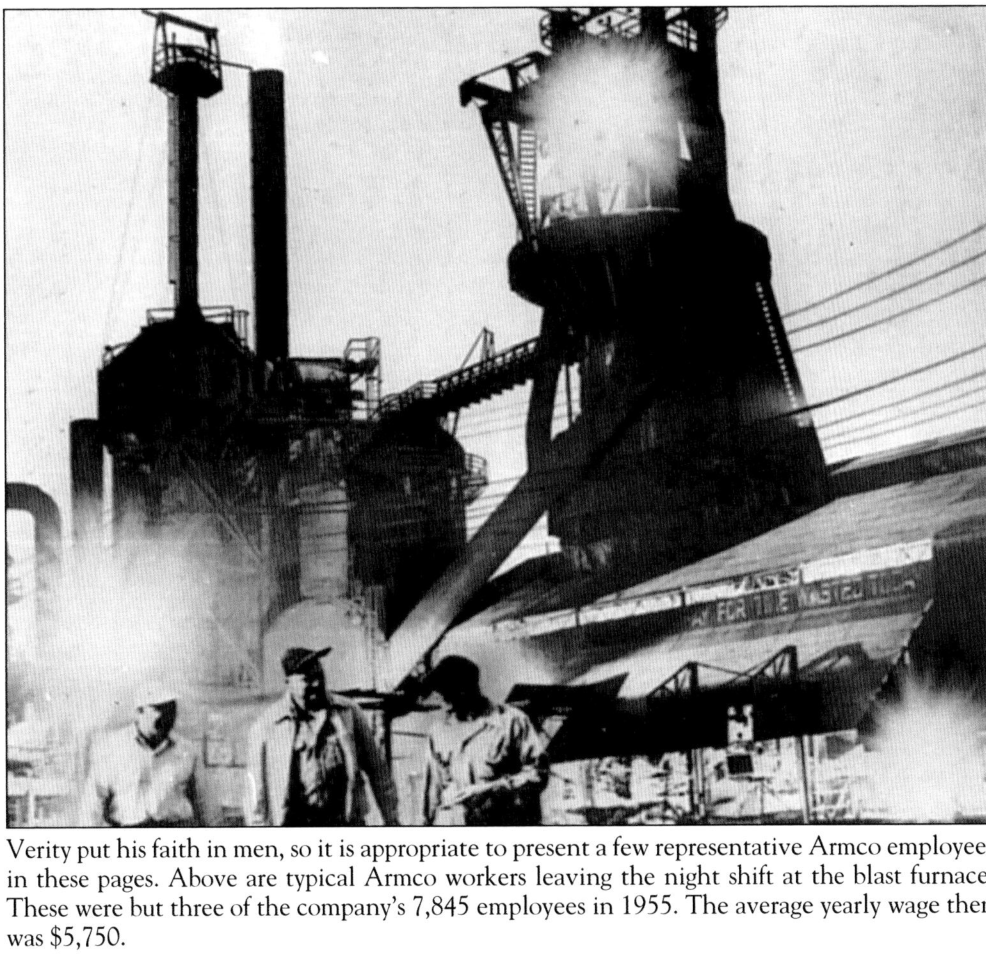

Verity put his faith in men, so it is appropriate to present a few representative Armco employees in these pages. Above are typical Armco workers leaving the night shift at the blast furnace. These were but three of the company's 7,845 employees in 1955. The average yearly wage then was $5,750.

Verity considered this man to be the best choice for an employee that he ever made. In November 1902, a young Charles R. Hook began his long association with Armco as night superintendent of the sheet mill. From that point he advanced to general superintendent, vice president, and in 1930, he became president of Armco. He ended his active career as chairman of the board (1948–1959). He continued on as a director until his death on November 15, 1963. During his lifetime he served on the board of directors of numerous other companies and national organizations, and won accolades for his public service work. His contributions both locally and nationally could fill a book; in fact, they do—in John Tebbel's biography *The Human Touch in Business*.

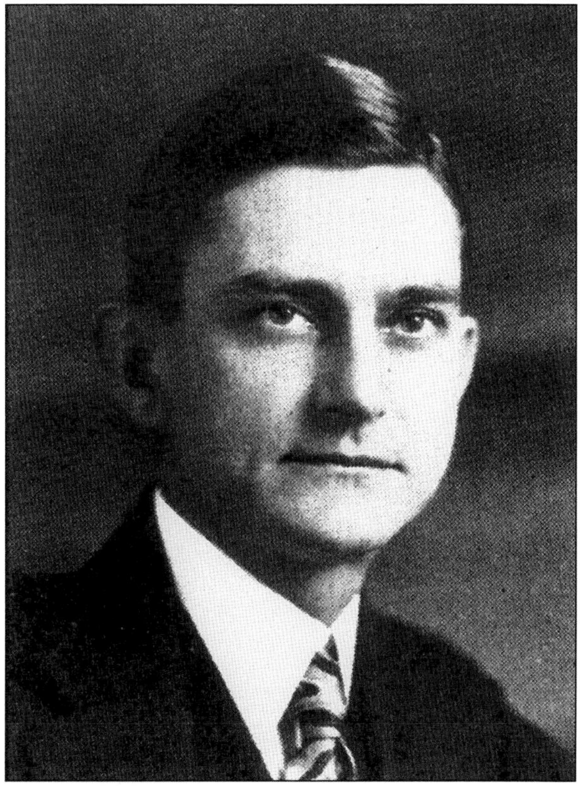

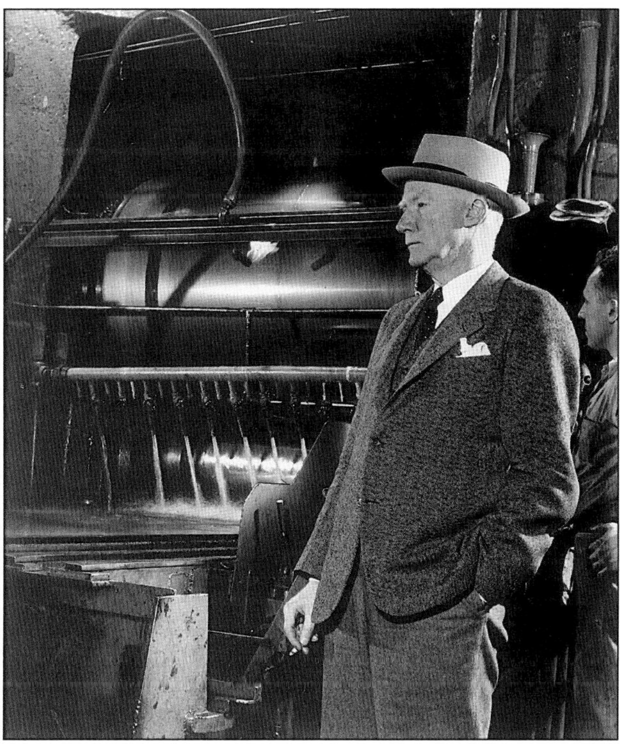

This man is surely the second most important man that Verity ever hired. Inventor John B. Tytus Jr. was a native of Middletown, born in 1875, and a Yale graduate. While working in his father's paper mill, he wondered why steel couldn't be made like paper. He drew up plans for building the first continuous rolling steel mill at Armco's Ashland Works in 1924. This invention revolutionized the steel industry by producing steel more cheaply, thus making it readily available for many uses, especially in appliances and automobiles.

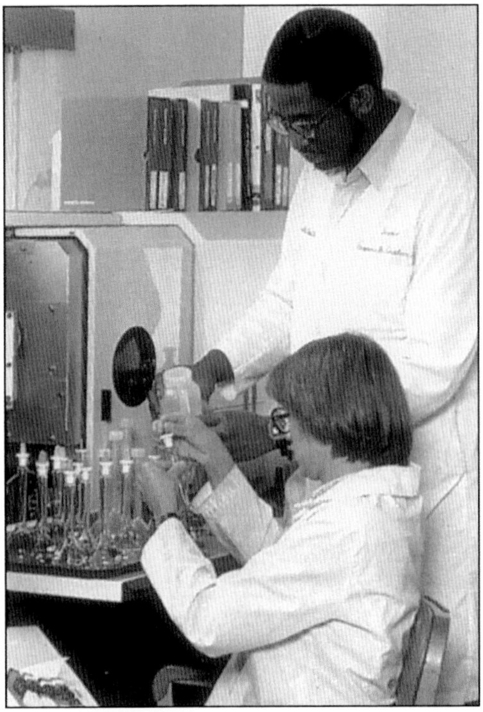

Here is a 1987 photograph taken inside the Armco Research and Technology Center, showing two scientists at work. This fully-equipped lab could provide complete analysis capabilities. At that time, the center employed one hundred fifty scientists and engineers, in addition to one hundred technicians and support personnel.

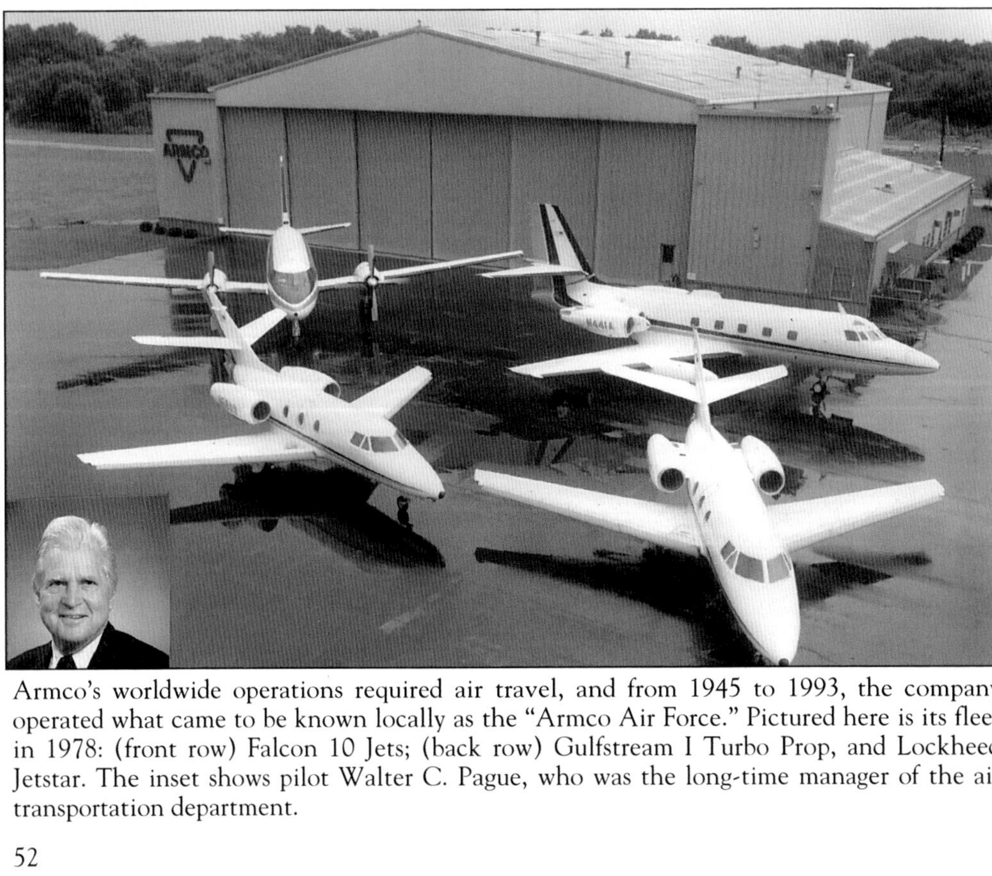

Armco's worldwide operations required air travel, and from 1945 to 1993, the company operated what came to be known locally as the "Armco Air Force." Pictured here is its fleet in 1978: (front row) Falcon 10 Jets; (back row) Gulfstream I Turbo Prop, and Lockheed Jetstar. The inset shows pilot Walter C. Pague, who was the long-time manager of the air transportation department.

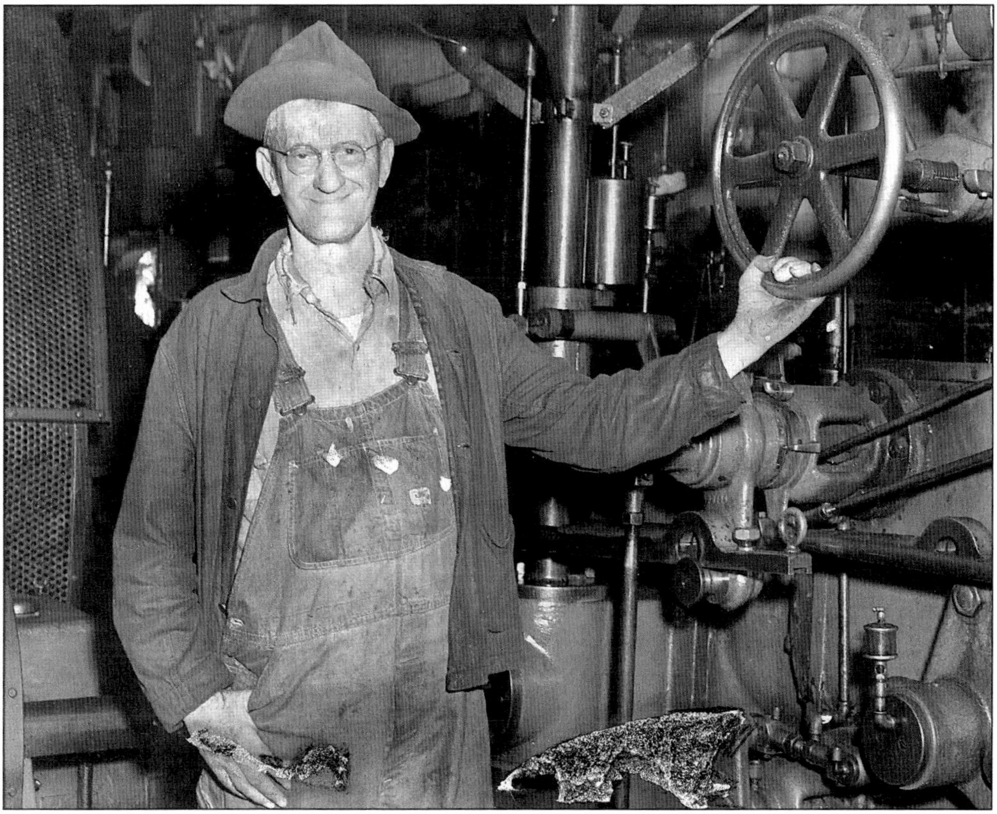

This is one of the 650 employees at the Hamilton plant in 1947. This plant produced pig iron for the Middletown works, which was sent in a molten state to the open hearth furnaces by "thermos cars."

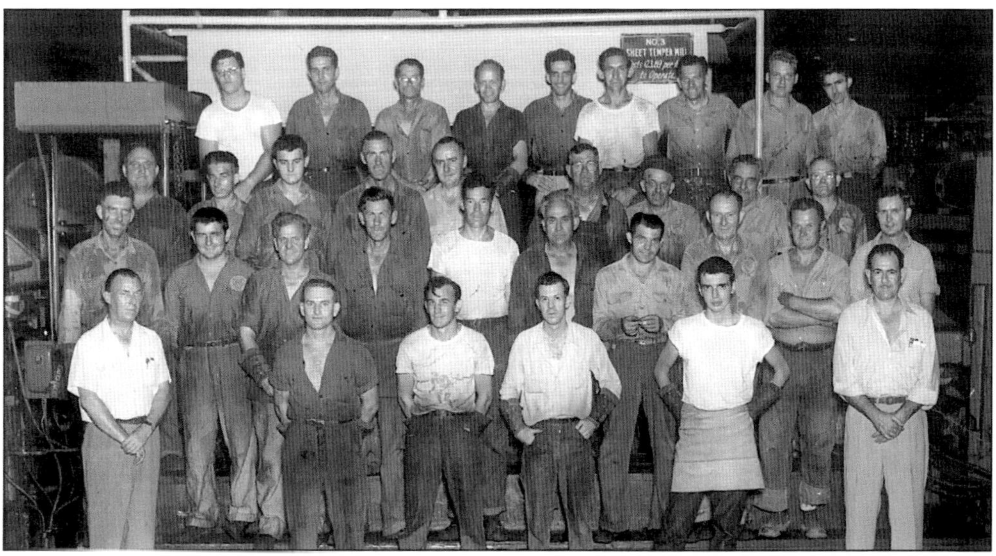

Here is the crew of the Number Three sheet temper mill in July 1952. The names recorded on the back of the photograph include Haskins, Rose, Thomas, Williams, Sherrett, Reynolds, and McClain, but a definitive identification has not been made.

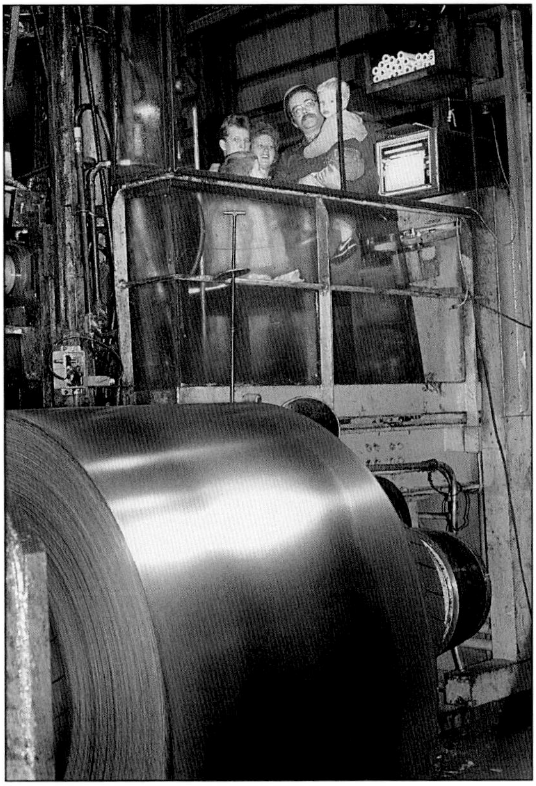

This photograph shows Bill Rogers, maintenance electrician, and his family at the Number Six coil temper mill roller's operating station on the occasion of east processing's 50th anniversary open house.

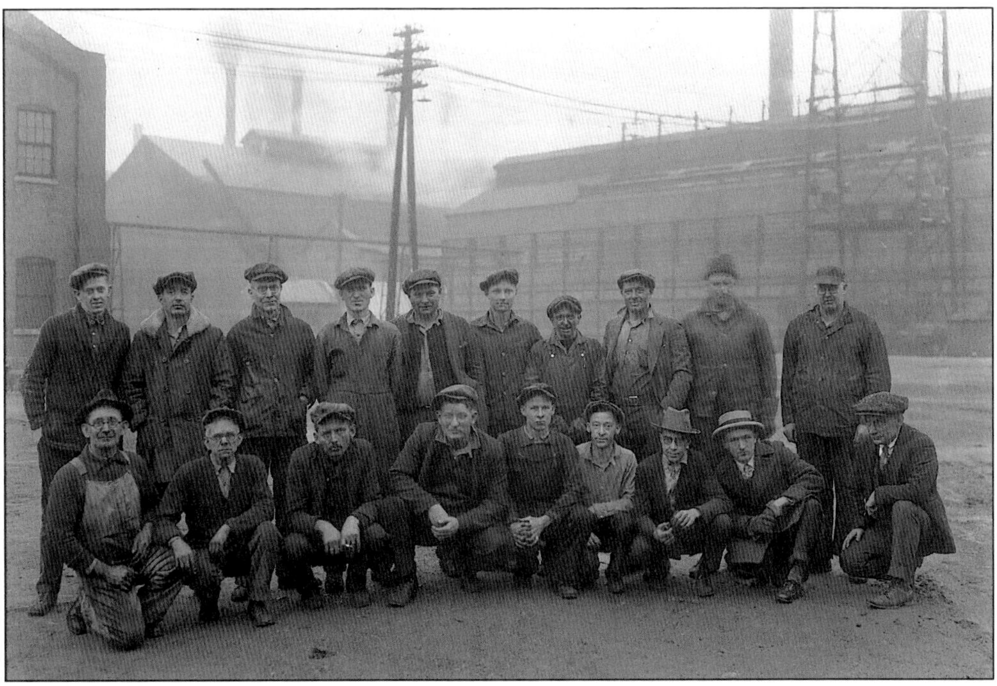

This hot strip mill crew has just completed its eight hours, and will soon be heading for home. This photo was taken one day in 1928 at East Works.

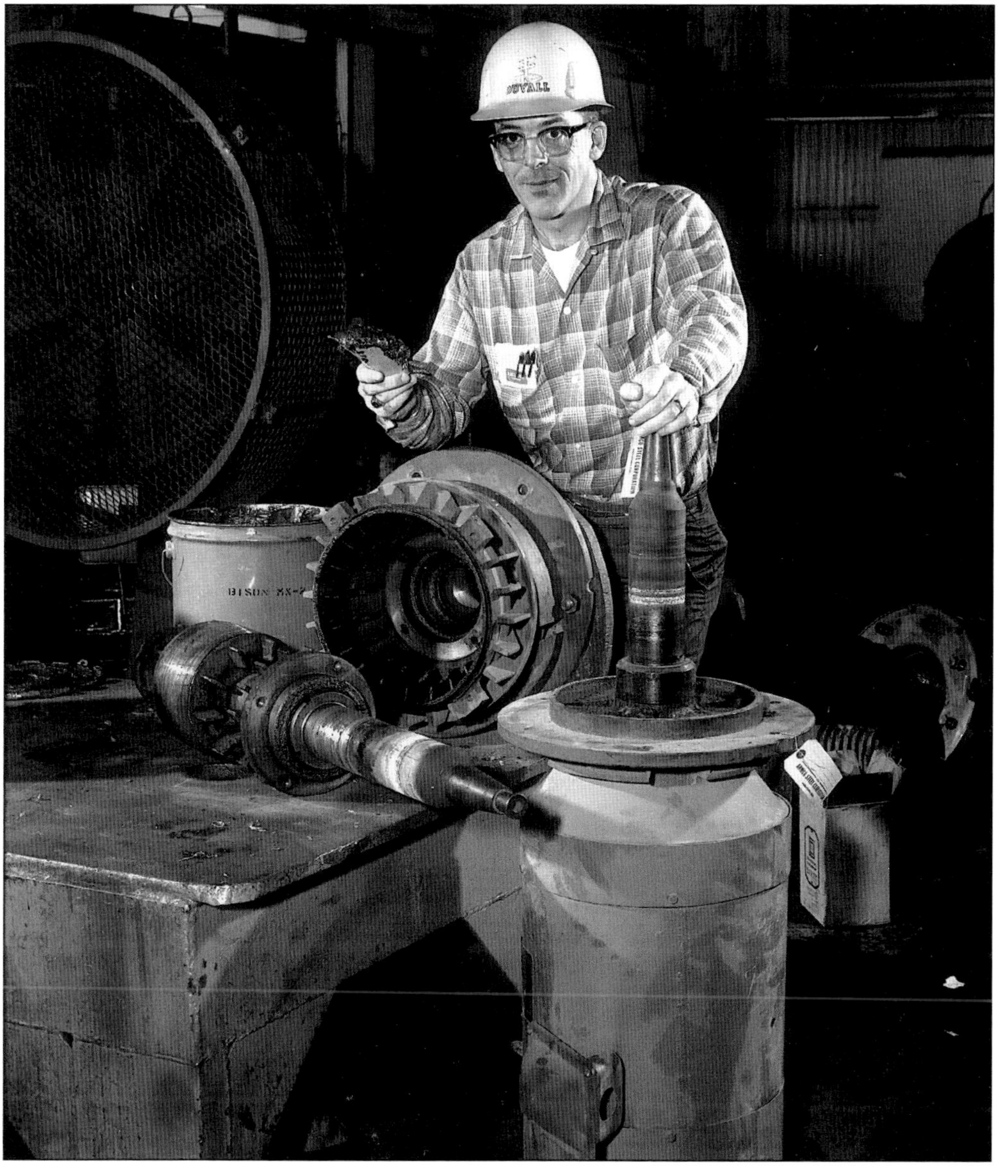

Herbert Duvall (1919–1992) was a representative Armco employee, spending his entire working career at the plant (1939–1981) with time out only for service in World War II and the Korean War. Like almost 20 percent of Armco workers, he was a member of the maintenance department. This group kept the complex machinery in operation 24 hours a day, 365 days a year. The section known as assigned maintenance did the routine work, while the shops department was made up of men skilled in various trades who worked on major repairs and breakdowns. There were ten such groups within this section.

Duvall worked in the electric repair shop. Above, he is shown repairing and oiling a blower motor for an annealing furnace. It was in connection with this work on motors that Duvall developed a cost-cutting idea for which the company gave him a special award.

Duvall's father-in-law, Dan Mokry, an Austrian emigrant to America, joined Armco in 1915 and retired in 1951. His son, Jack Mokry, also became an Armco employee and furnished several photos for this book.

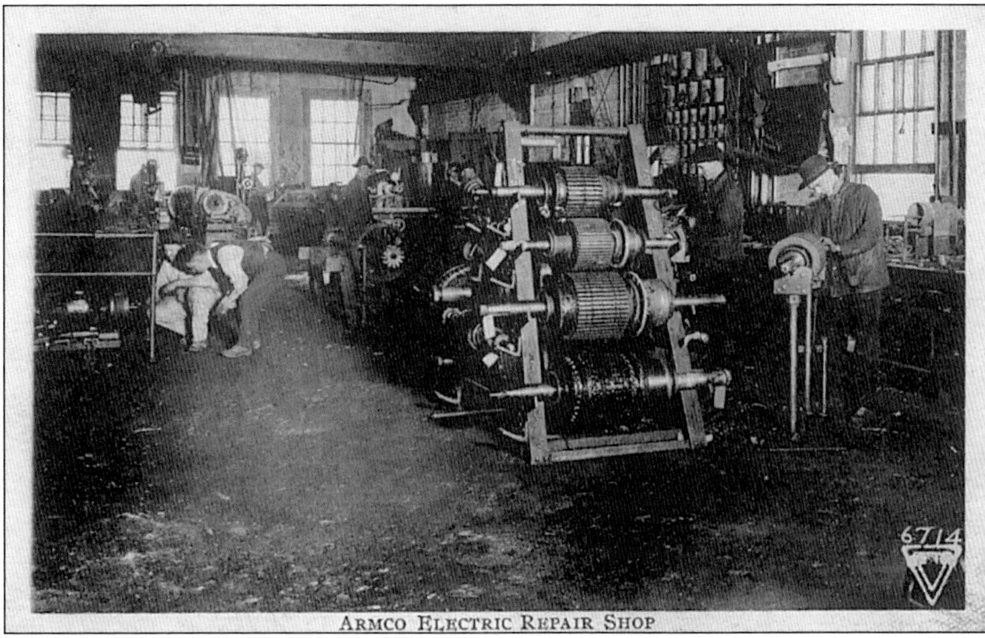

Inside the electric repair shop, the men are rebuilding armatures that are used in the hundreds of electric motors throughout the mill. The photo was taken in 1920, and the building housing this shop was built in 1916.

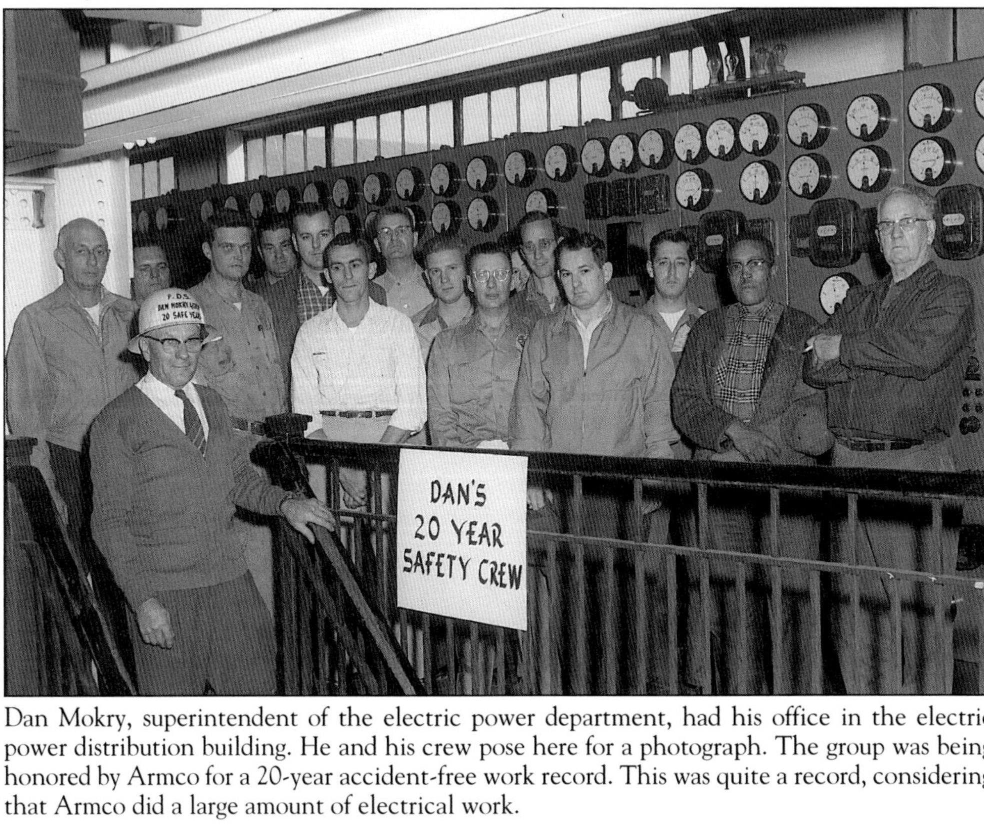

Dan Mokry, superintendent of the electric power department, had his office in the electric power distribution building. He and his crew pose here for a photograph. The group was being honored by Armco for a 20-year accident-free work record. This was quite a record, considering that Armco did a large amount of electrical work.

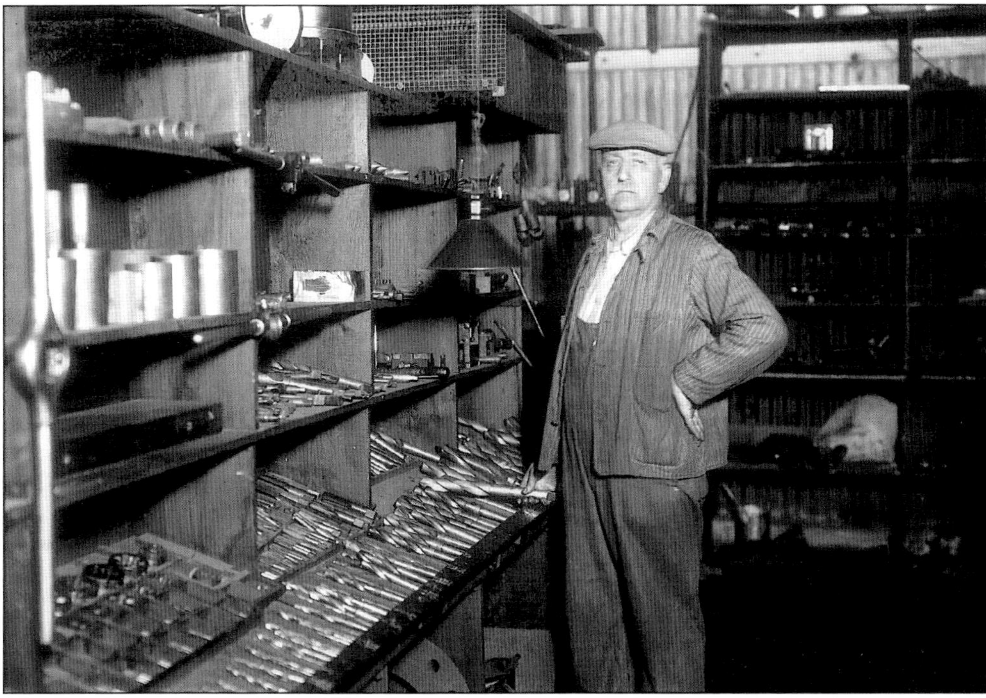

Charles Metty is caught by a photographer as he comes into the machine shop tool room at Armco. The large company machine shop had just about anything needed to repair equipment that failed, unless it was a major breakdown that required external rebuilding.

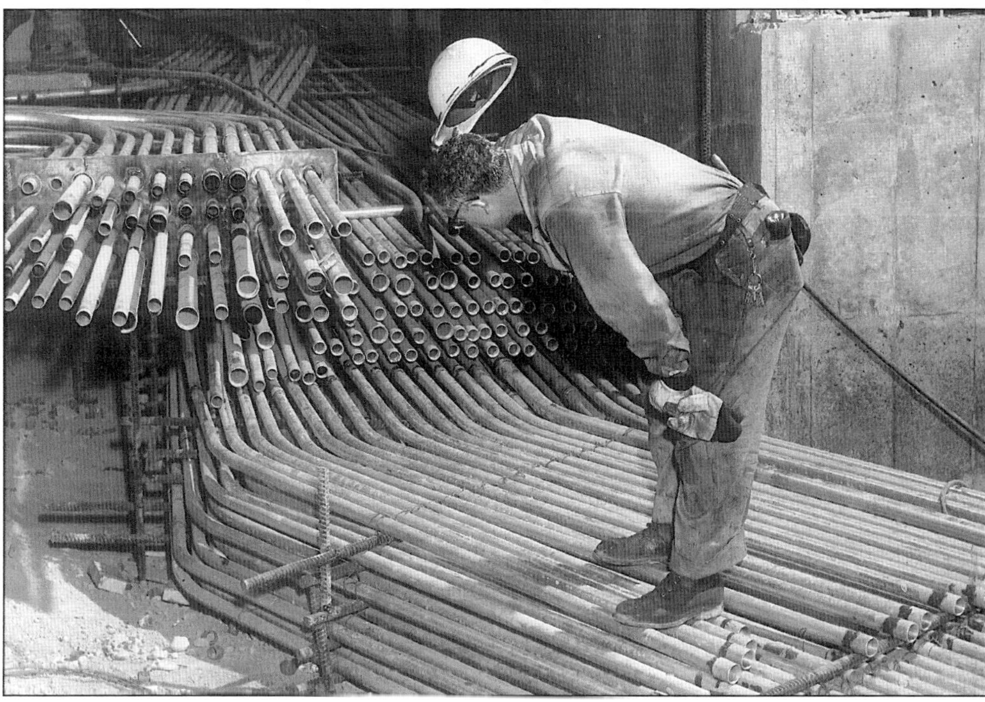

Lee Miller, a Middletown Works electrician, is shown studying where which wires will go into each conduit in the new Number Three zinc grip-coating line, which was built in August, 1960.

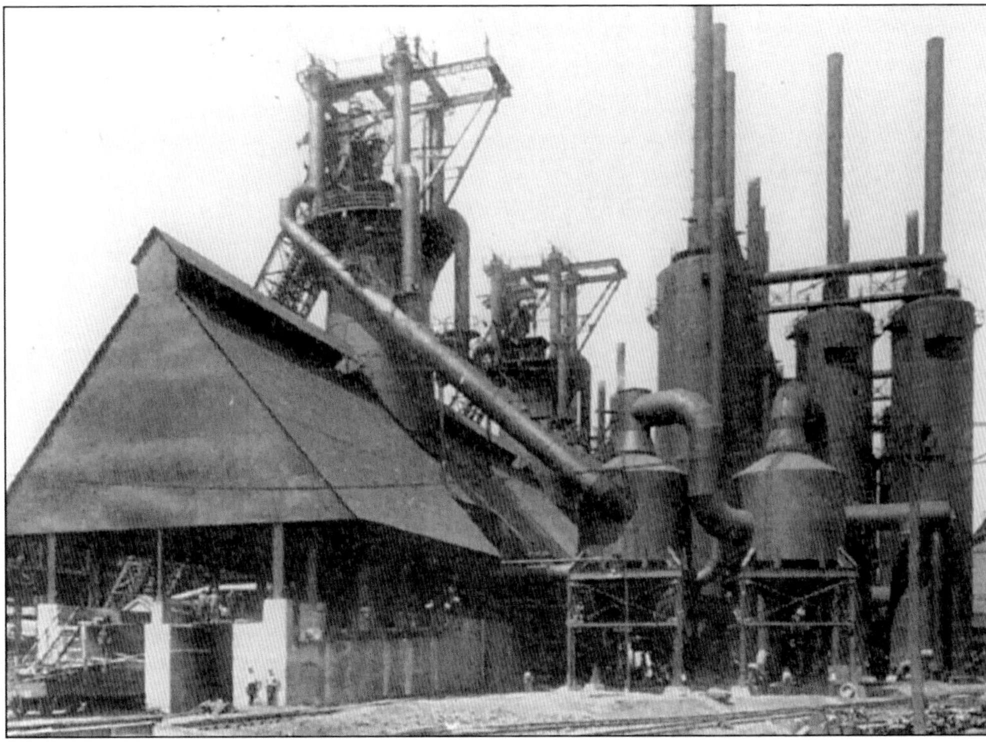

As Armco did not have a blast furnace in Middletown until 1953, it required a source of pig iron. As already noted, the Kopper's plant in New Miami helped supply that need, as did the Columbus Iron and Steel Company, which Armco acquired in 1917. Here is the first Columbus blast furnace, which came on line in 1900, just in time for Armco's start up.

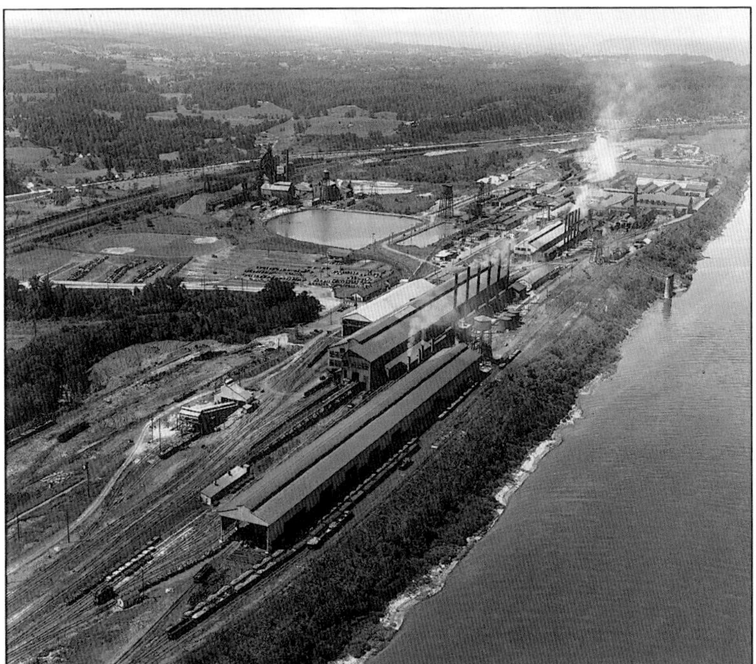

On December 31, 1921, Armco purchased the Ashland (Kentucky) Iron and Mining Company which had two blast furnaces, six open hearth furnaces, blooming, and sheet mills. Here is a 1949 view of the Ashland Plant along the Ohio River. Ashland's slabs are still vital to the Middletown Works.

Three

ARMCO AND ITS INDUSTRIAL NEIGHBORS

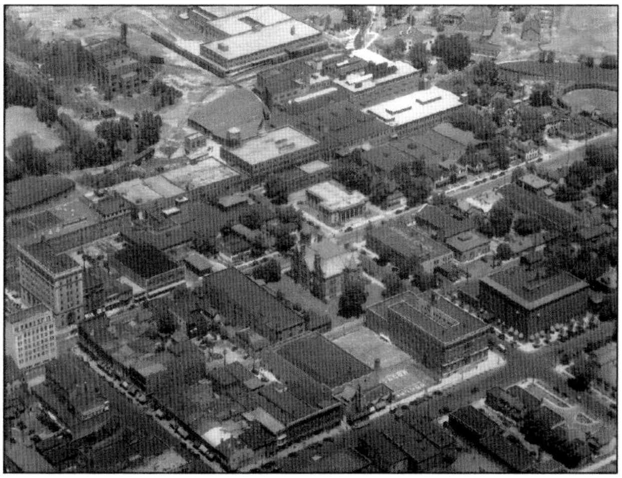

Middletown has been fortunate throughout its history to have a diversified industrial base and industries willing to cooperate in the best interests of the city. For many years, this was accomplished through the organization of an Industrial Council. However, much of the credit must also go to the hardworking, loyal employees who were willing to sit down with management to settle problems.

By 1910, Middletown had shed its nickname of the previous 50 years as the "Paper City," adopting the sobriquet of the "TIP City"—tobacco, iron, and paper. The steel industry grew rapidly to become the city's major employer. A year after Armco began operations (1901), it had 415 men on the payroll; by 1905, 688; and by 1920, 1,516. During World War I employment reached 5,638. However, employment in other local industries held steady. As late as 1938, employment statistics counted 5,396 workers at Armco, while 2,412 were employed in the paper industry, and 1,078 were still engaged in tobacco processing.

While industrial employment fluctuated during the past century, steel and steel-related industries accounted for about 50 percent of the local jobs, while other manufacturers provided the other half. For example, in 1940, employment figures revealed that 20 percent of the workers were in the paper industry and 10 percent in tobacco processing plants. The remaining employees worked in the manufacture and repair of machinery and services. This chapter is devoted to the story of the industries other than steel.

This aerial photo (Mayfield collection, 1946) shows the old Sorg Paper Company complex north of Central Avenue and west of Main Street (upper right sector of photo). On March 15, 2000, its owners, the Wausau-Mosimee Paper Company, announced the closing of Sorg. However, in 1989, what once had been Sorg Mill Number Three was rebuilt and split off from Sorg, and became the Bay West Division of Wausau-Mosimee (shown in the upper sector, near the river). It will continue in operation.

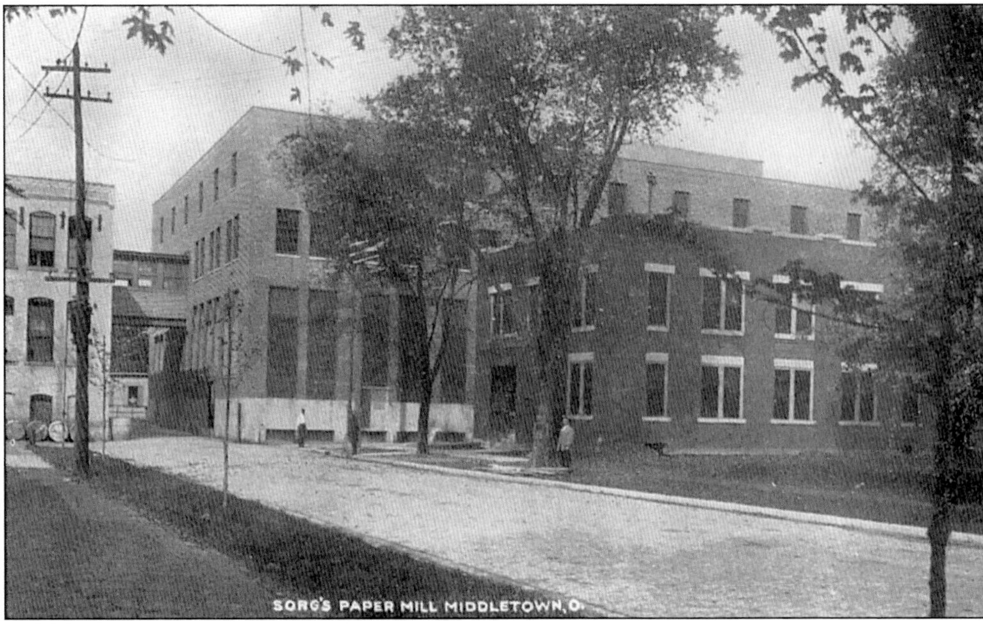

The Sorg Paper Company was born in 1899. Paul J. Sorg purchased the mill (built in 1852 by the Erwin Brothers) that was along the new Middletown Hydraulic, used for power. As a result of mergers in 1931, Sorg ran three big mills. In 1983, Sorg became a subsidiary of the Mosimee Paper Company, presently Wausau-Mosimee. Sadly, it closed May 15, 2000.

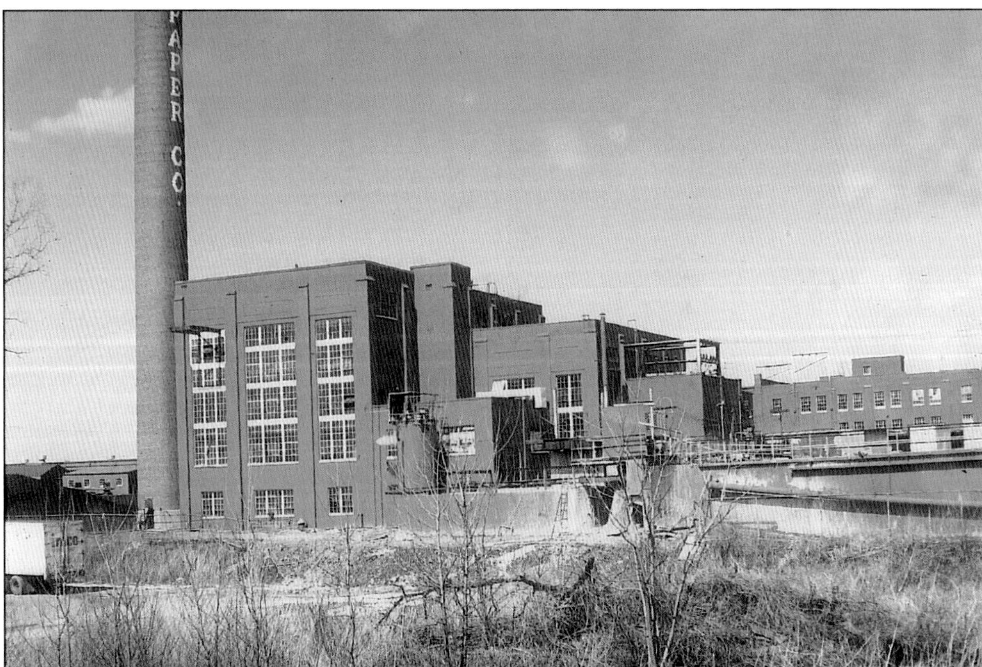

Here is a view of the Sorg Paper Company's power plant, which at one time furnished steam to several large buildings downtown for heating. Its main purpose, however, was for the Sorg complex, part of which is shown in this photo.

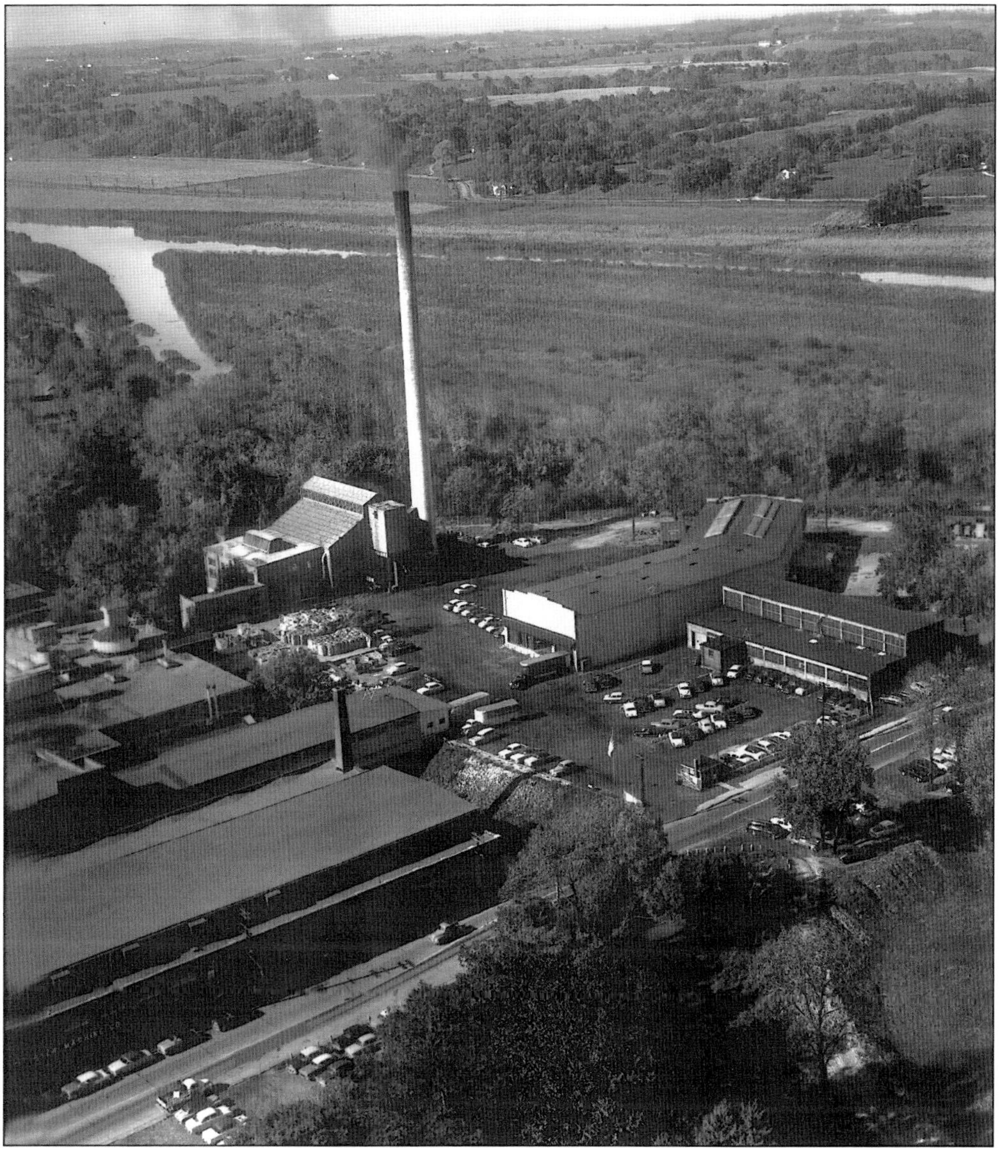

In 1900, there were seven paper companies making various grades of paper and paperboard. The biggest mill was the Tytus Paper Company—once the largest paper mill in the west—which evolved into the Tytus-Gardner Company, and finally became known as just Gardner. This aerial photo shows the original plant by the smokestack.

In the twentieth century, the company went through several corporate changes, from Gardner Board and Carton to Gardner Richardson. It then became part of Diamond (later Diamond International) in 1957. In 1982, the plant was acquired by the Jefferson Smurfit group of Dublin, Ireland. After a merger in 1999, the company became the Smurfit-Stone Container Corporation.

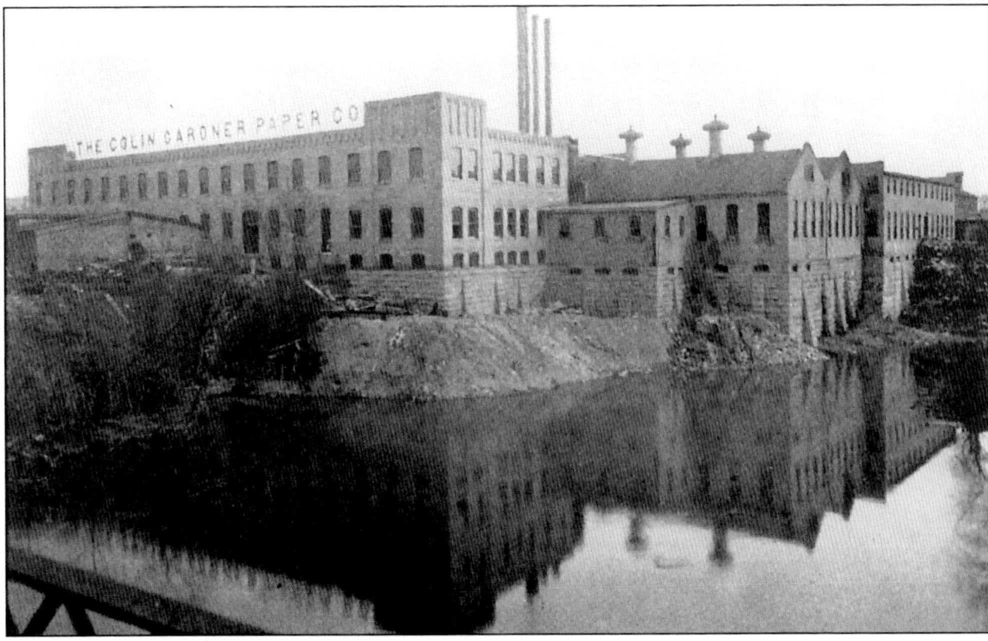

The historic plant shown in the above photo was Mill Number One of Gardner. It closed April 12, 1980, after one hundred years of operation.

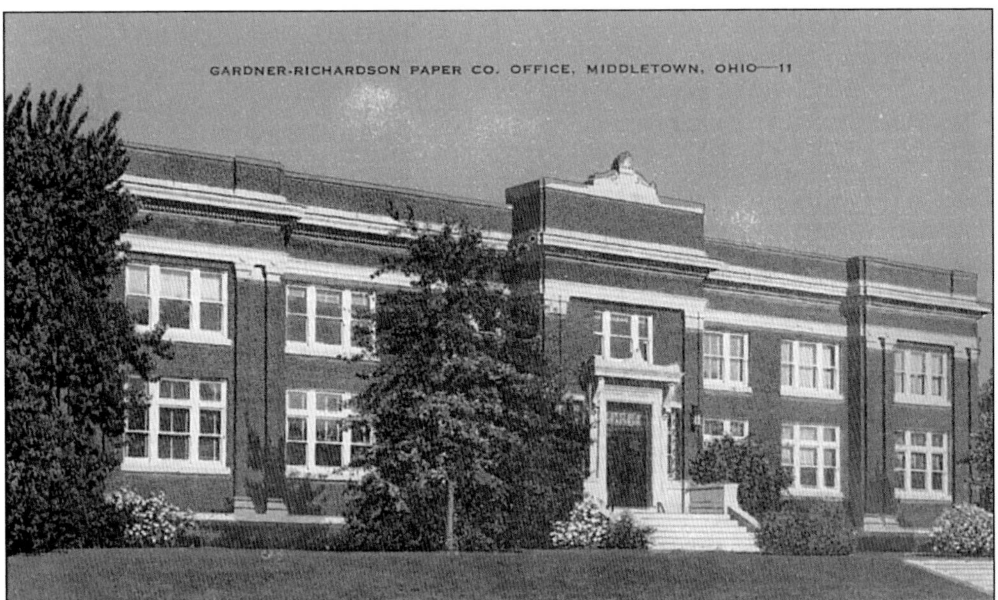

This photo shows the general office of Gardner, while at its peak at mid-century of operations as an individual company. At that time it employed some 1,000 employees, and was deeply involved in community affairs.

Gardner specialized in making paperboard. By 1950, it operated five big machines, which produced over a railroad carload of paper every hour. One of the machines that produced 10-foot-wide paperboard is shown here, as the paperboard speeds toward the "dry end".

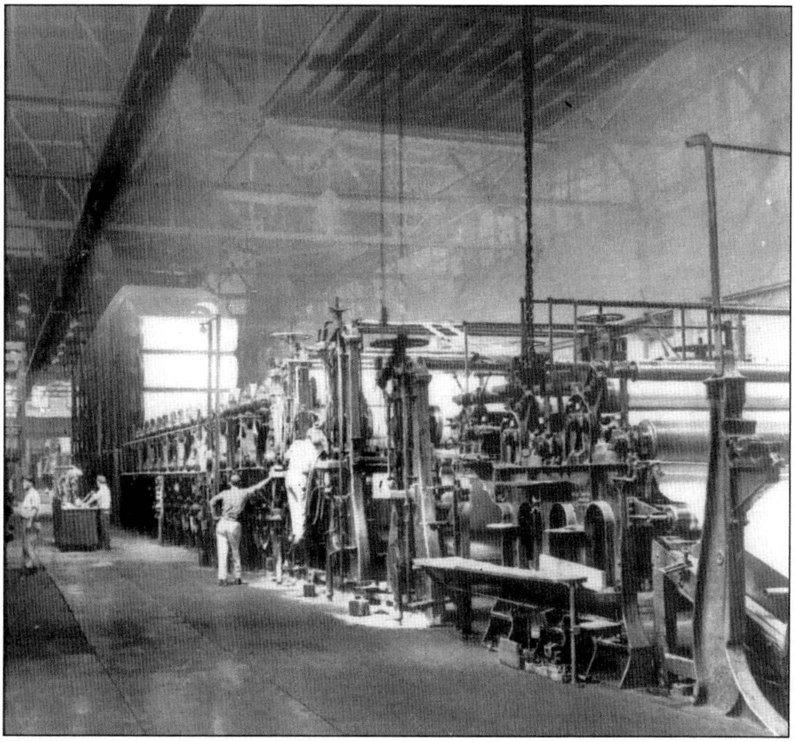

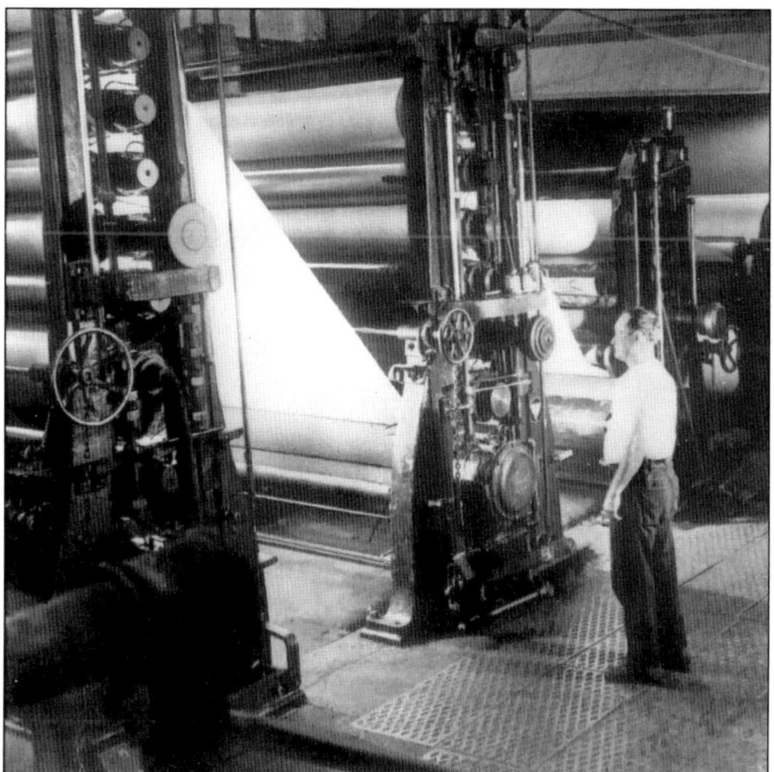

The paperboard, after going through the last dryer stack, is shown here entering the calendar section, which added the desired finish. On this sheet, fine screen half-tones were printed.

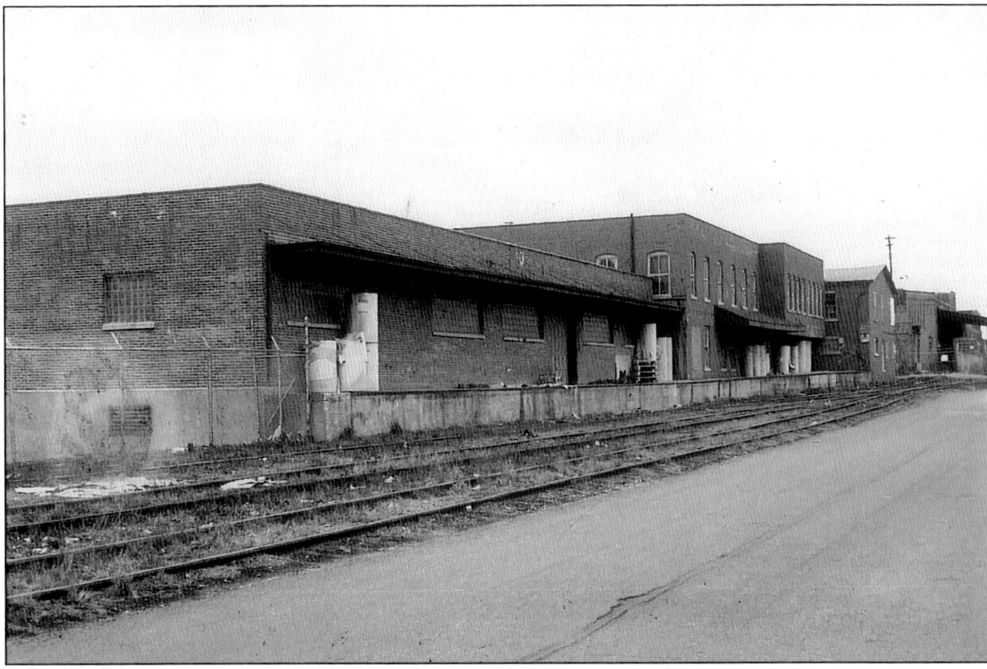

The Wrenn Paper Company, which specialized in blotting papers, was founded in 1858. Its plant, along the old Hydraulic, used water power. In 1958, it merged with Mead Corporation. It went into another line, selling the blotting paper machine to Sorg. Wrenn closed in 1974.

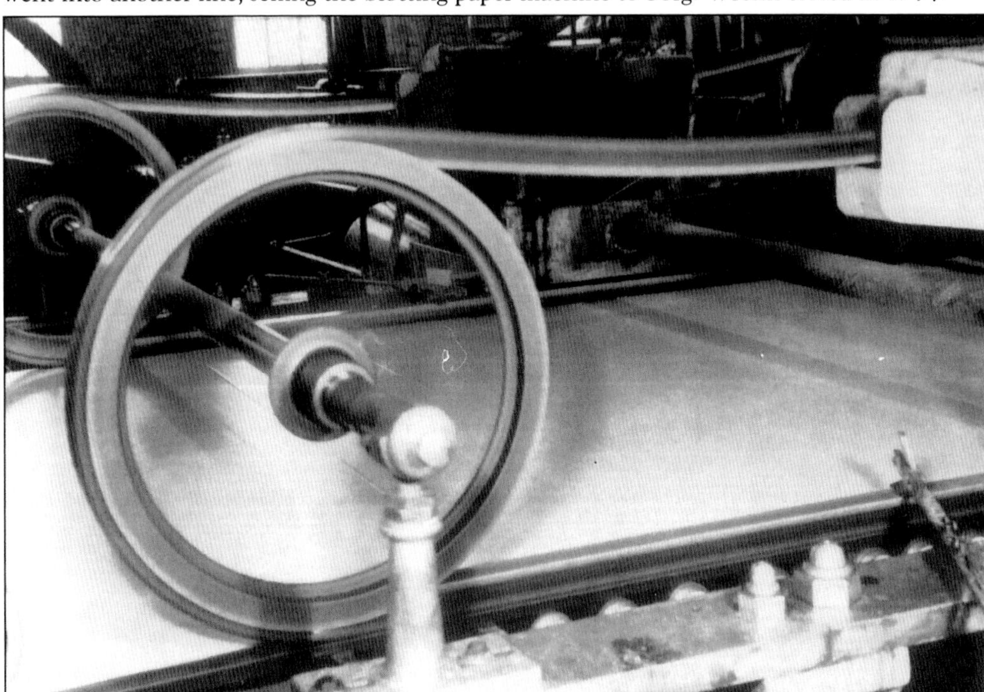

This photo was taken inside the Wrenn Paper Company plant. The screened blotting mix flowed along on mesh copper cloth called "the wire." Here, the sheet is being formed.

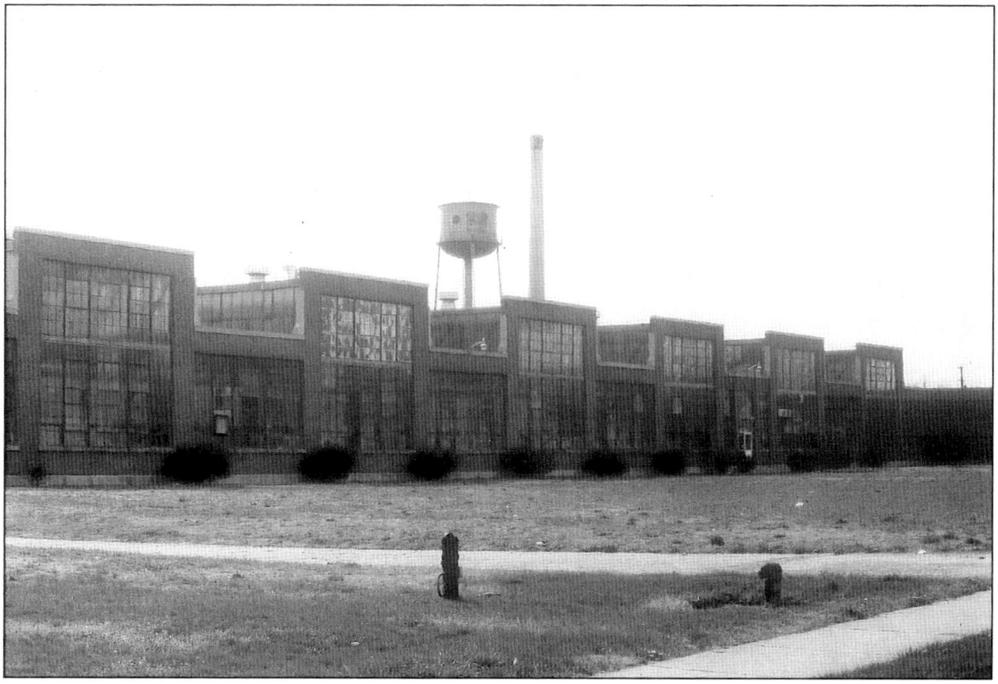

The Raymond Bag Company moved to Middletown from Cincinnati in 1910, after local financier James Lawrence gained controlling interest and became its president. At one time it employed 850 people. In 1920, Lawrence also organized the Lawrence Bag Company. Raymond Bag was later sold, first to Albemarle, then to Hoerner-Waldorf, and finally to Champion before it closed. Since 1986, the old site has been owned by Akers Packaging.

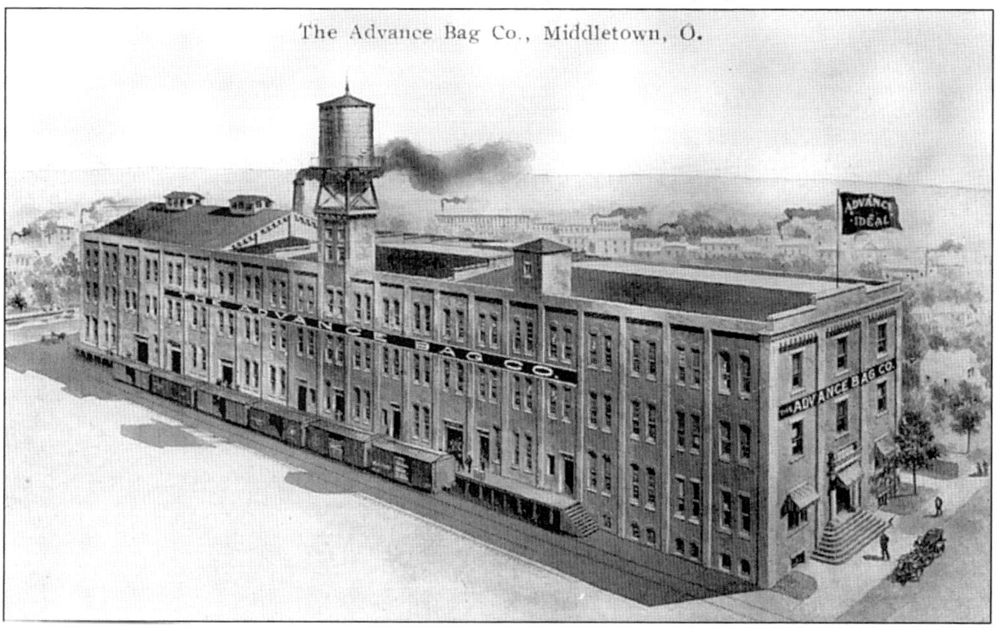

Organized in 1889, the Advance Bag Company became the largest plant of its kind in the United States. Morris W. Renick served as its president from 1909 to 1921, and a few years later it was absorbed by the paper-bag trust. The old building still stands at Main and Verity Streets.

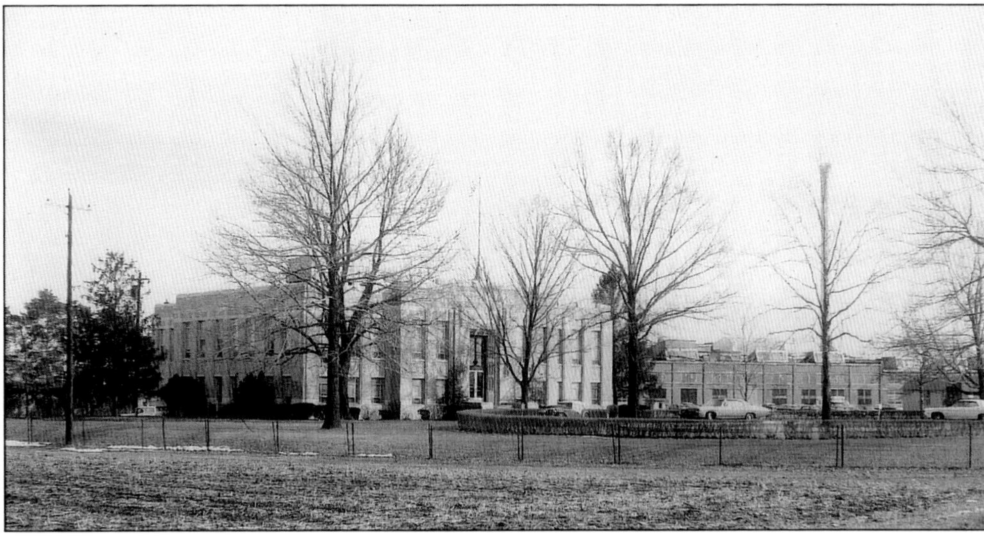

The Crystal Tissue Company, now part of Akers Packaging, can trace the start of its paper-making era back to 1886, although it had been a manufacturing site since 1827. A small, straw-board mill evolved into the manufacture of lightweight tissue and waxed papers. It became noted for its beautiful Christmas wrapping papers, and remains famous for its tissue paper products to this day.

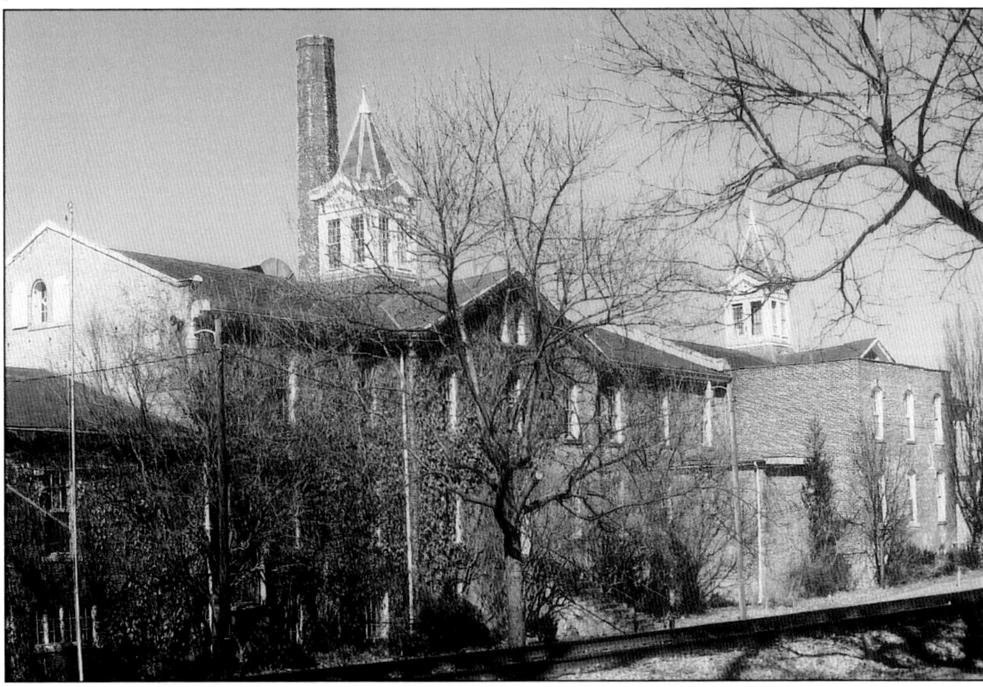

The historic Harding-Jones Paper Company at Excello was founded by A.E. Harding in 1865, and specialized in the manufacture of fine, water-marked writing papers with high rag content. Over six hundred dandy rolls, each containing a different company trademark, were run each year. The advent of the computer ended this kind of business correspondence. After several corporate changes, and most recently known as Simpson Papers, it closed April 30, 1990. The building still stands, but all paper machinery is gone.

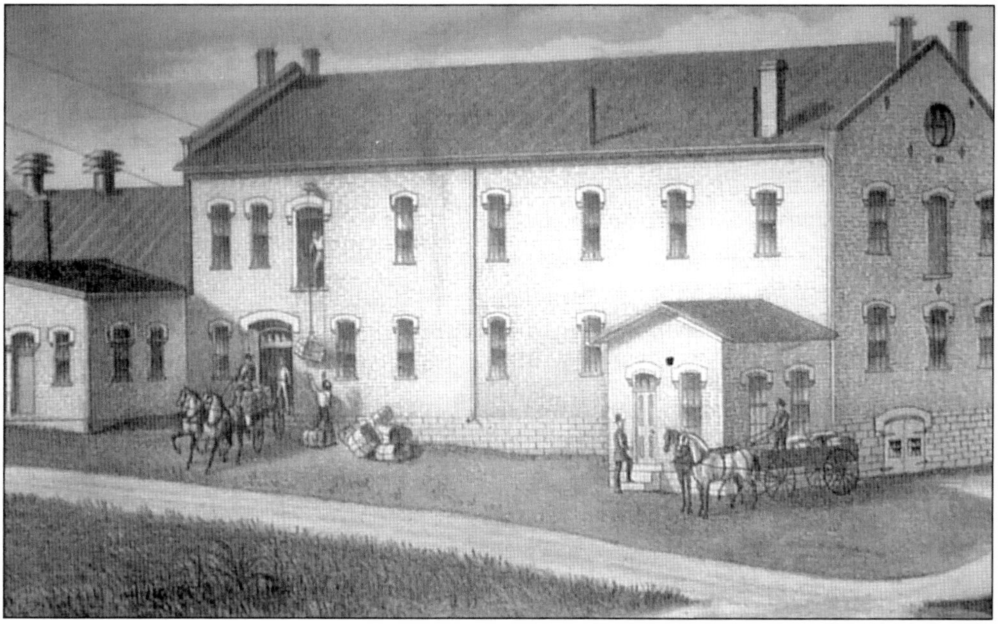

The Middletown Paperboard Company at 427 Vanderveer Street produces boxboard from recycled paper, and is known for its paperboard specialties. This very old mill site dates back to 1827, when a grist mill's waterwheel was turned by canal waters. In 1873, C.H. Wardlow and J.K. Thomas built a new paper mill on the site, producing manila and bag paper.

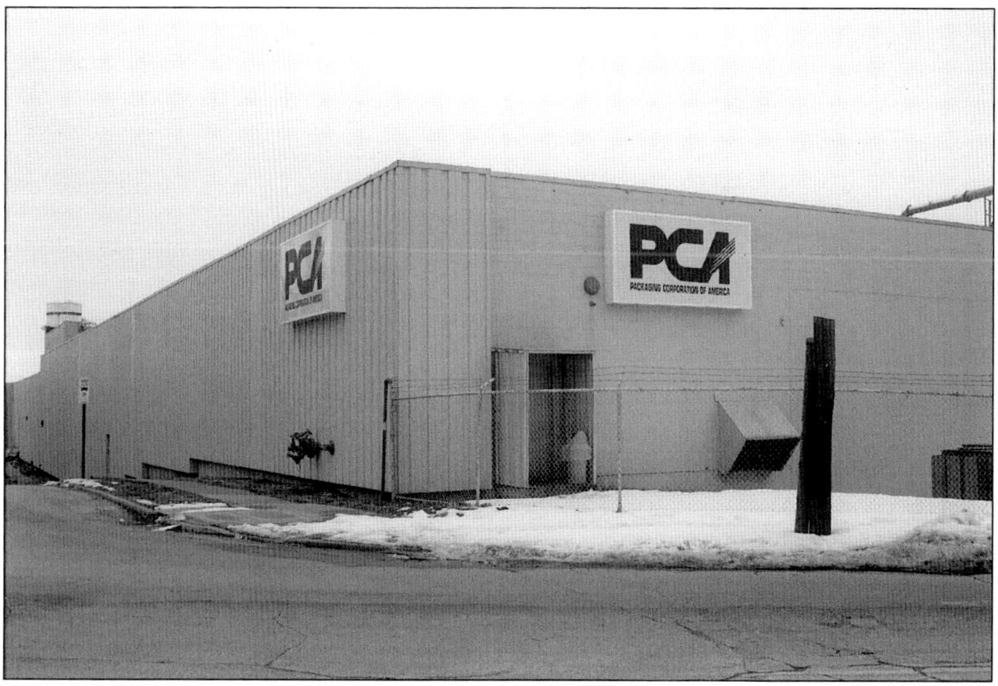

Fairbanks Fiber was organized in 1909 by C.B. Oglesby, and was sold in 1912 to Frank C. Carley, who ran it for many decades. Eventually it moved and became first a part of Ohio Boxboard, then the Packaging Corporation of America, which produced millions of corrugated cardboard boxes a year.

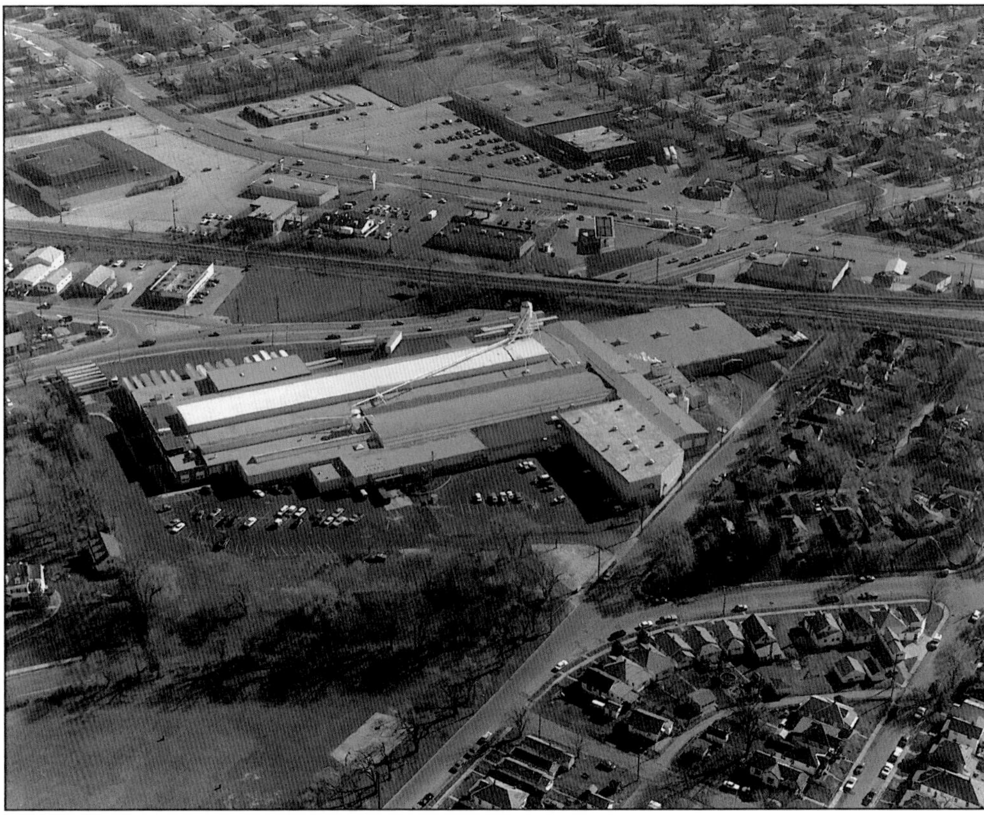

This is an aerial view of Inland Paperboard Packaging, Inc. The company was founded by E.T. Gardner and George H. Harvey in 1928, but due to the Depression, the plant was sold to Inland. Since its beginning at 912 Nelbar Street, this carefully-integrated operation has kept the production line of corrugated boxes and shipping containers moving despite corporate changes.

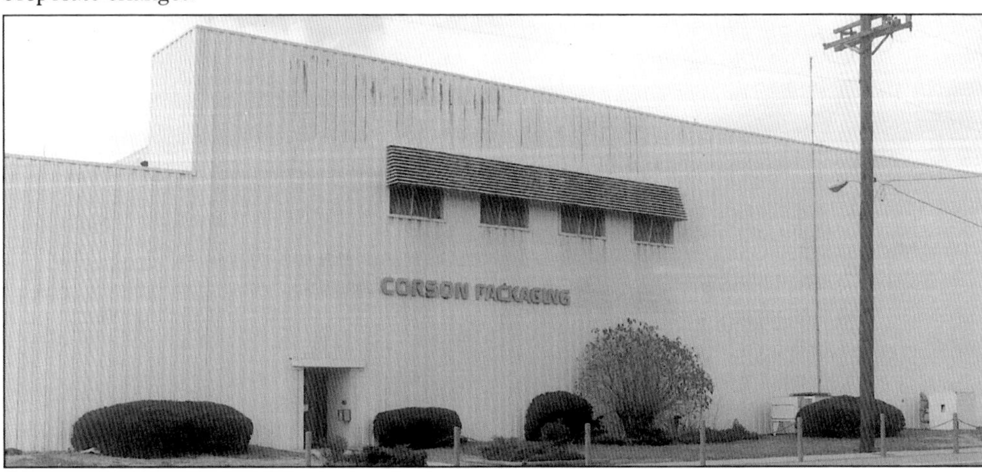

Corson Packaging started as the Interstate Folding Box Company at 300 South Verity Parkway in the early 1900s and grew under the direction of its president, Frank Bergstein. In 1981, it was acquired by American Packaging, and in 1993, by Corson Packaging. It was known for its folding paperboard cartons. Corson closed the plant during the summer of 2000.

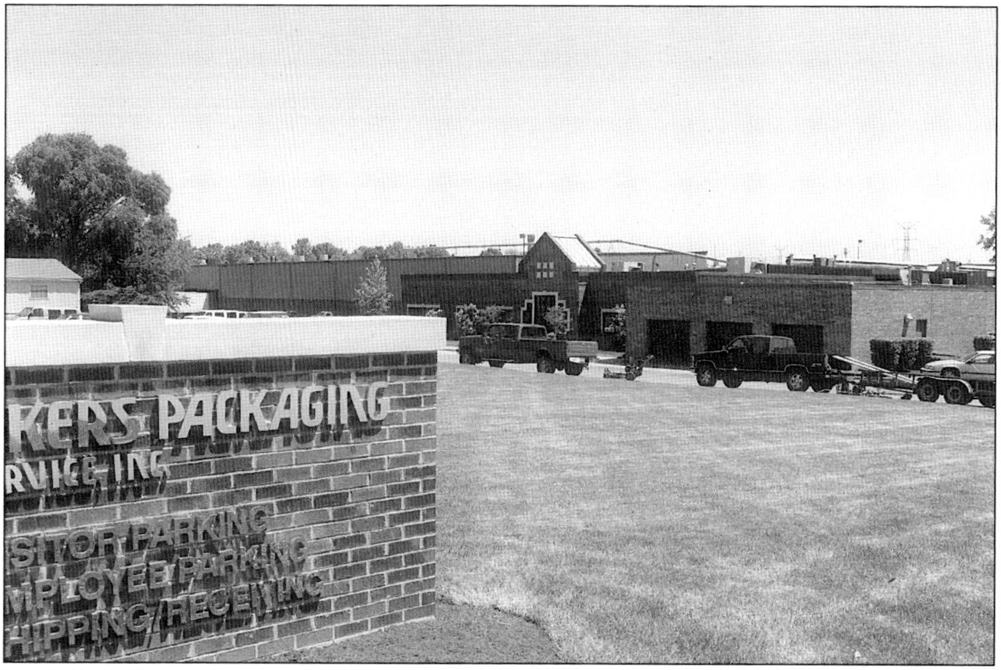

In 1963, William Akers, who had worked at Inland, decided to start his own Akers Packaging plant specializing in custom-made corrugated boxes, packaging materials, and die-cut containers. The plant on Lefferson Road has experienced rapid growth and has undergone several expansions. In 1995, a 100,000 square-foot addition doubled the size of the building.

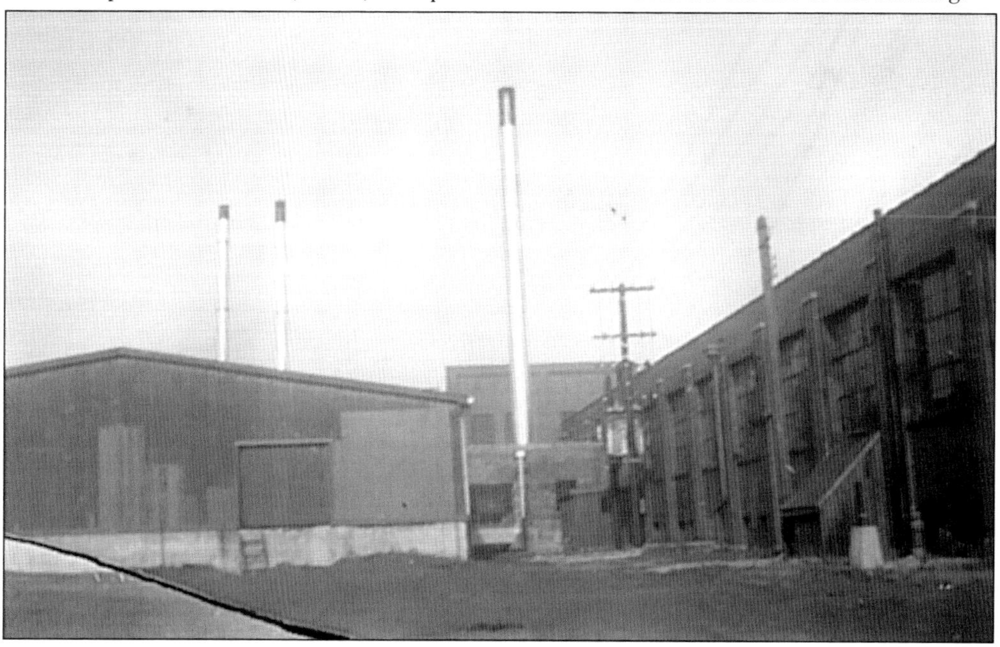
The Middletown Packaging Corporation is located on Reinartz Boulevard. It has long been a part of the city, starting in the early 1900s as the Nashua Coated Paper plant. It later became Ohio Waterproof, and finally St. Regis (Pollock Division). It is known for its printed, coated, and waxed papers.

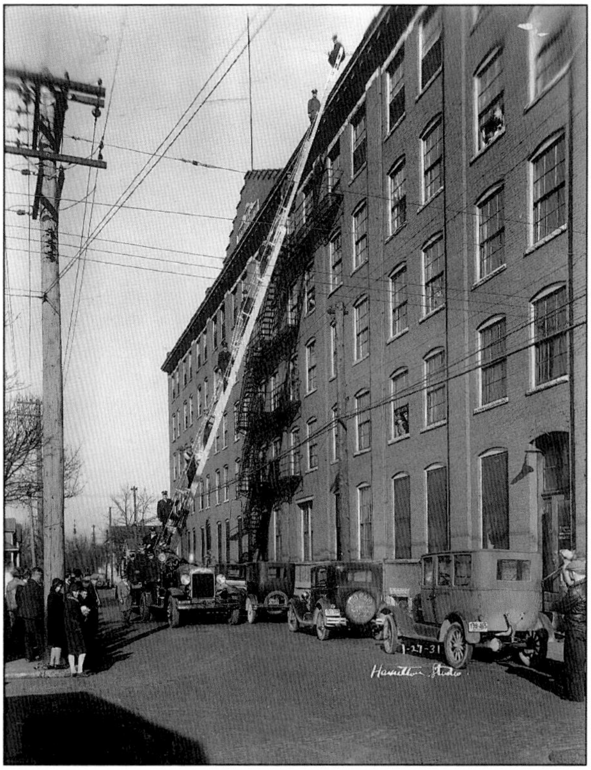

While collectively the paper mills were the city's largest employer at the beginning of the twentieth century, the largest single workplace was that of the American Tobacco Company, successor to Sorg Tobacco. In 1912, the government broke up American Tobacco, and the local plant became P. Lorillard. Its only building filled an entire city block. The plant was closed in 1951 and was razed in 1958. This photo was taken January 24, 1931, and shows the Middletown Fire Department trying out their new motor-powered aerial truck.

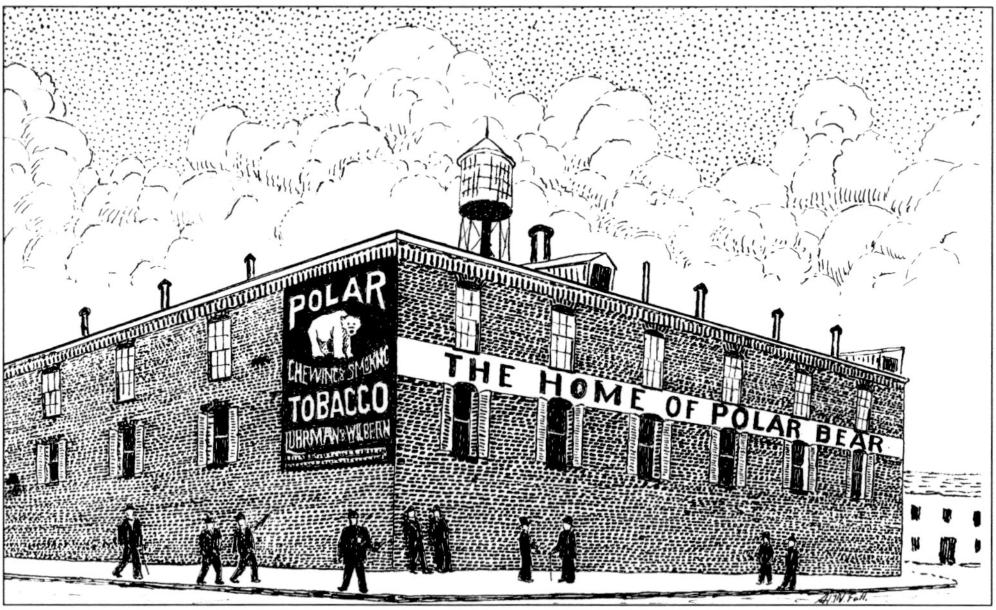

The oldest section of the complex was the one in which the company's most popular brand of chewing tobacco was manufactured. As it was located across from the Big Four Railroad depot, it could be seen from the railroad coaches as they approached the stop. The conductor only had to call out "Polar Bear" (the brand of tobacco) and everyone knew the train had arrived in Middletown.

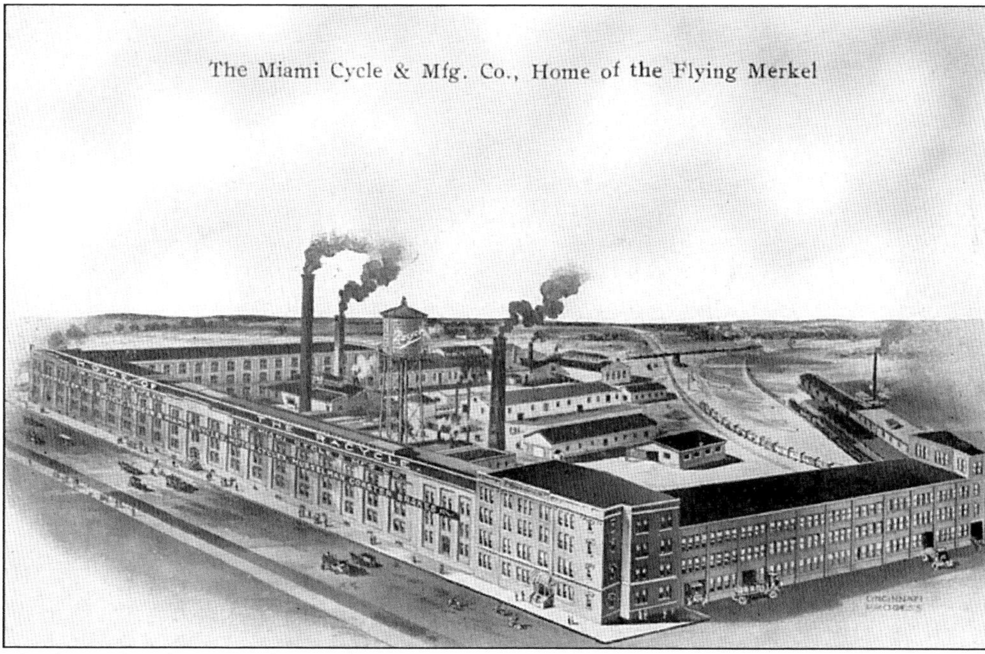

This large plant began as the McSherry Manufacturing Company, which made farm implements. Most of the plant, once one of the city's major industries, was destroyed by a raging fire on March 11, 1972. At times as many as 1,500 people worked in the huge structure. It later became the Miami Cycle and Manufacturing Company.

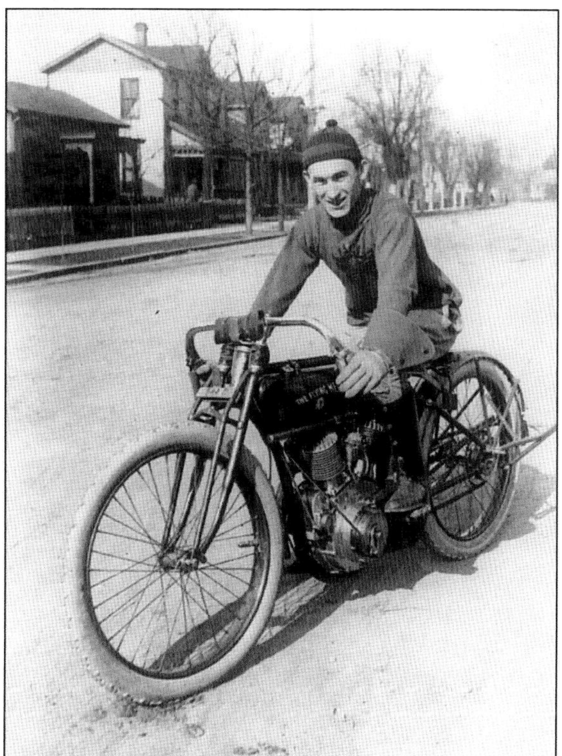

As Miami Cycle, it manufactured millions of bicycles and motorcycles. During World War I, it was converted to a large munitions factory but returned to the production of motorcycles and bicycles after the war. However, due to the popularity of the automobile, that market soon faded away. The company then became Miami Cabinet. Here, William Weikel is shown on the company's most famous product—the "Flying Merkel" motorcycle.

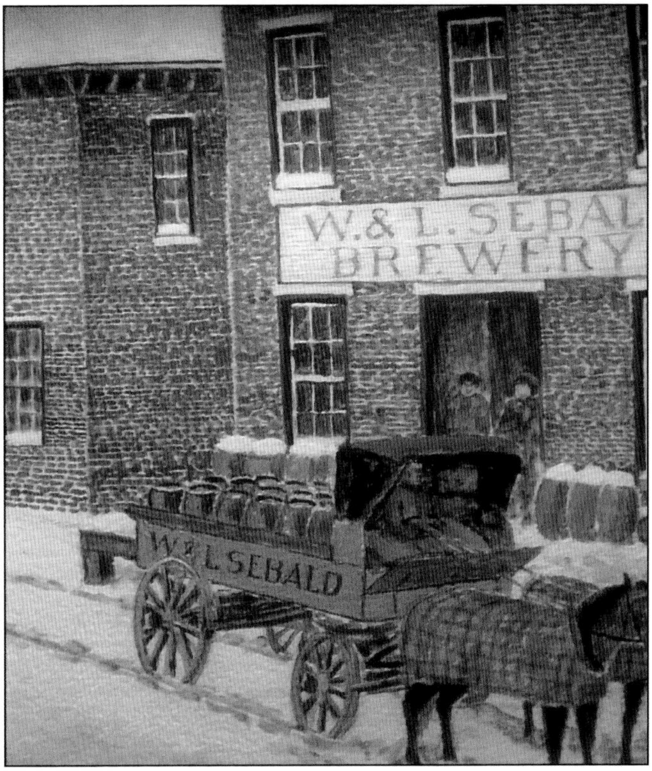

The William and Louis Sebald Brewing Company, which opened in 1866, was another large industry that grew to cover almost a block along the old canal on Verity Parkway, between Central and First Avenues. It used grain from nearby farms to make fine beers. The national Prohibition law closed it down in 1919. Above, a Sebald delivery wagon begins its rounds in 1900.

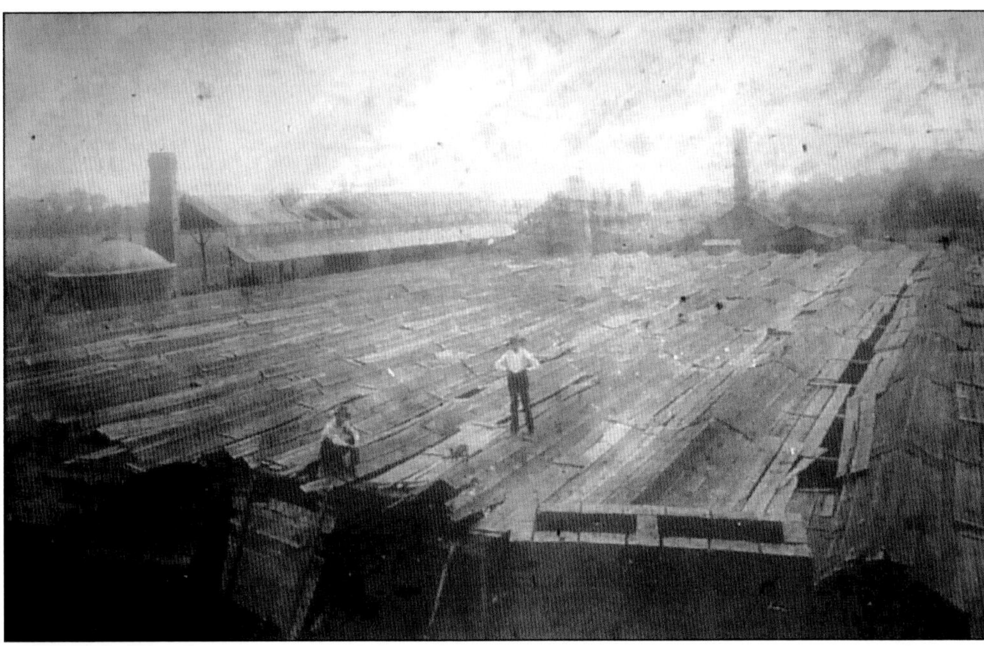

In 1887, William Smith, a local contractor, began to manufacture bricks to use in his business. He opened a brickyard on North Main Street along the canal, in what is now Smith Park. There was a large clay deposit there that he dug out of the ground, leaving the present pond that is now stocked with fish.

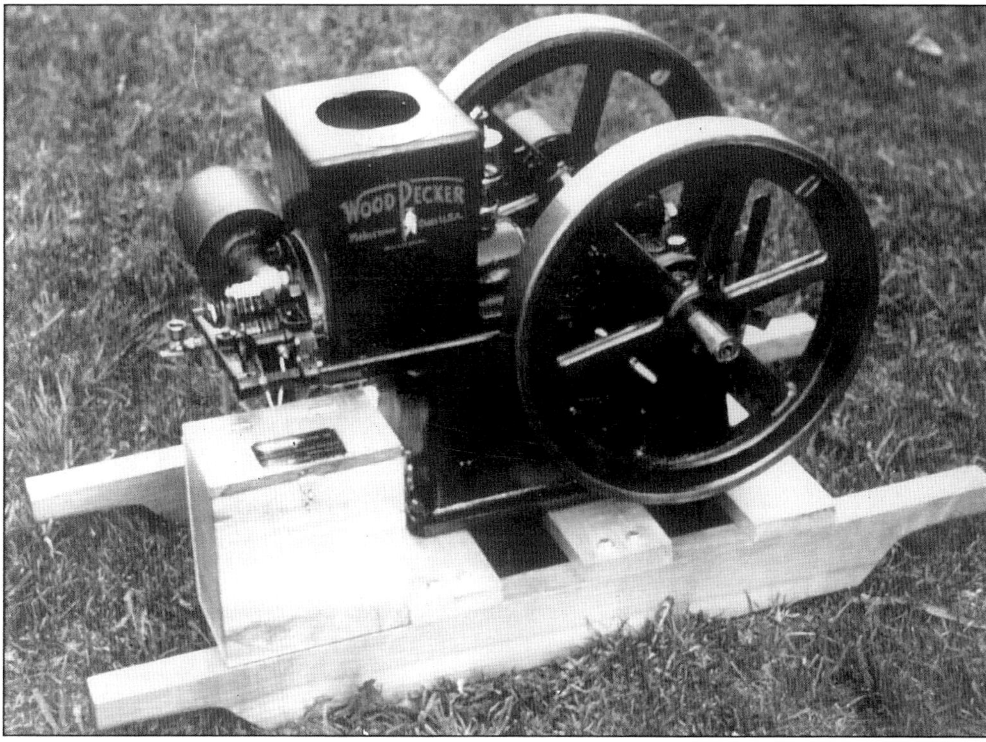

By 1905, a 60-man work force was producing 1,800 gasoline engines of various sizes each year at the Middletown Machine Company along the Big Four tracks. The "Woodpecker," as the engines were called, are now antiques in great demand among collectors. Pictured here is one restored engine in a private collection.

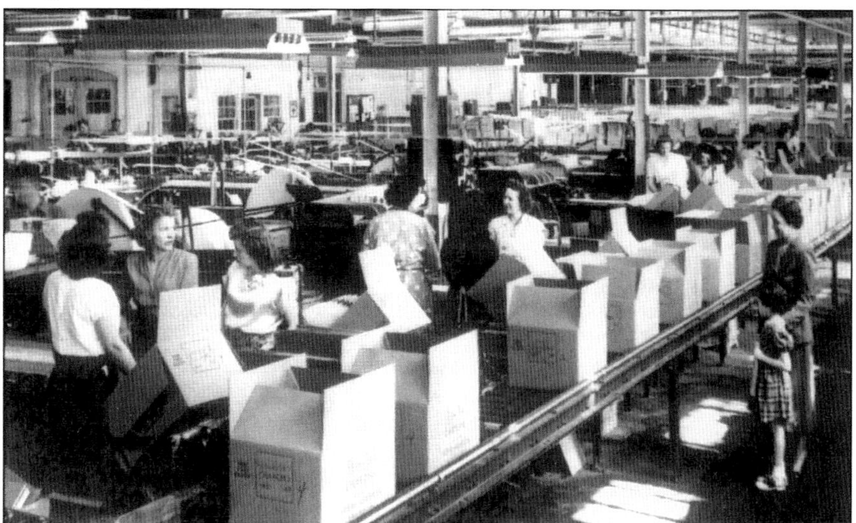

The previously mentioned Gardner had two major subsidiaries. One, Manchester Machine, provided the repair for its mill equipment. Under new management, it closed in 2000. The second has moved to other locations, but it brought about a major change in merchandising that began in 1935—milk and juice bottles made from paraffin-coated paperboard. Above is a view from inside the new plant along Charles Street.

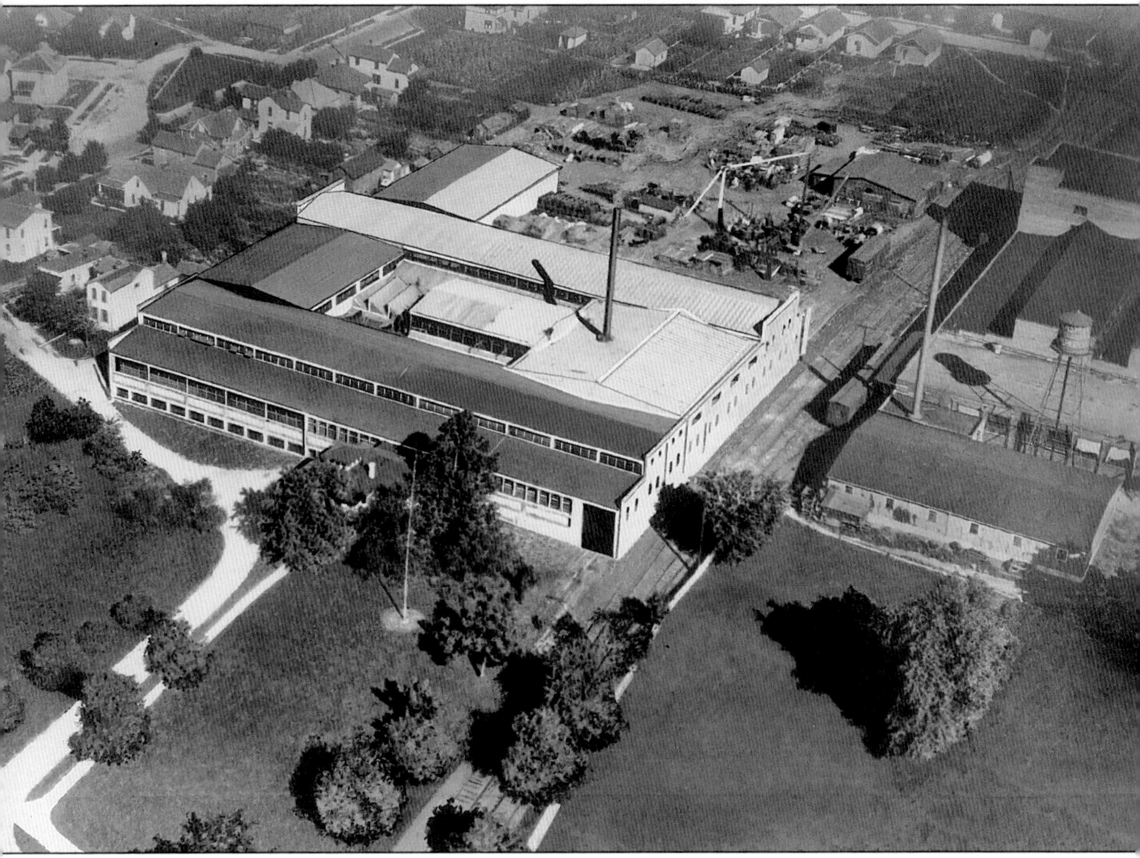

An early aerial view (Mayfield collection) reveals the Shartle plant in 1924. Across the railroad tracks, on the right side, is a glimpse of the then Nashua Paper Company.

Black-Clawson became the world's largest manufacturer of pulp and paper machinery. It developed the "Hydrapulper," and was used in paper recycling systems. In 1997, the paper machine division was sold, and the local operation became centered largely on research. The firm is now known as Thermo Black Clawson, Inc.

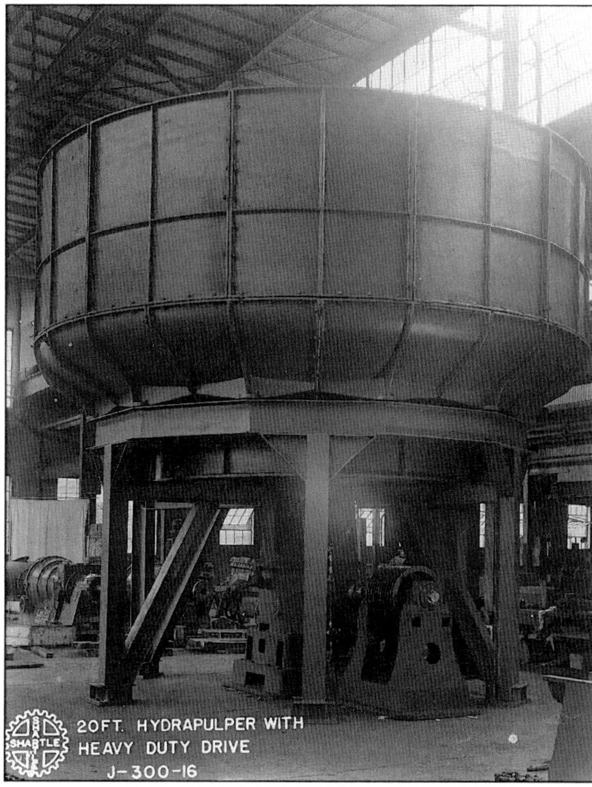

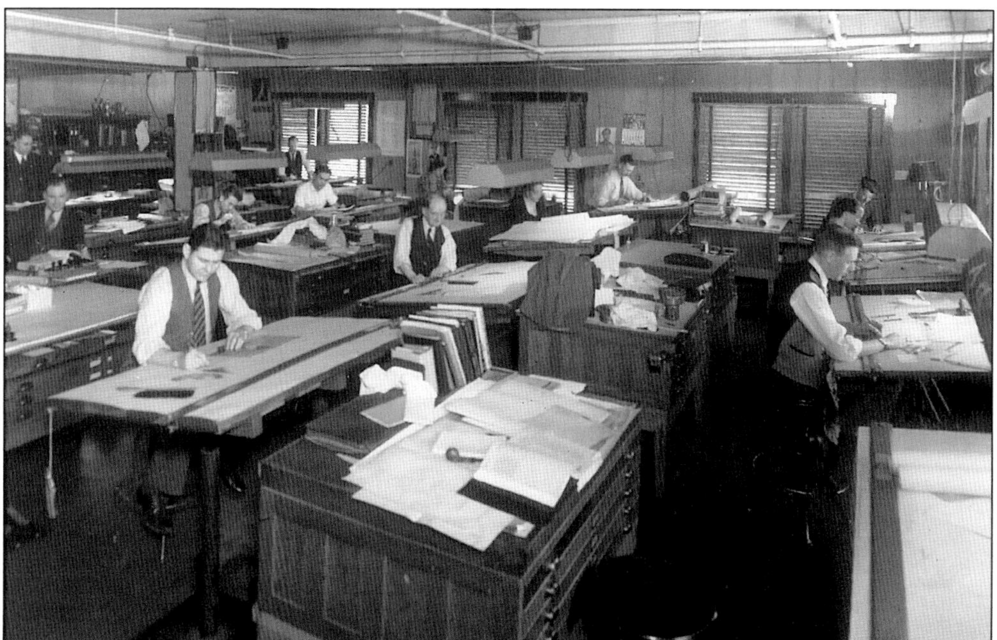

This view shows the inside of the engineering department at Black Clawson in 1944. The company was a leader in paper technology research for many years, and 80 percent of all paper recycled in the United States was processed with their equipment.

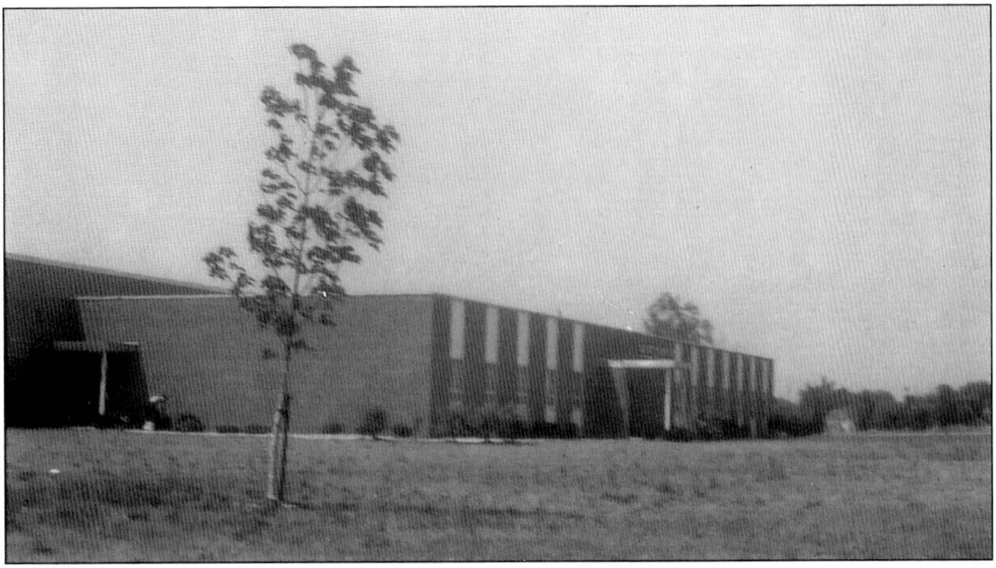

The Square D Company began here in 1904 as the Barkelew Electric Manufacturing Company, and made electrical switches. They moved from Canal Street to Flemming Road at the railroad, then to the new plant on South University Boulevard. It became part of the Square D group in 1967, which became a holding of the giant French electrical equipment firm—Groupe Schneider.

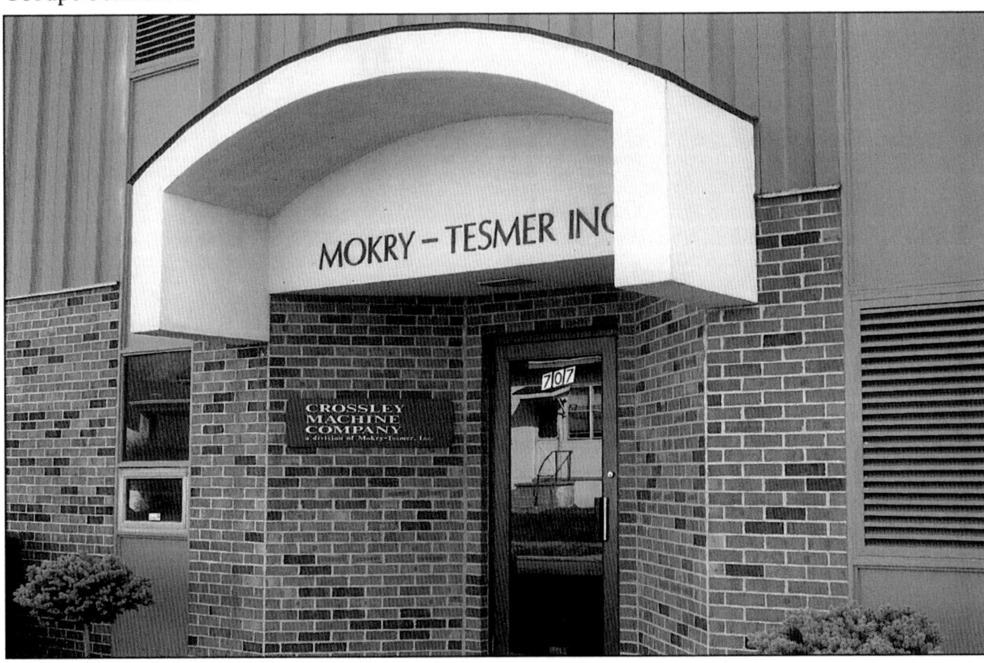

Mokry-Tesmer, Inc., at 707 Mary Etta Street, is a specialized, well-equipped machine shop serving both the metalworking and paper industry. They specialize in industrial machining, especially in rolls for the steel, paper, and textile industries. The company offers a long list of repair services for area industries. While a small plant, its equipment is state-of-the-art. It was founded in 1919 by August Mokry, a master mechanic from Vienna, Austria. William Tesmer joined him in a partnership in 1920.

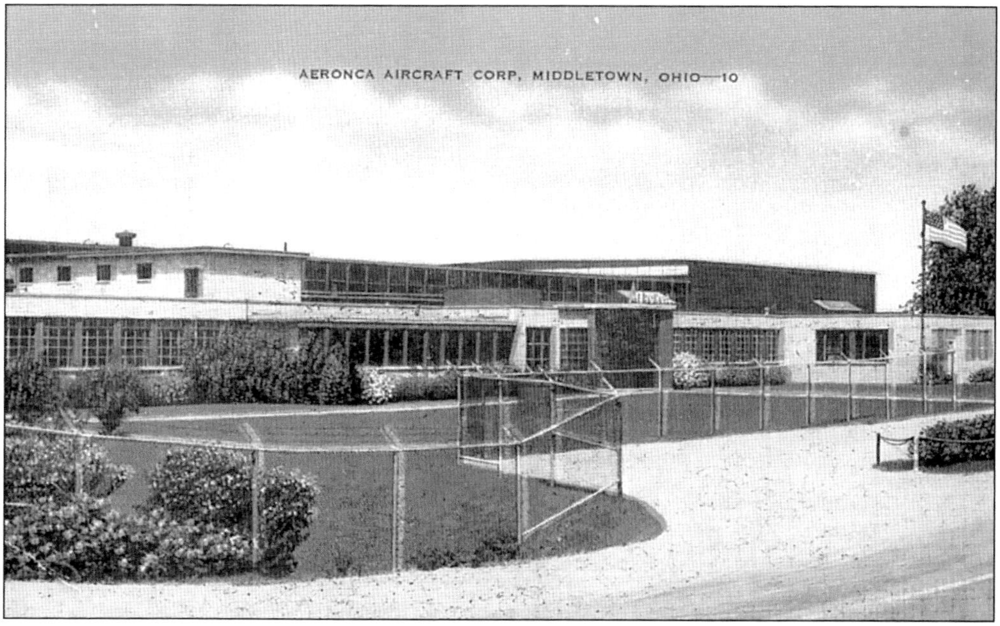

In June 1940, the Aeronautical Corporation of America—Aeronca—began production of a lightweight plane in a new factory on Germantown Road, adjacent to the airport. Above is its longtime corporate headquarters. It is now a division of Magellan Aerospace Corporation of Ontario, Canada.

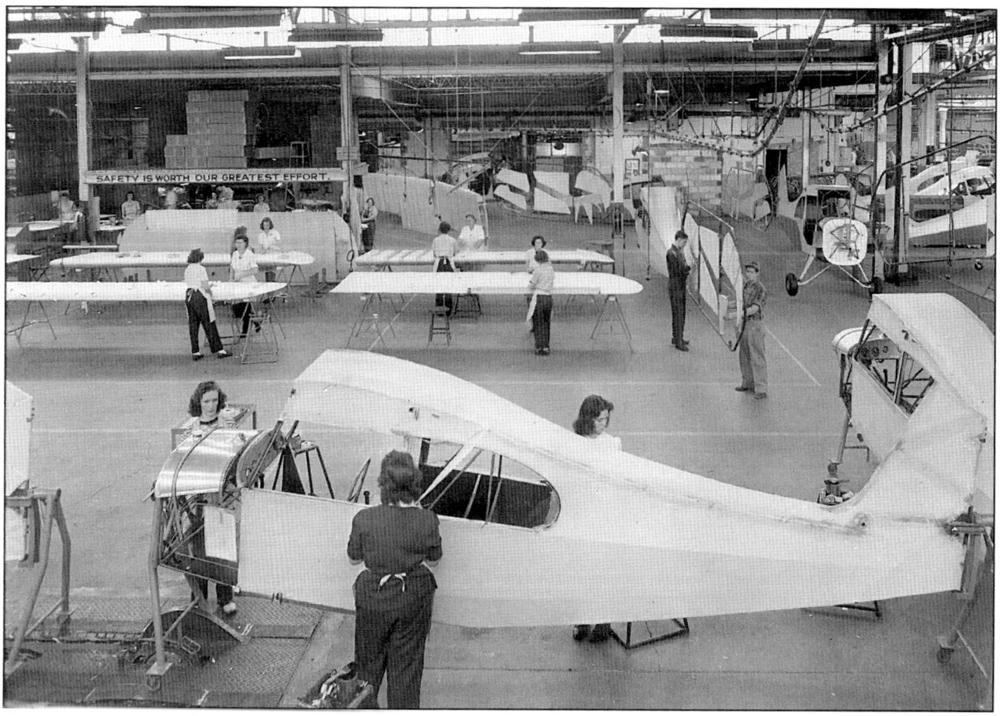

Between 1929 and 1950, Aeronca produced 17,408 light aircraft. During World War II, it made special training planes as well as gliders. After the war, Aeronca began to supply parts for larger aircraft, missiles, and space shuttles.

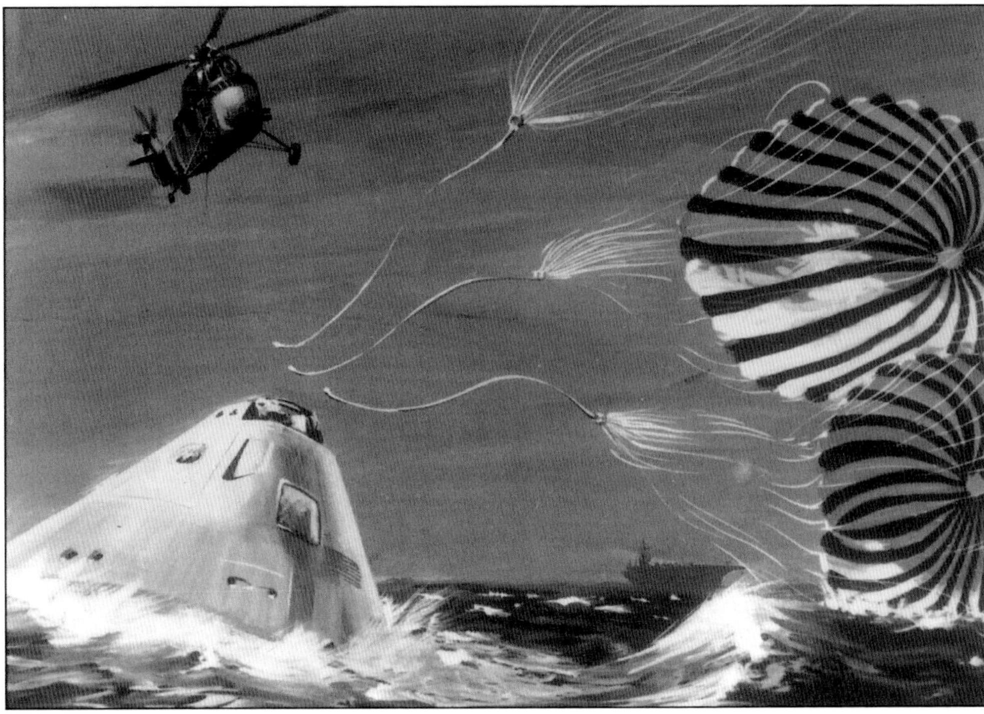

One of Aeronca's specialties was the making of brazed honeycomb stainless steel panels, used for the entire outer shell and heat shield of command modules. Aeronca, using Armco special stainless steel, helped put man on the moon on July 20, 1969.

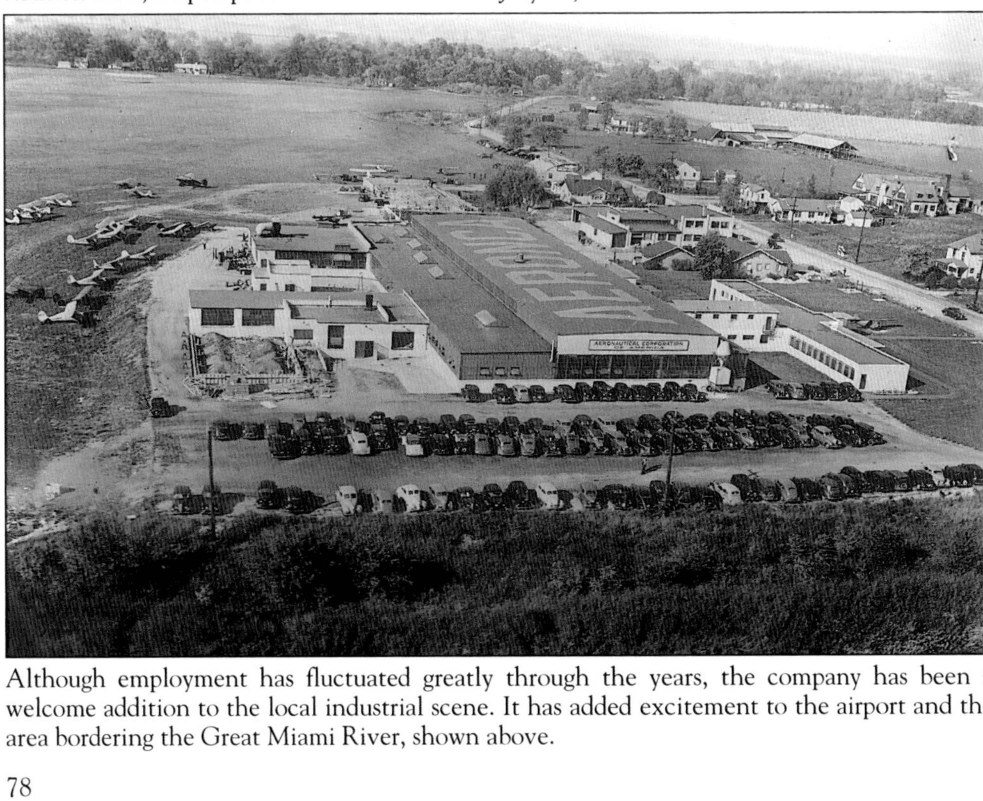

Although employment has fluctuated greatly through the years, the company has been a welcome addition to the local industrial scene. It has added excitement to the airport and the area bordering the Great Miami River, shown above.

Four

Postcards From Armco

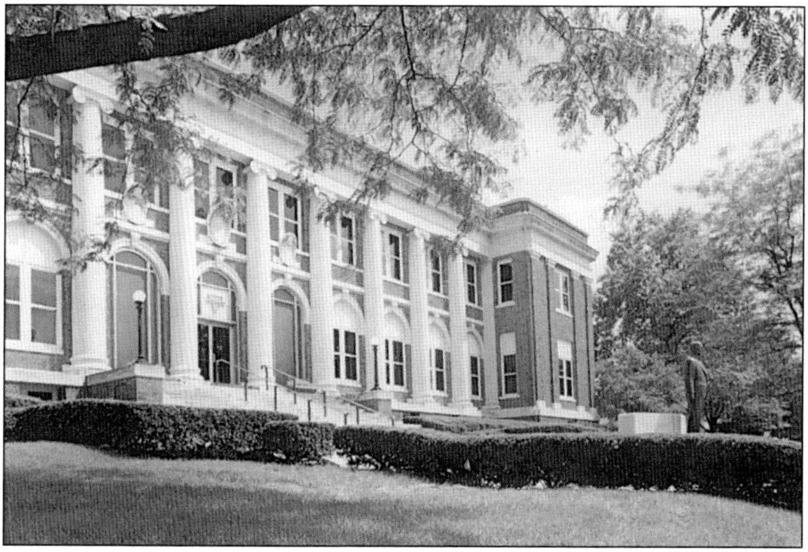

The last set of local cards, published in 1982, included a postcard of the Armco general office. Someone once stated that this landmark building, erected in 1916, is to Middletown what the Capitol Building is to the nation. For almost half a century it had been officially known as the headquarters of the American Rolling Mill Company, but on April 15, 1948, shareholders approved an amendment to the Articles of Incorporation that changed the name to Armco Steel Corporation. For many years, this had been the company's advertised trademark on all its products. In announcing the change, the company recognized that the popular acronym had, in fact, already been adopted by the public, and stated that "millions of people changed our name."

On April 27, 1978, another name change left it simply "Armco, Incorporated." According to officials, this action was taken due to diversification into new areas. Armco had become more than just a steel company, and one-third of its 1977 income came from new ventures. In the winter of 1985, it was a great shock to the city when Armco moved its corporate offices from Curtis Street to Morristown, and then Parsippany, New Jersey. In 1993, the offices moved again, this time to Pittsburgh. However, when the corporate office left, it took only 20 top officials to its new offices. The balance of the staff was left in Middletown to run the Eastern Steel Division. In 1989, Armco sold half-interest in this division (the Middletown and Ashland plants) when it entered into a joint venture with the Kawasaki Steel Corporation of Japan, thus creating the Armco Steel Company, L.P. (Limited Partnership). This new company set up its corporate offices in the building on Curtis Street. On April 7, 1994, after another corporate change, the joint venture became AK Steel Corporation.

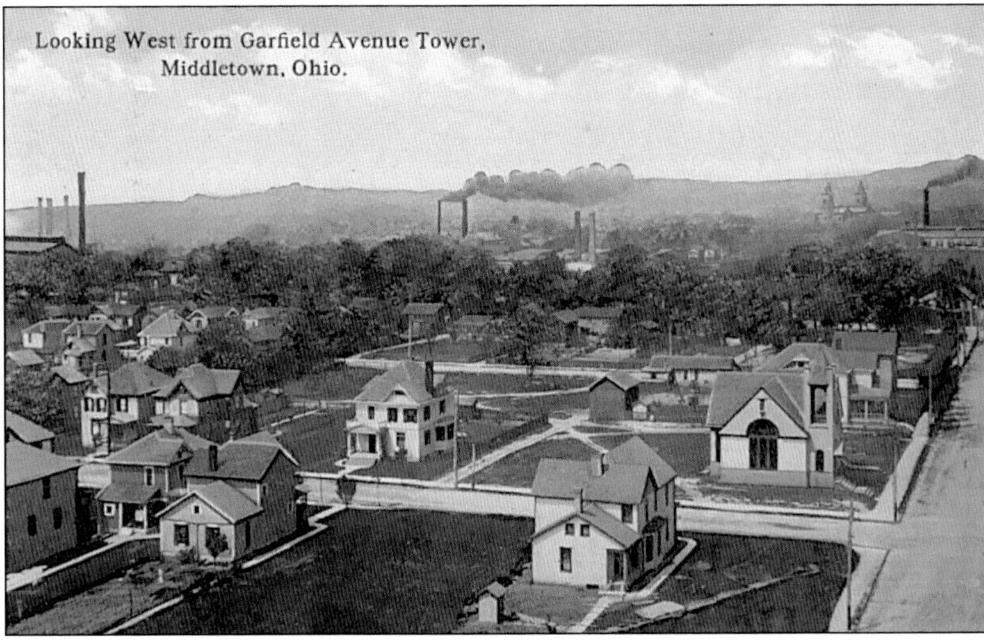

Postcards were very popular during the early years of the century. Around 1915 a new set appeared, with a bird's-eye-view of the then east end, showing the smokestacks of the old Armco Central Works in the background. The photo was snapped from atop the old light tower at Girard and Garfield Streets.

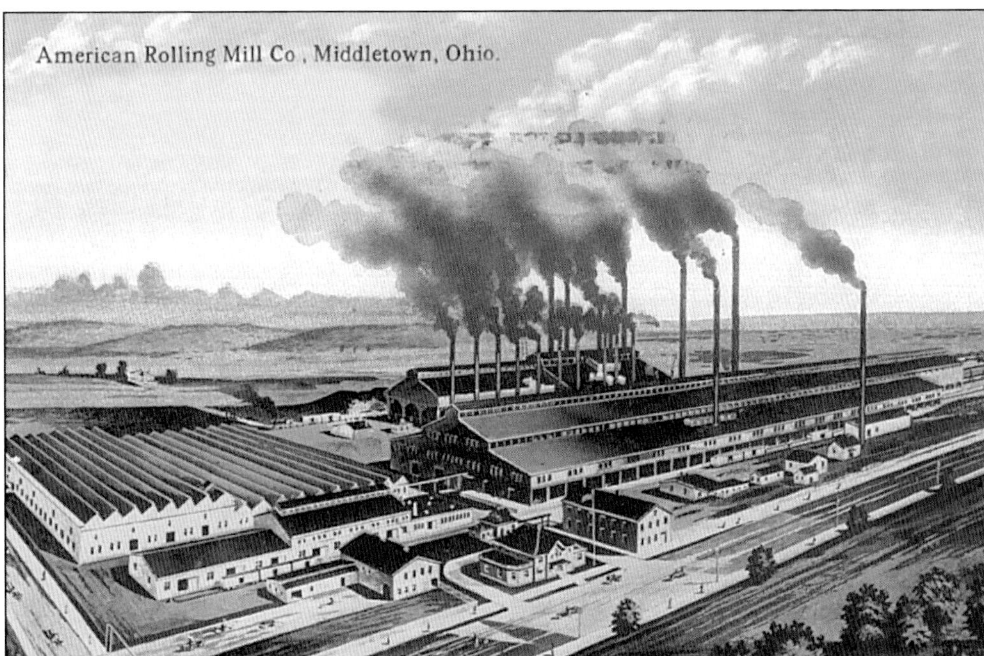

This set also included a card of the Central Works on Curtis Street. Note the original office building on the west side of Curtis, and in the far background, the Miami-Erie Canal, still flowing at that time.

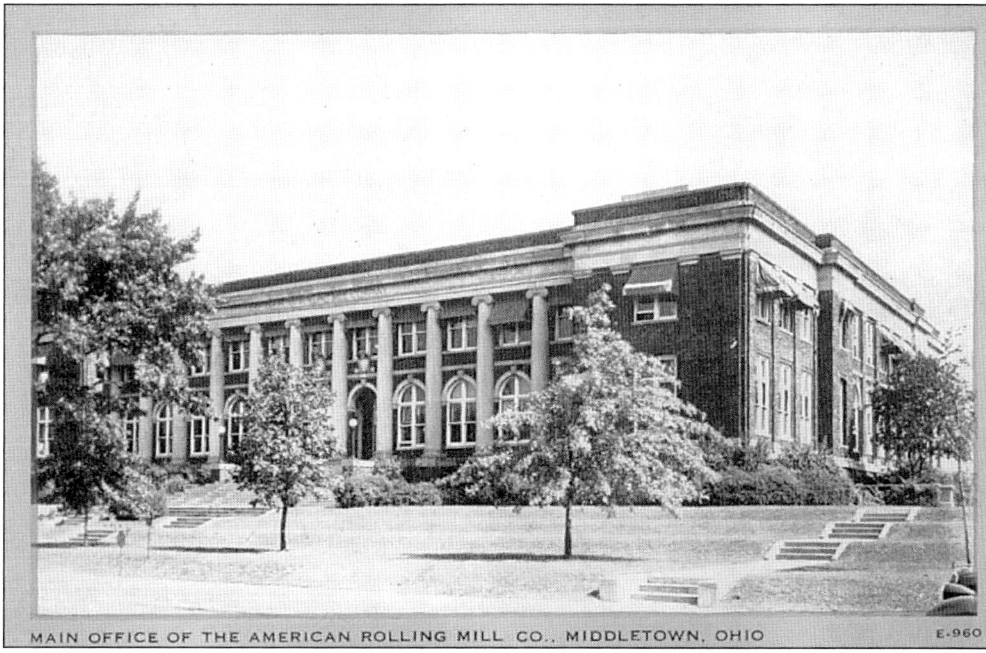

On June 25, 1918, Armco officials moved into their finally completed (delayed by World War I shortages) general office building on the east side of Curtis Street. Armco was so proud of the building that in 1925, they entertained the editors of major industrial publications here. It is remembered that one editor praised the spacious lobby.

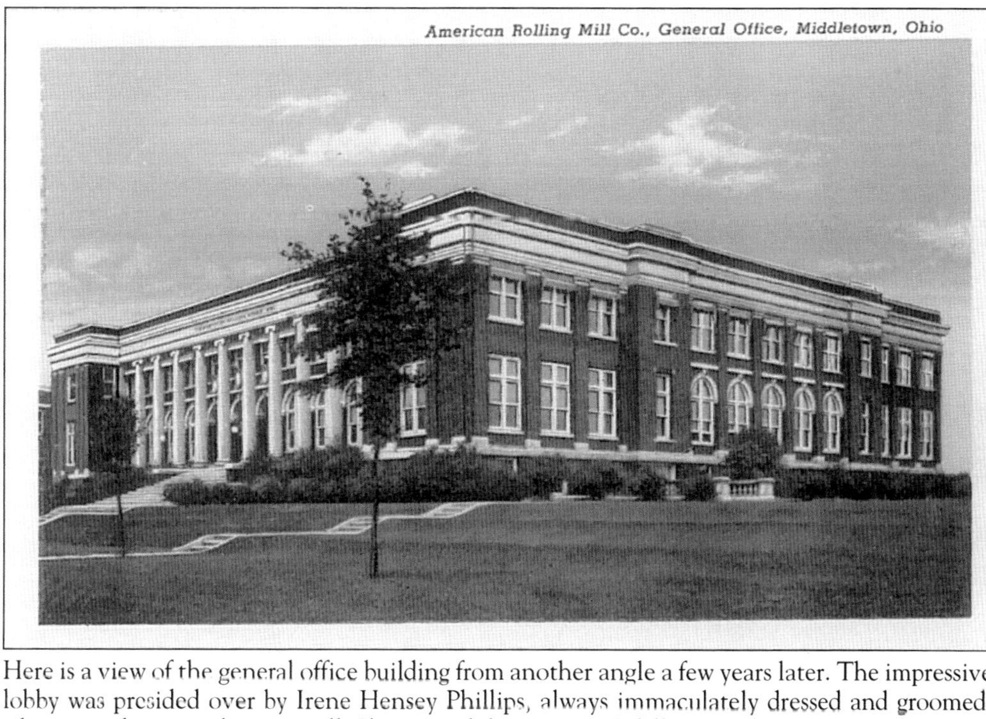

Here is a view of the general office building from another angle a few years later. The impressive lobby was presided over by Irene Hensey Phillips, always immaculately dressed and groomed, who gave a happy welcome to all. She arrived there in 1926, following Elmina McKnight Kinne and Isabel Jones. She had a long tenure.

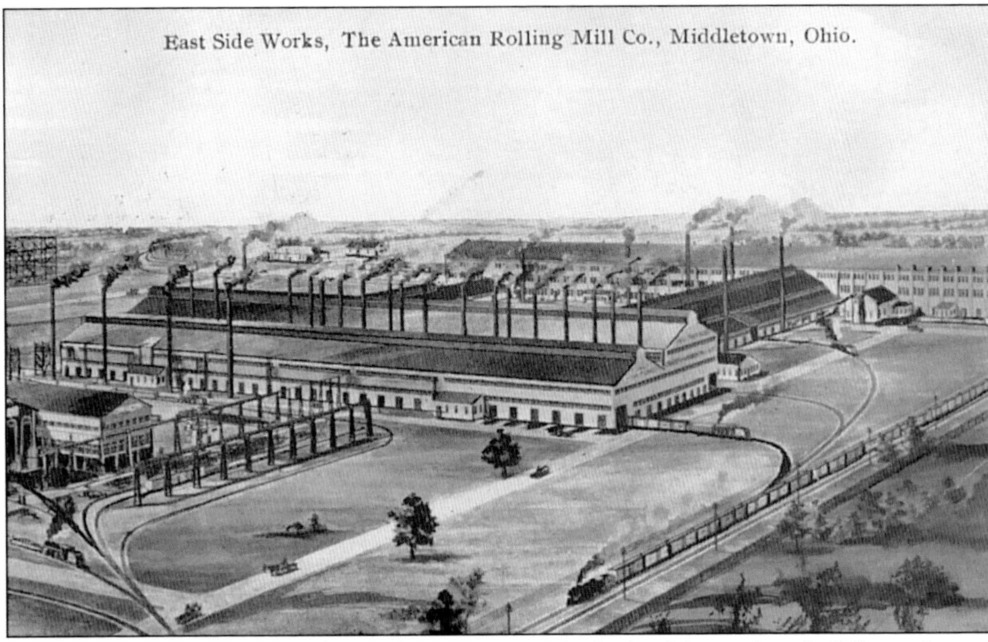

The East Side Works is shown here. The message on the back of the card reads: "This is the mill I work in, but not half of the works is shown...you can imagine the size of this place."

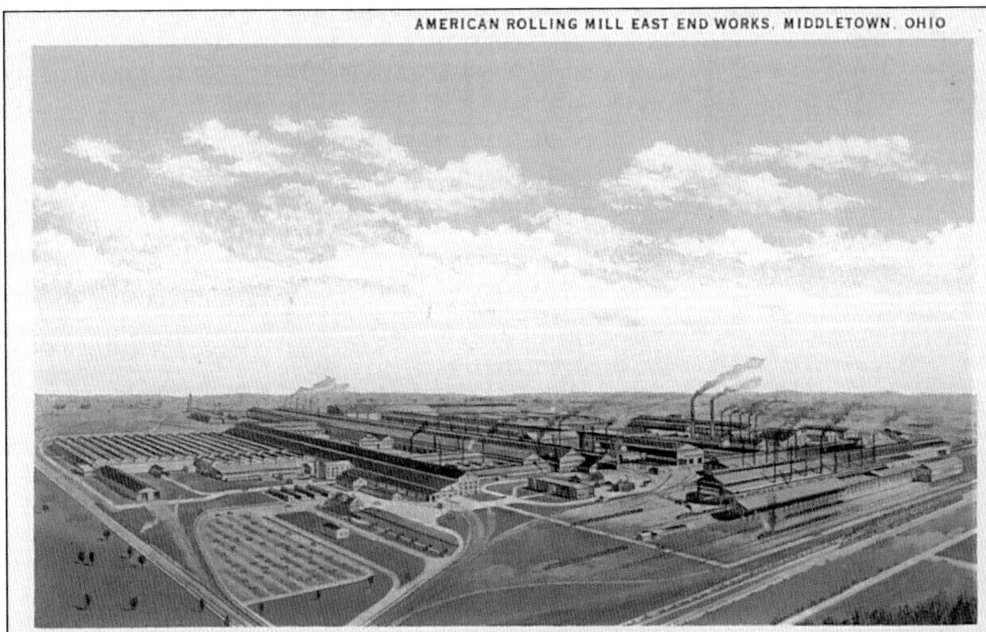

Another card revealed the size of the site. It covered 560 acres of farm land, formerly planted with corn. The mill began operations in September 1911, and the original Curtis Street plant became known as Central Works.

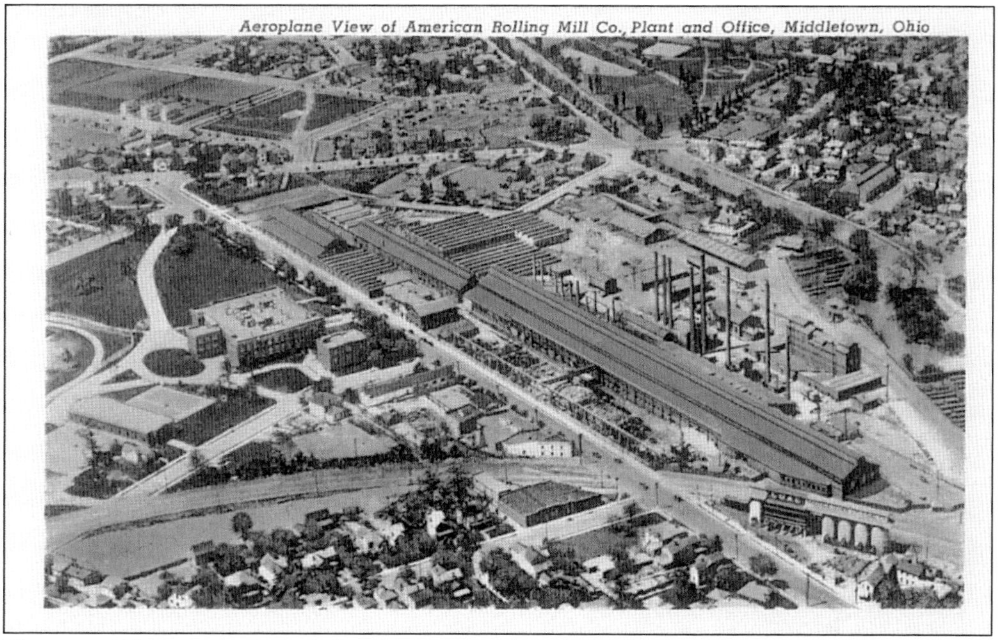

This is a 1920 aerial view of the Central Works taken by a photographer for the Mayfield collection. Note the new general office building and the adjacent small research building.

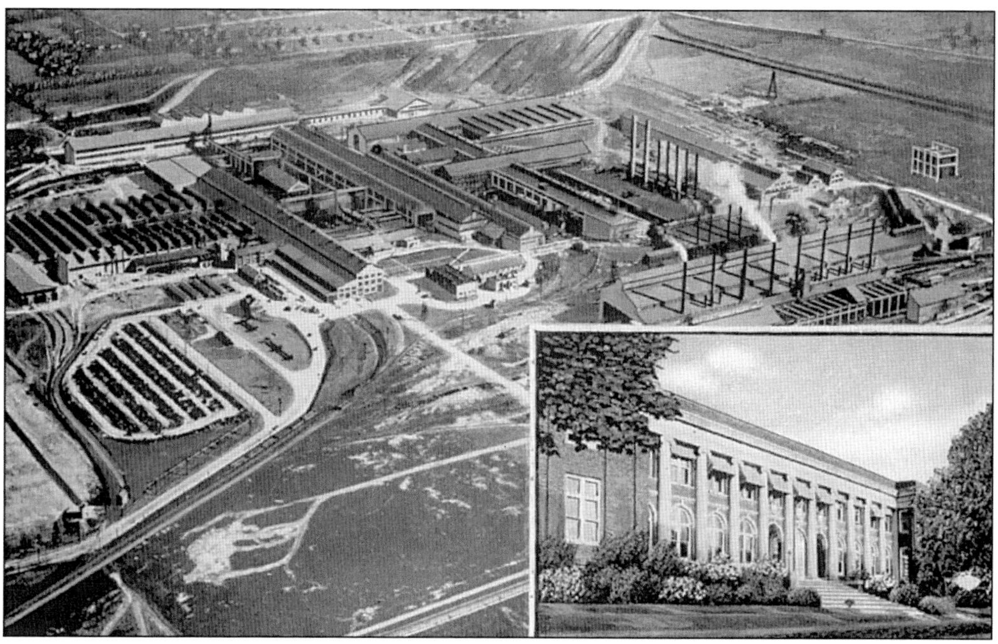

Here is an aerial view of East Works, published by the Middletown Post Card Company (the insert is the general office). The works at the time contained four, 60-ton open hearth furnaces, soaking pits, a blooming mill, a bar mill, a sheet mill, a jobbing mill, and a finishing department.

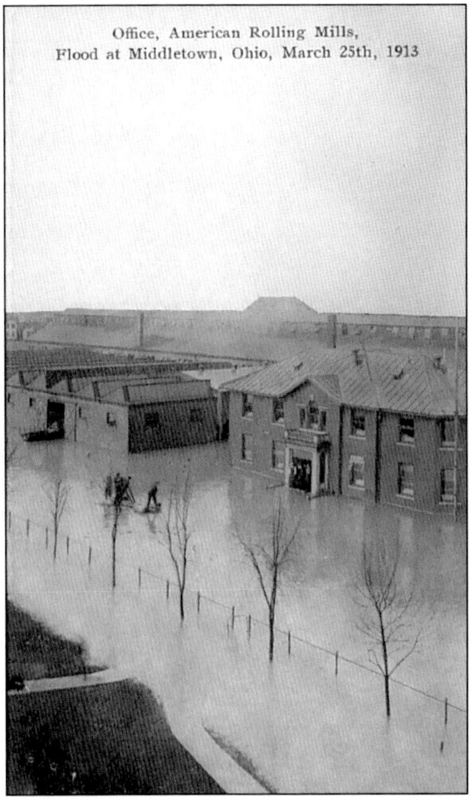

From March 25 to March 26, 1913, a devastating flood hit southwestern Ohio. Middletown was hit hard, as was Armco's Central Works, situated along the old Miami-Erie Canal, whose waters merged with those of the Great Miami River to the west.

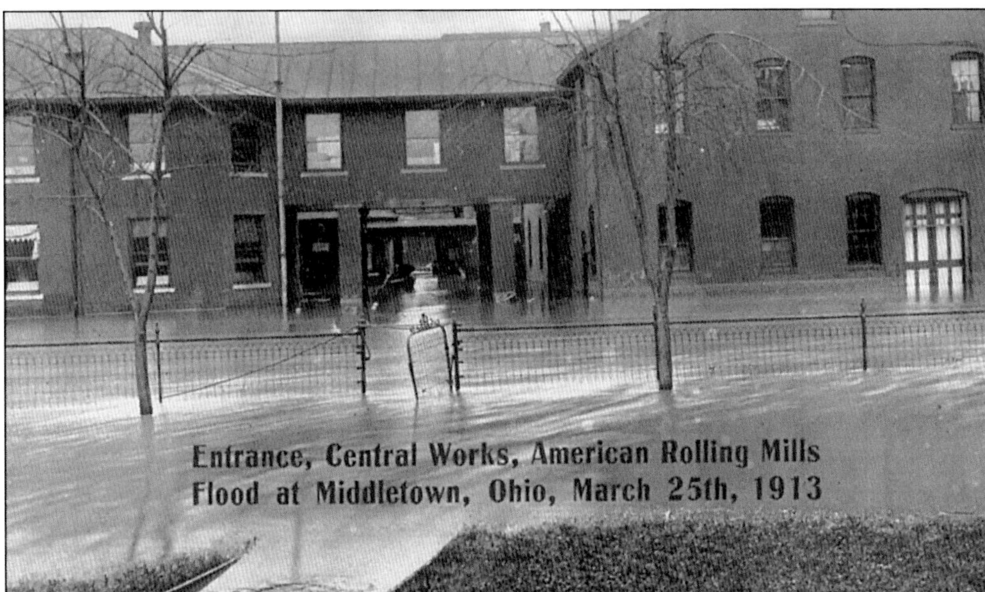

Only heroic effort amidst the confusion saved the day. At the time, furnaces Number Two and Three were ready to tap, and One and Four were almost melted. Workers built a dam at the north end of the plant, giving men time to pour the heats. Only the quick work prevented explosions as loyal workers outwitted the flood with their small improvised dams.

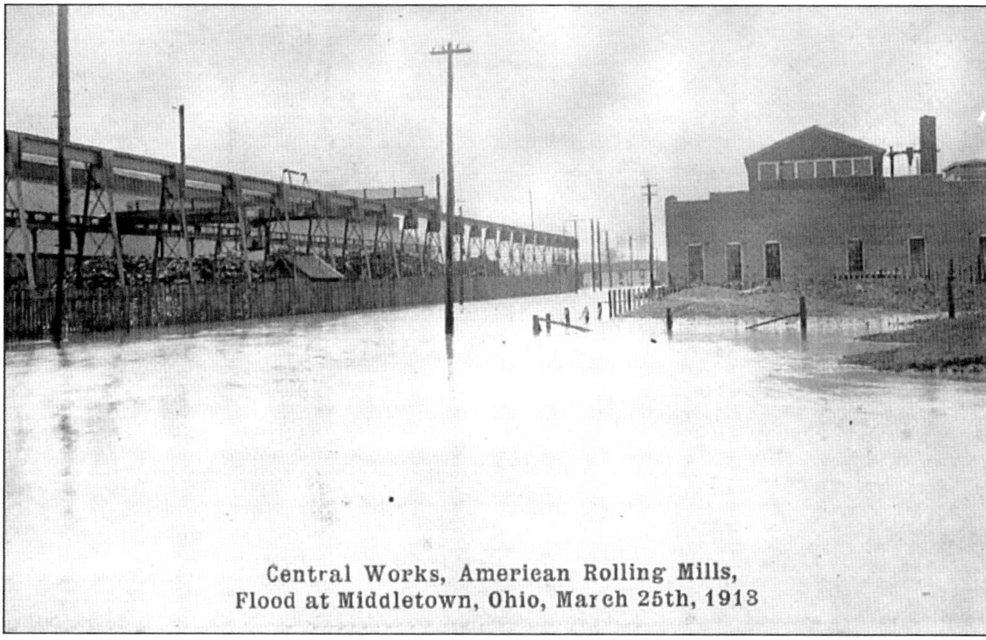

By March 29, 1913, after the floodwaters had gone down, the Central Works had to be cleaned of the slime and mud that coated everything. All four furnaces were damaged and had to be rebuilt. Formaldehyde was scattered everywhere to prevent disease among the men.

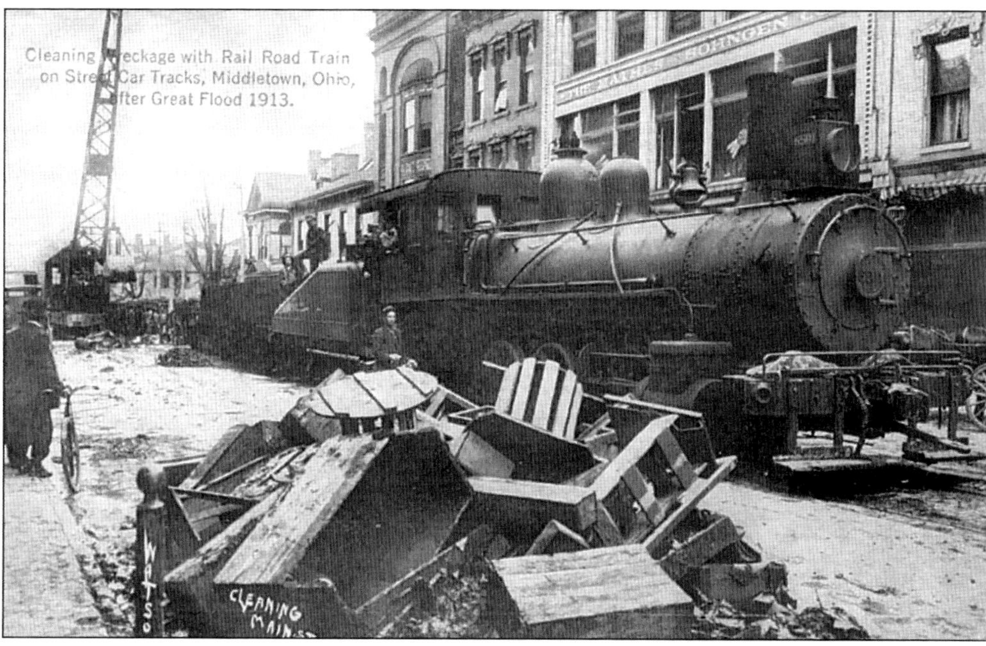

On Verity's orders, Charles R. Hook, his assistant, arranged for Armco to help the city clean up the debris. Following George LaFayette's suggestion, the traction car tracks on Main Street were connected so an Armco locomotive, followed by a crane and dump cars, could help carry away the trash. Middletown was the first city in the area to recover from the deluge.

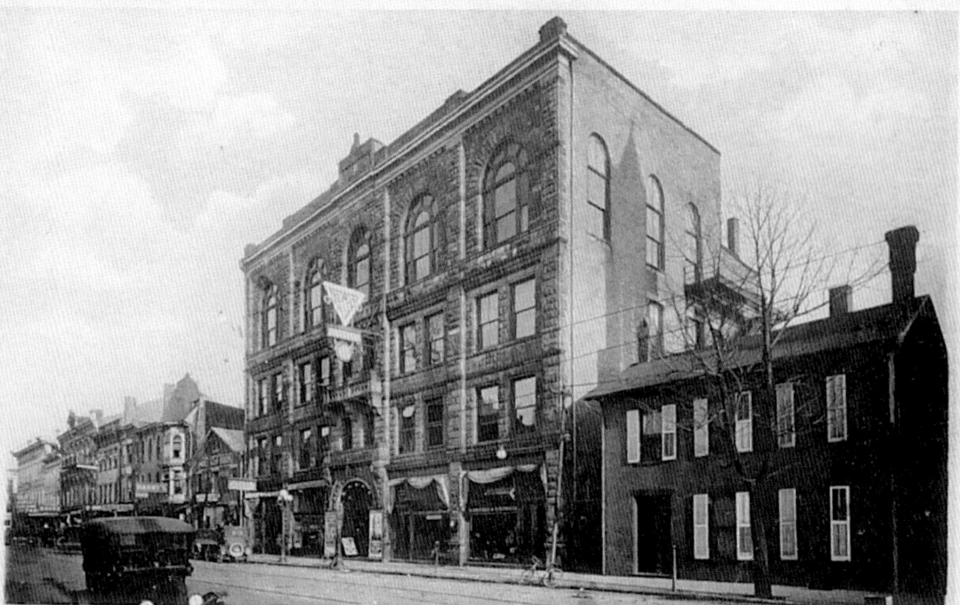

ARMCO ASSOCIATION CLUB ROOMS

In 1920, the official Armco photographer, Thomas Portsmouth, collaborated with Bennett Chapple on an Armco publication, *Armco in Picture and Fact*. Some of the photographs were reproduced on postcards. One in this set shows the Armco Association Club rooms when they were located on the third and fourth floors of the Sorg Opera House building on Main Street.

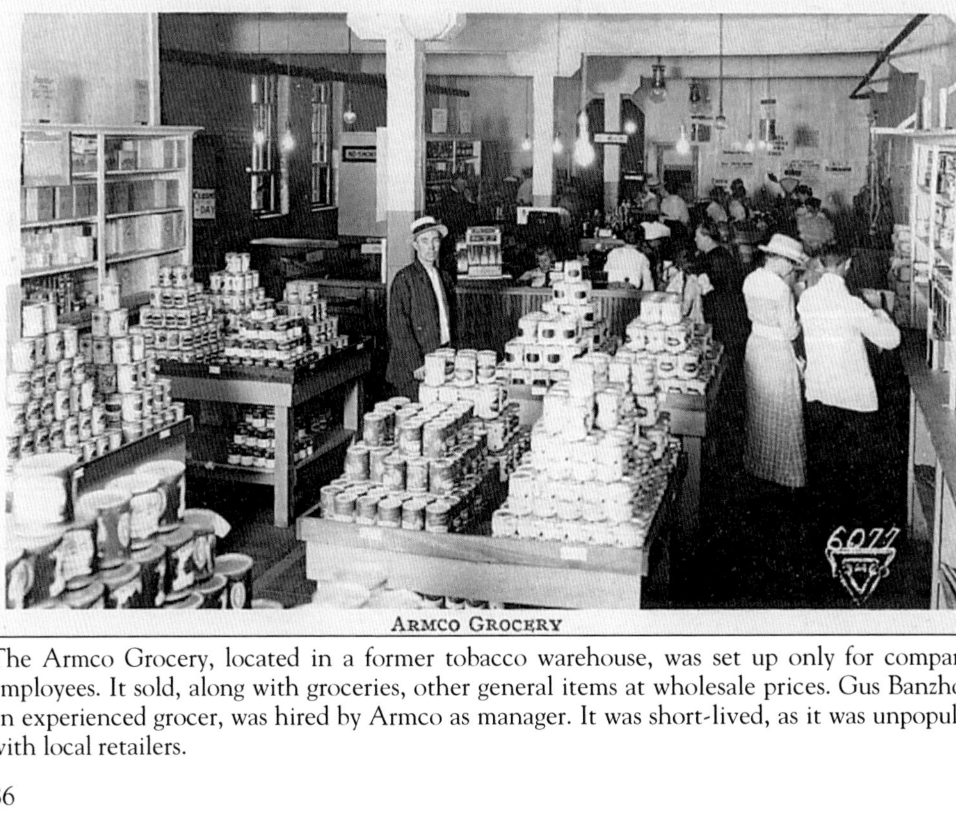

ARMCO GROCERY

The Armco Grocery, located in a former tobacco warehouse, was set up only for company employees. It sold, along with groceries, other general items at wholesale prices. Gus Banzhof, an experienced grocer, was hired by Armco as manager. It was short-lived, as it was unpopular with local retailers.

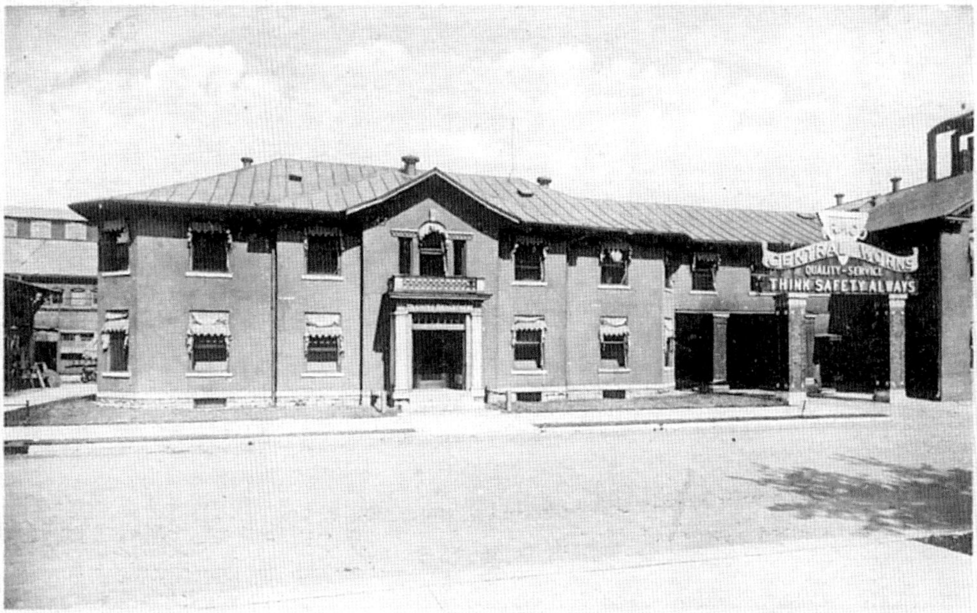

ARMCO SCHOOL

The Armco School, or training department, was located in the old general office building, where all educational activities were brought under one roof. The school offered apprenticeship courses in the steel-making trade as well as office training, salesmanship, and technical courses.

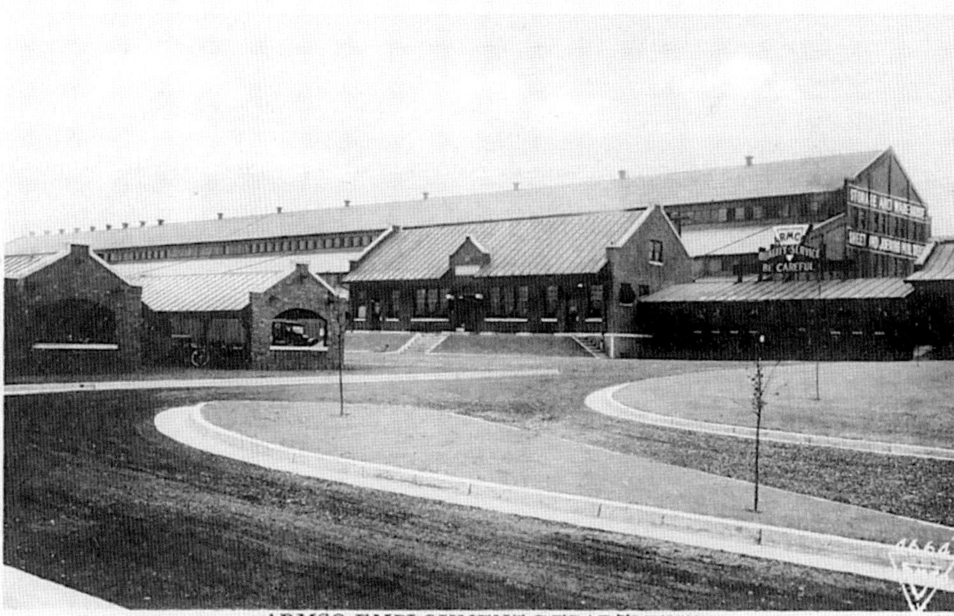

ARMCO EMPLOYMENT DEPARTMENT

The employment department had personnel who interviewed each applicant to learn what skills he possessed that were pertinent to Armco's needs. Past work records were also reviewed. Through this process, the foreman or department head would hire new employees.

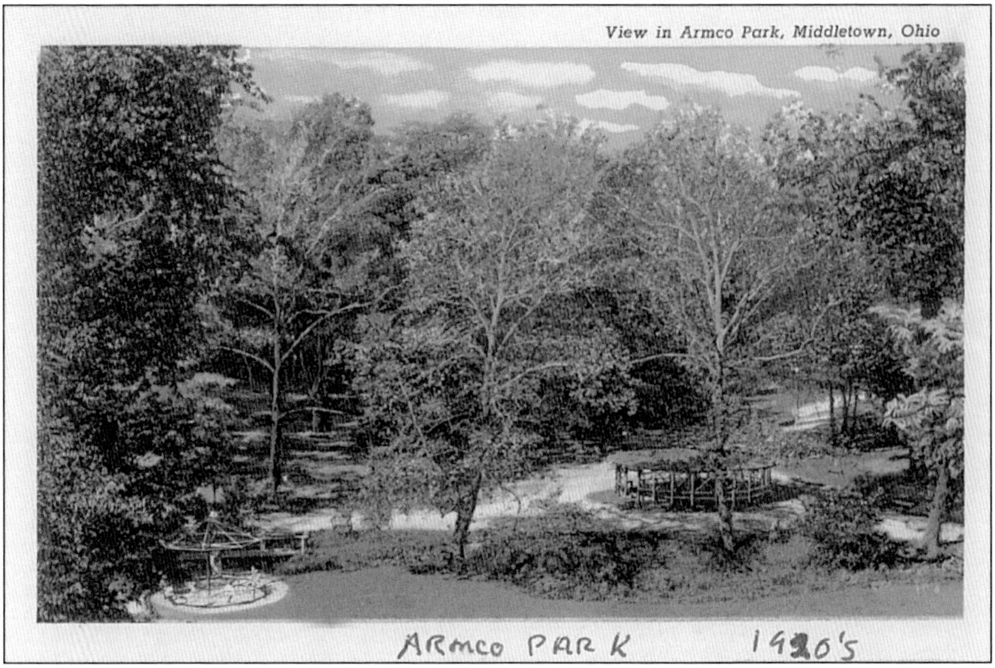

In 1922, the board of directors authorized the purchase of 435 acres of hilly farmland and woodland east of Middletown. The area, which had been known as Cooch's Woods, became Armco Park. It was open to employees and townspeople alike. Above is the road through Sycamore Glen to Bunny Hollow.

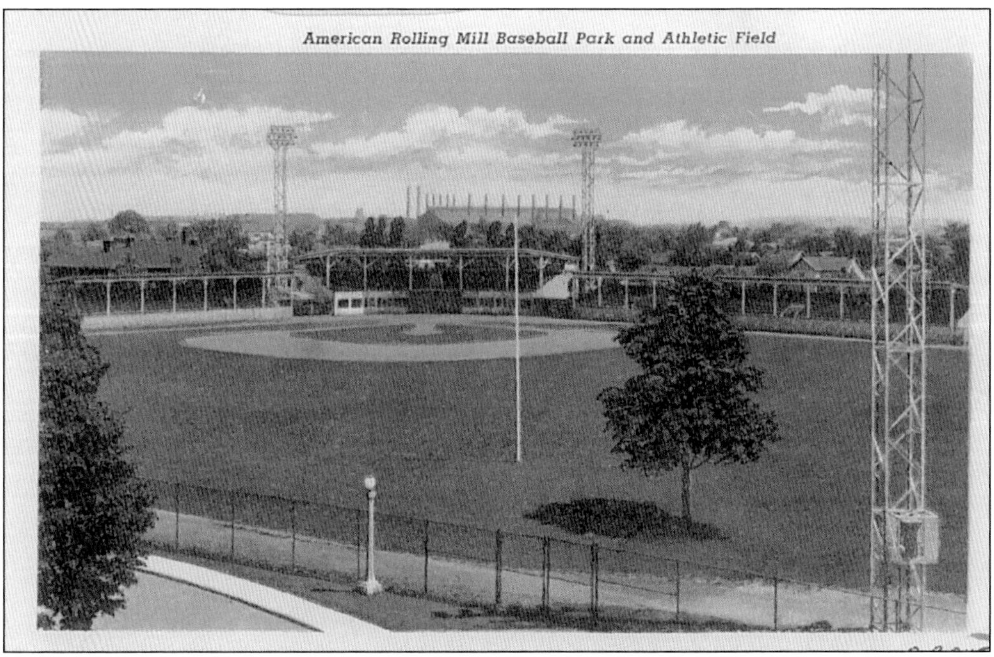

Southeast of the general office building, Armco built a baseball park and athletic field. The company sponsored many teams including baseball, basketball, and football (in season), as well as other activities to encourage physical fitness. It also had a substantial grandstand.

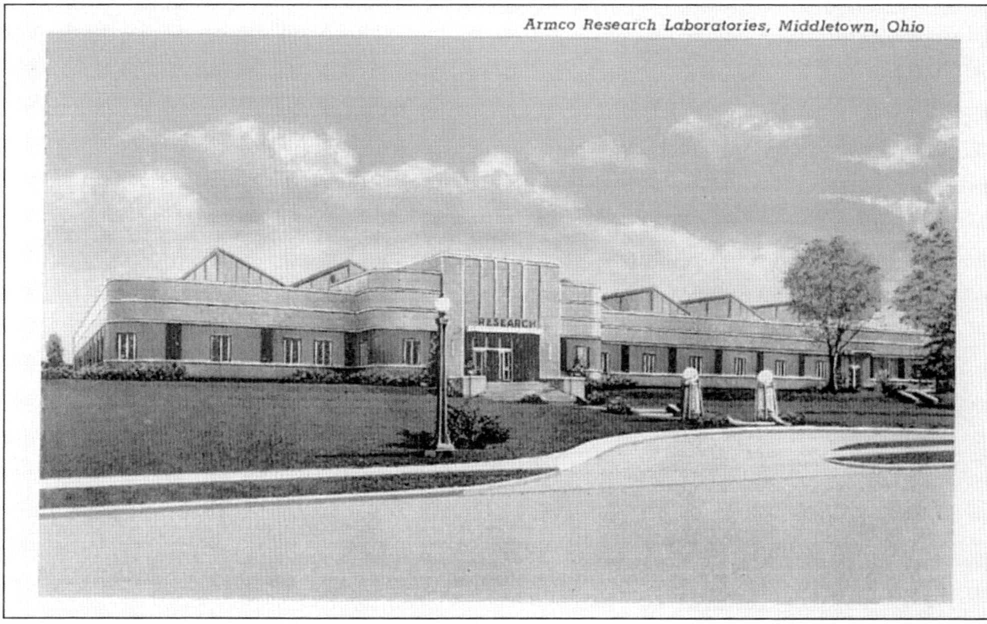

Armco's first research building (pictured elsewhere) was destroyed by a gas explosion in 1935. Fortunately, the explosion occurred at night, so no one was injured. The new, modern research laboratory was dedicated November 5, 1937.

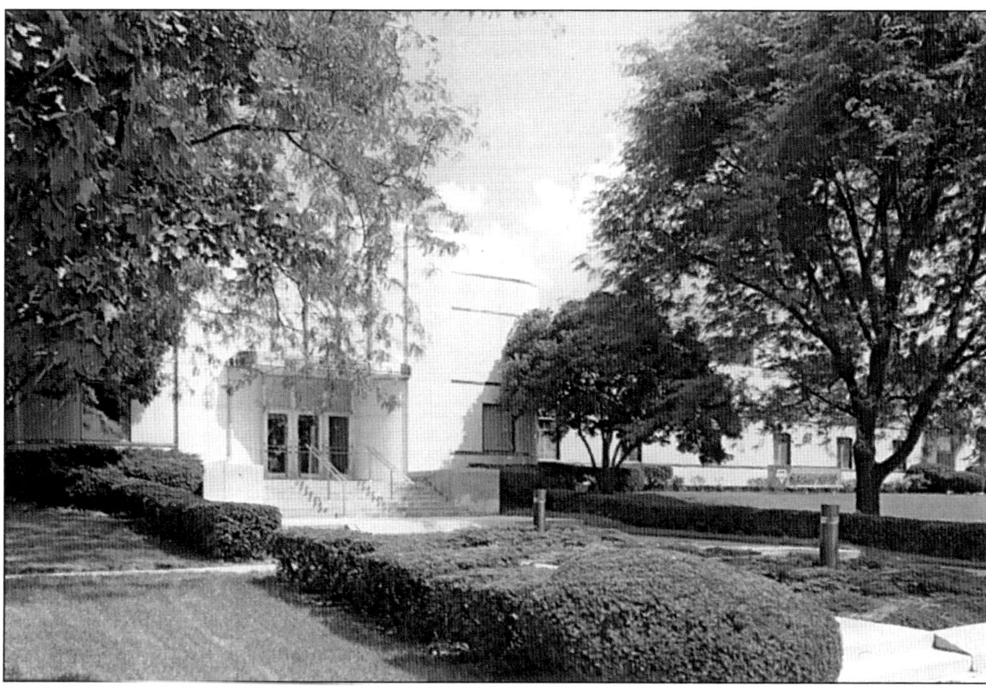

Later known as the research center, the building more than doubled in area in 1961, and took on another major addition in 1976. It was an innovation when built, and used paneled Steelox walls developed by Armco, architectural vitreous enamel, stainless steel trim, and glass brick.

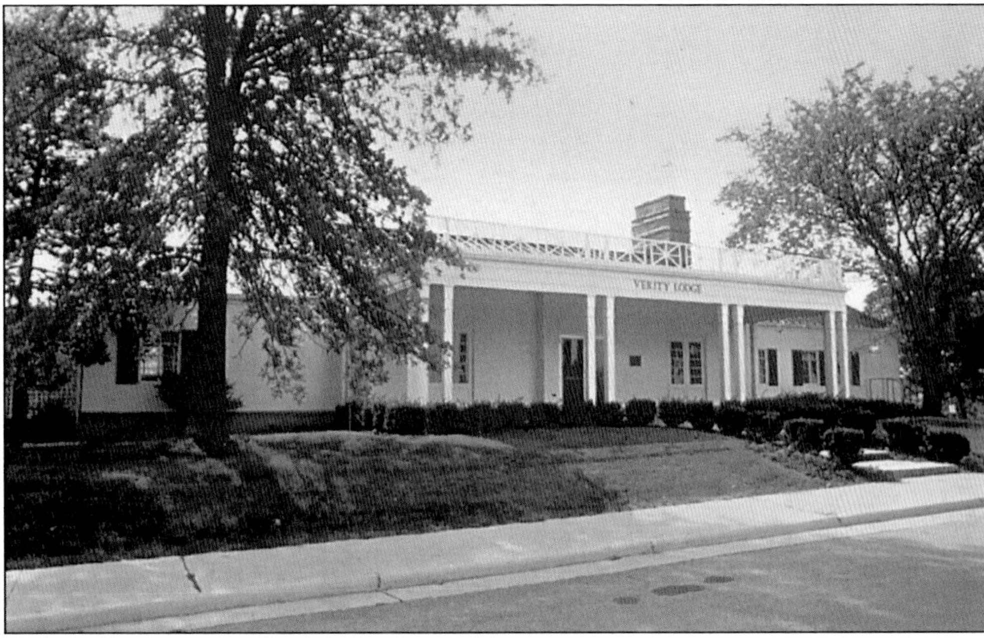

Verity Lodge is now the student center for the Middletown campus of Miami University. It was originally a gift from Armco to the Armco Girls' Association, organized March 31, 1919. The clubhouse was dedicated September 24, 1942. Armco, who also donated the land for the local campus, included this building for student use and provided another facility for the women.

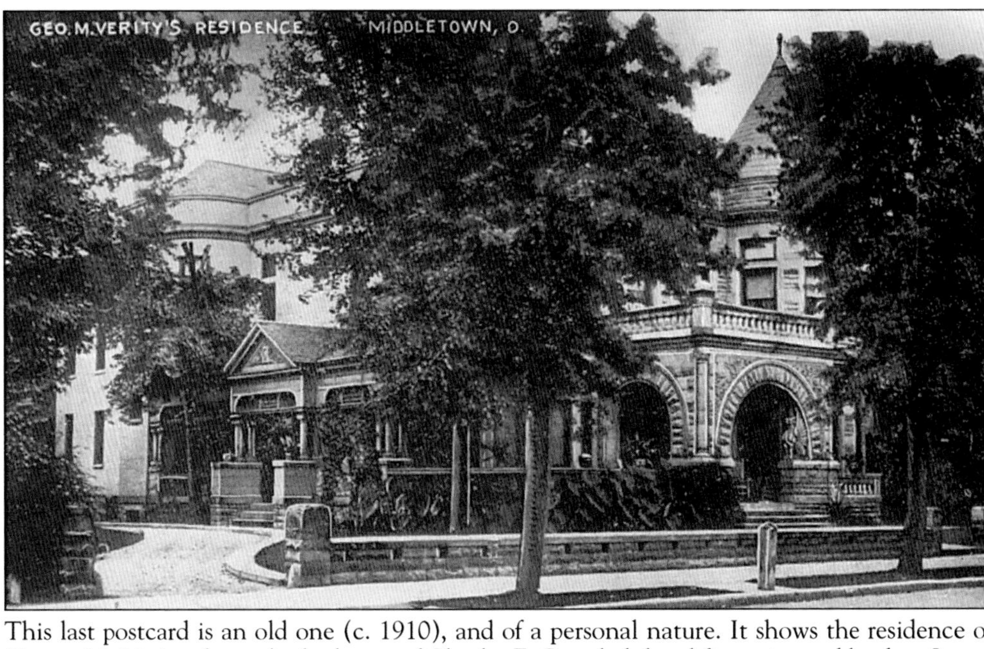

This last postcard is an old one (c. 1910), and of a personal nature. It shows the residence of George M. Verity, formerly the home of Charles F. Gunckel, local financier and banker. It was purchased from the Gunckel estate and extensively remodeled by Verity, who lived there until his death in 1942. This card was a bestseller for many years at Levy's Postcard Shop, located at 129 East Third Street (Central Avenue).

Five

Armco—The Good Citizen

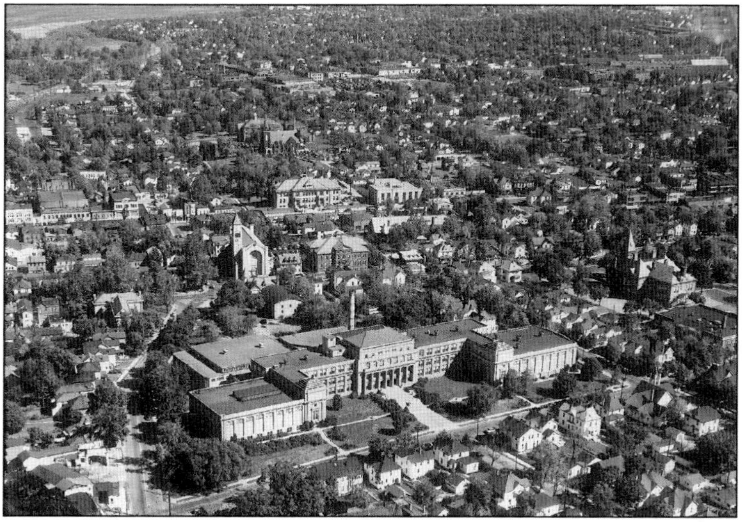

During the last century, the phrase "Middletown is Armco, Armco is Middletown" was often heard. Some approved, while others felt it displayed a note of paternalism and implied too much company control over civic affairs. Since Armco employed half the workers in the city by the middle of the twentieth century, the company naturally exerted a strong presence, although an altruistic one. In 1919, George M. Verity had published "Armco Policies," in which he encouraged employees to take part in local affairs. Verity believed in a working partnership between company management, company workers, and the community at large. Thus, Armco officials, from the president down, were active participants in all aspects of the social and cultural life of Middletown. The photographs in this chapter illustrate how closely Armco was involved in the life of Steel City.

Armco was deeply concerned about the welfare of its own employees. In 1900, steel workers had little protection in the work place. Safety practices were commonly ignored. Armco introduced new benefits for its workers, many of which spread throughout the industry. These improved working conditions made for better communities.

Armco's original plant in Middletown was located at the south end of Curtis Street at Yankee Road. Surrounding it was an attractive, middle-class neighborhood. Respecting this, Armco's policy was to make its plant attractive and to be a good neighbor. Within a mile of the plant there was a fine high school, a library, elementary schools, and churches. This aerial photograph from the Mayfield collection shows a view of the neighborhood to the north of the general office and Central Works. Although taken in 1955, many landmarks remain today.

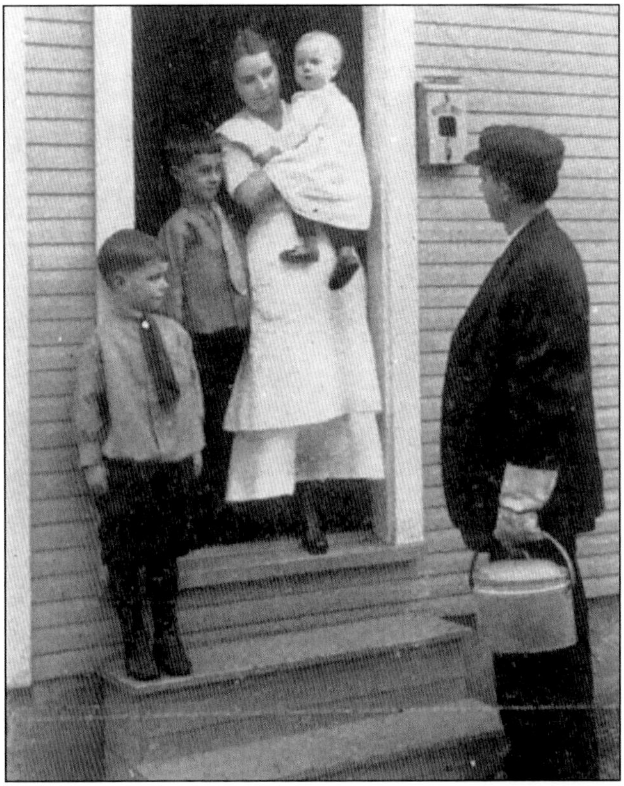

In this photo, Earl Otterbein, a typical early Armco employee, bids his family goodbye as he heads for work. He will be protected by an Equitable life insurance policy, the first such policy ever written in the hazardous steel industry, and the premiums will be paid by Armco. He will work an eight-hour day, as Armco was the first steel company to initiate such a policy in an industry based on the 12-hour shift.

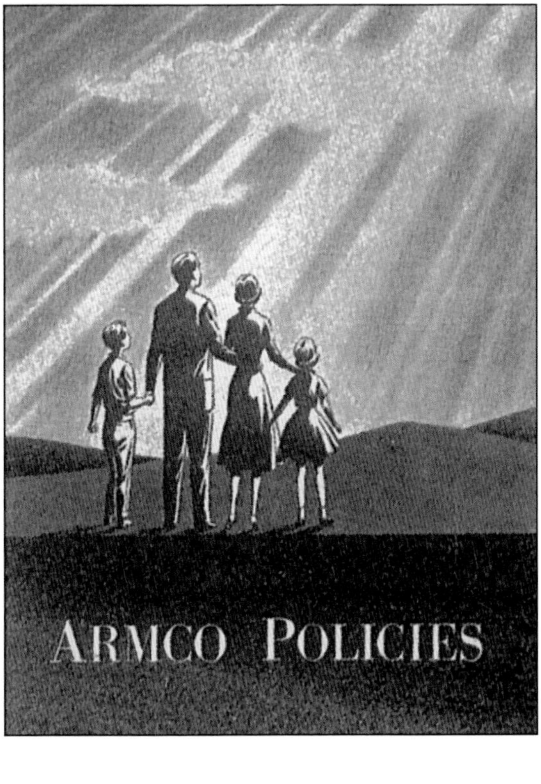

Written by George M. Verity and adopted by the board of directors, all workers were protected by what Verity called the "Armco Constitution." It set up a partnership between the company, its workers, and the community. It promised all workers a square deal, incentives to do the best job possible, and opportunities for promotions. Verity truly based the company on his faith in men.

In order to promote safety, Armco commissioned the Iron Man statue. Each year it was awarded to the plant that had the best safety performance of that year. Armco was an early supporter and member of the National Safety Council founded in Milwaukee, Wisconsin, in 1912. Armco led the movement to start a local chapter.

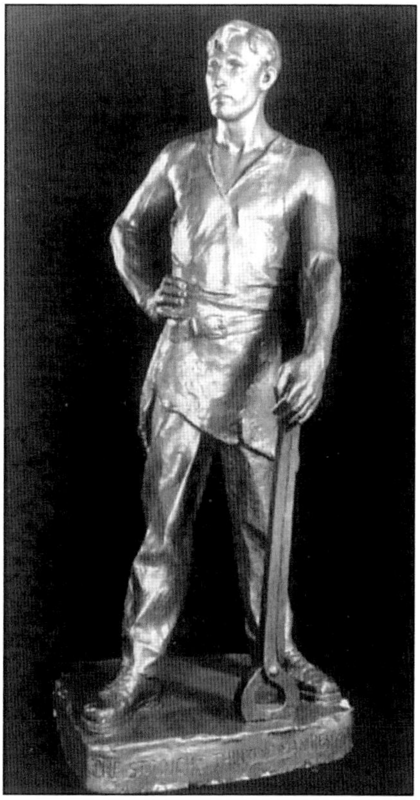

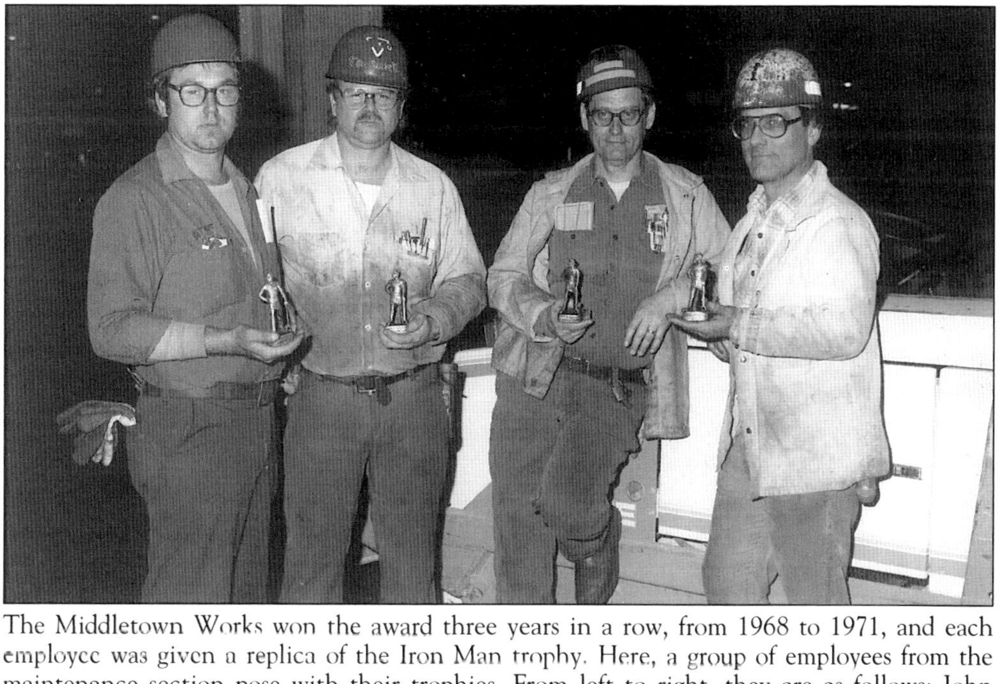

The Middletown Works won the award three years in a row, from 1968 to 1971, and each employee was given a replica of the Iron Man trophy. Here, a group of employees from the maintenance section pose with their trophies. From left to right, they are as follows: John Crowe, Tom Sorrell, Steve Countryman, and Tim Bechtel.

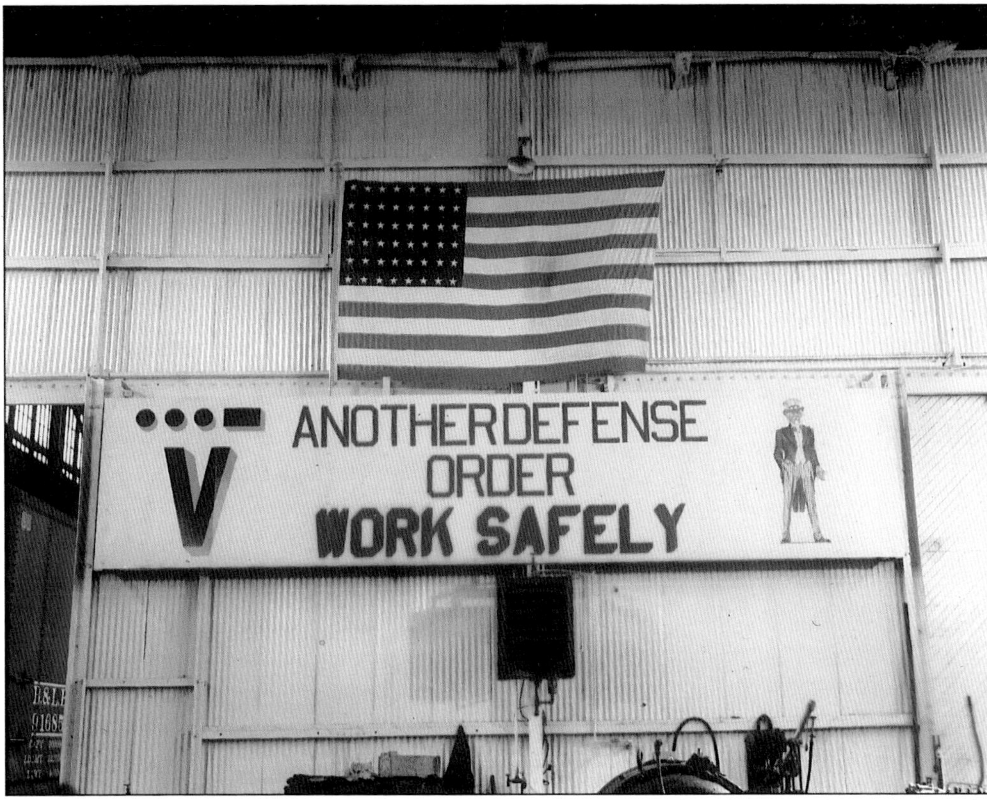

Even during those hectic days of World War II, Armco put "safety first," as shown here. The company was dedicated to saving lives. In addition to keeping workers on the job, it produced tons of steel used to win the war.

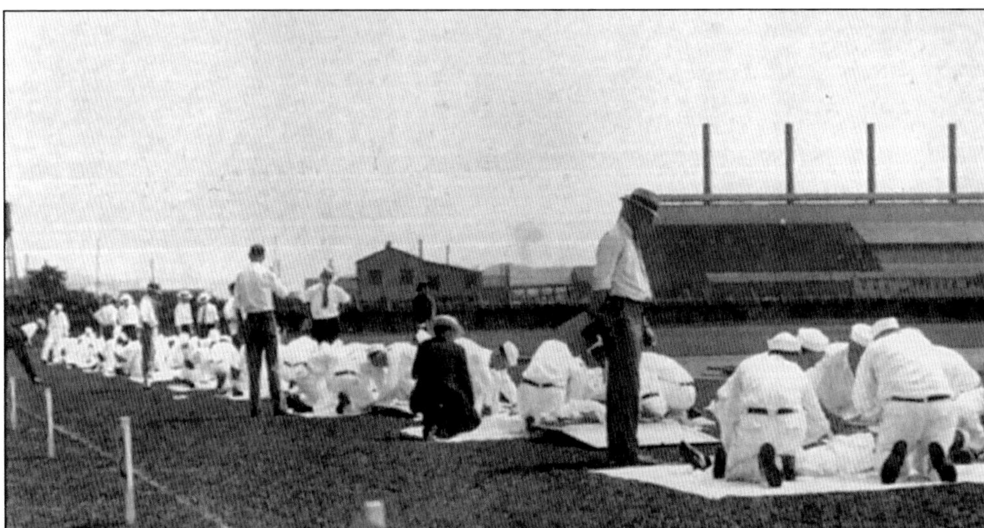
For many years, in preparation for an accident, Armco sponsored an annual contest at the Middletown plant known as the "First Aid Meet." Here, representatives of each Armco facility met for an event billed as one that would "vie with sports as an exciting contest".

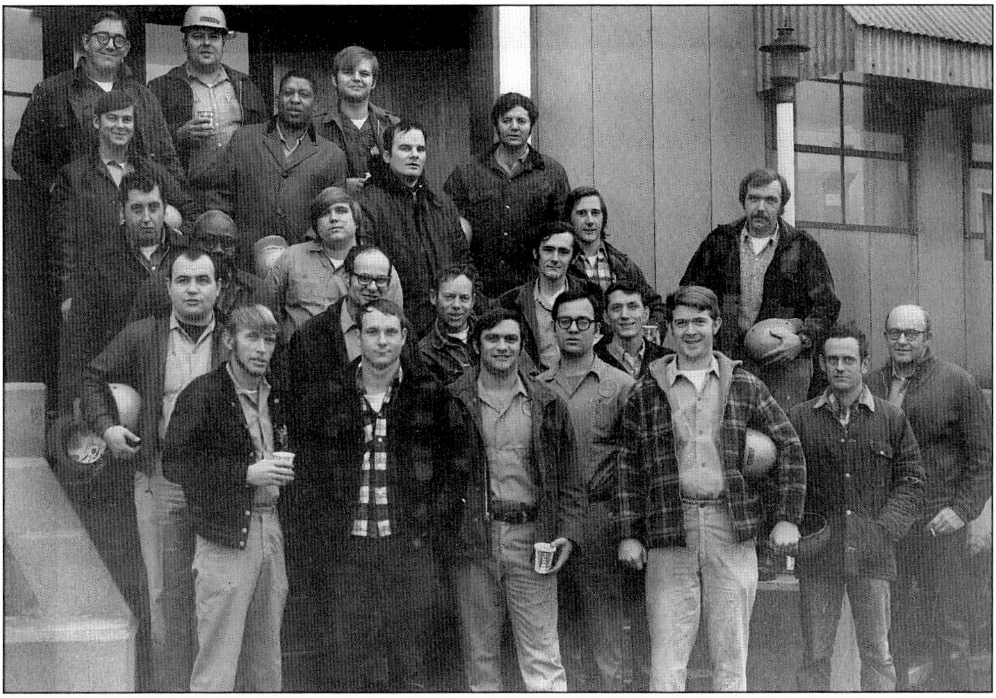

An Armco maintenance training class is shown in front of the training building in 1972. Roger Miller was a member of this class. For many years, Armco's technical training school was the biggest in the area, and every Armco worker was given an opportunity to work toward advancement.

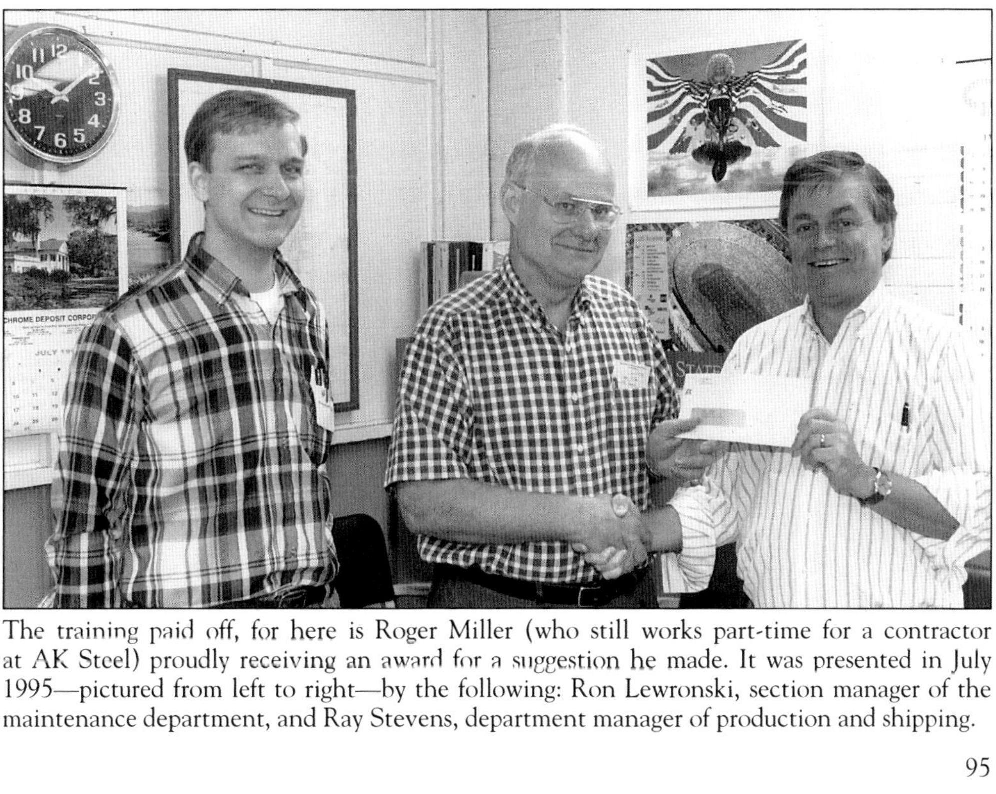

The training paid off, for here is Roger Miller (who still works part-time for a contractor at AK Steel) proudly receiving an award for a suggestion he made. It was presented in July 1995—pictured from left to right—by the following: Ron Lewronski, section manager of the maintenance department, and Ray Stevens, department manager of production and shipping.

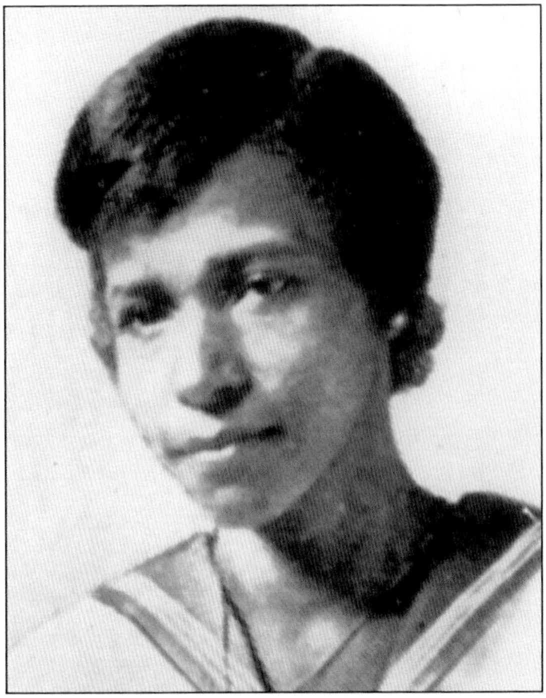

Willymay Durant, a graduate of the Tuskegee Institute in Social Work and Education, was employed by Armco in 1918 to counsel women and children. She taught the public school's first kindergarten class, and organized a Mothers' Club.

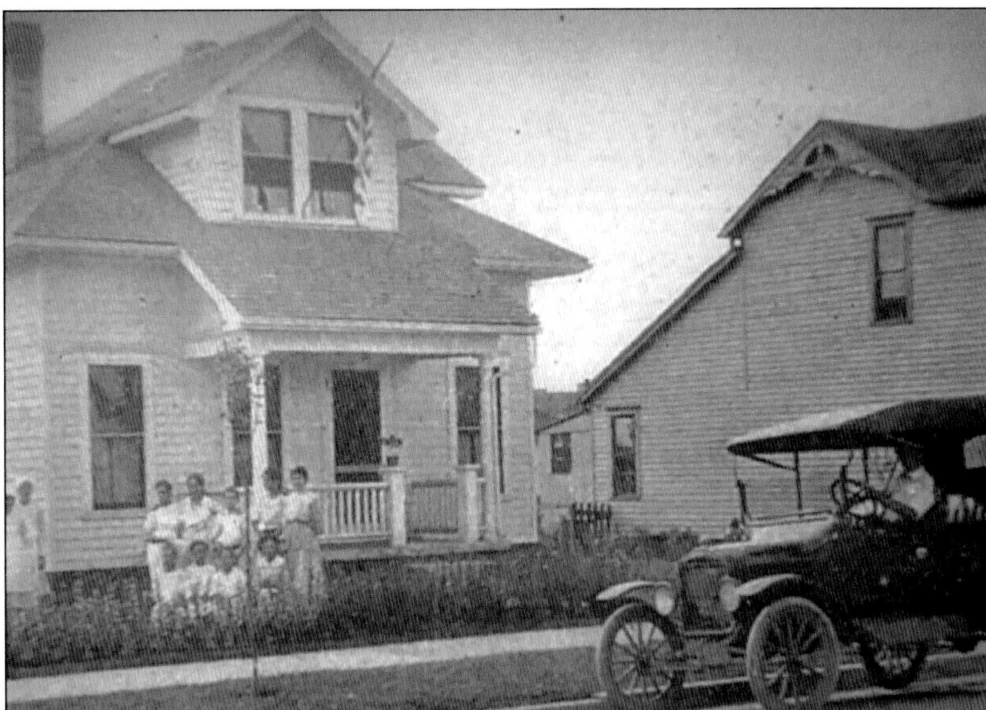

Armco's social services department had its headquarters in this house in the city's southern section, where many African Americans and recent European immigrants first settled. For Armco employees, it was a convenient area in which to live.

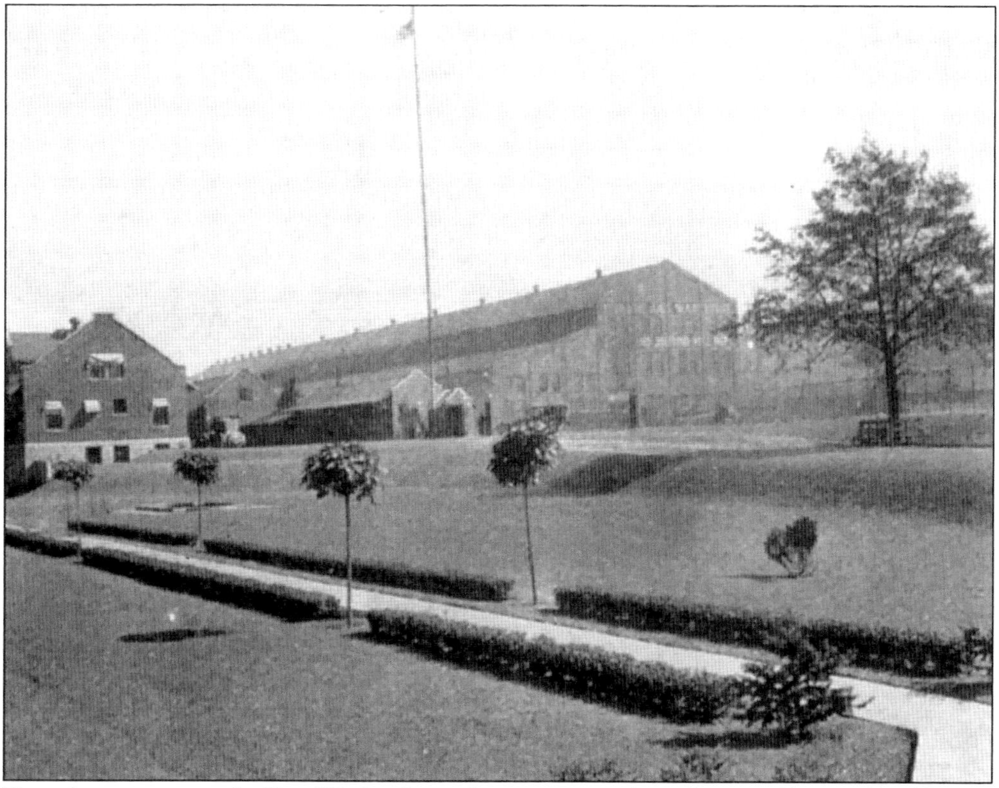

Near the entrance to the East Works, shown here, was a modern, fire-proof hospital building. It was completely equipped to care for injuries. Surgeons were on duty, as well as trained nurses. Armco also provided its own ambulance staffed with trained personnel.

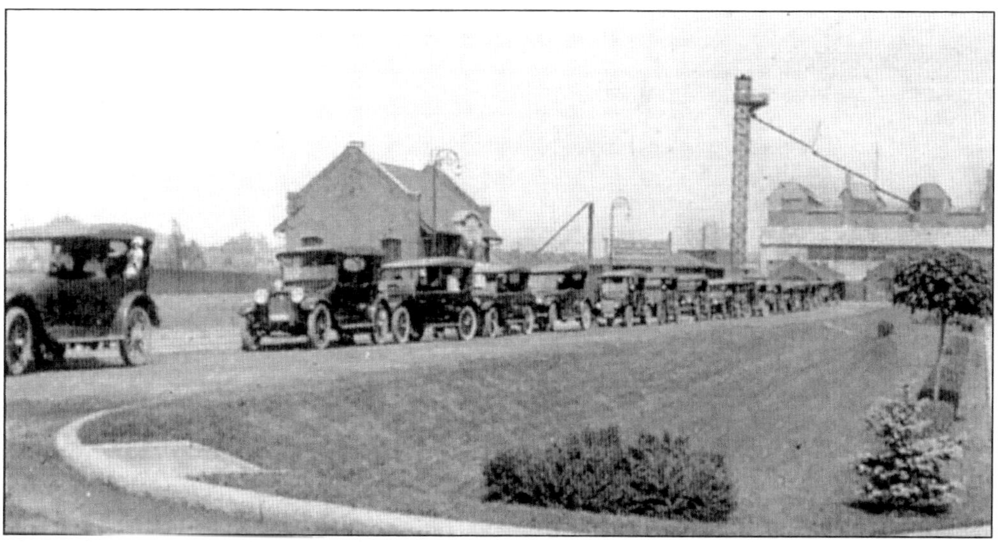

Shown here is a view of the Armco Bank on a payday in 1920. It was located just outside the entrance to the East Works for the convenience of employees. The Armco Bank was a branch of the local American Trust and Savings Bank.

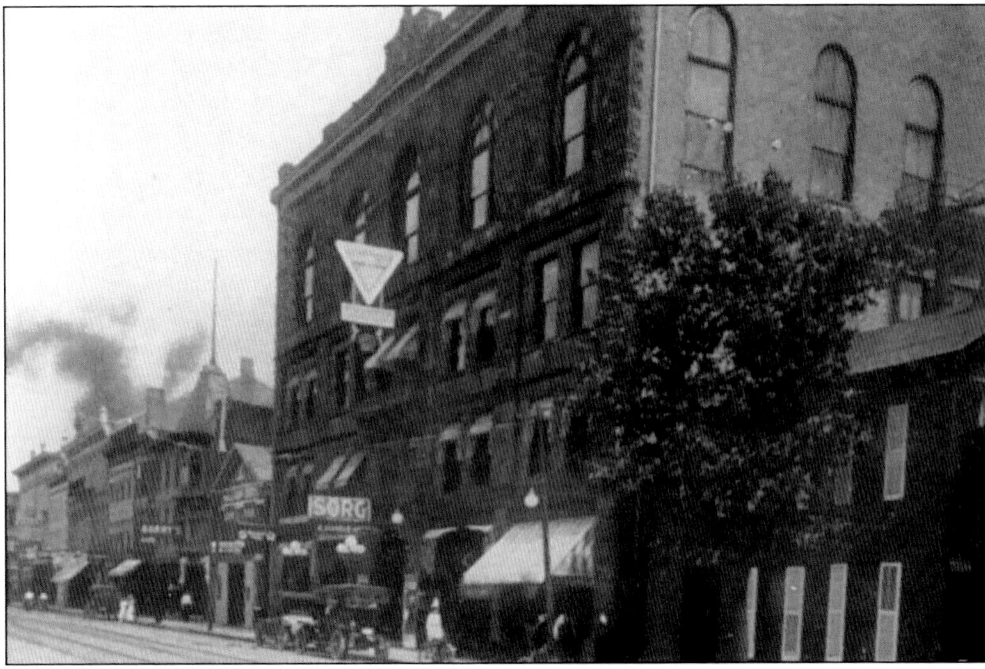

The Armco Association got its start in 1903. It was an employees' mutual benefit organization originally located in the Sorg Building. Later, it moved to a small office at the Middletown Works, where Mark Walke, its long-time secretary-treasurer, is remembered for his efficient handling of sick benefits and wise financial counsel.

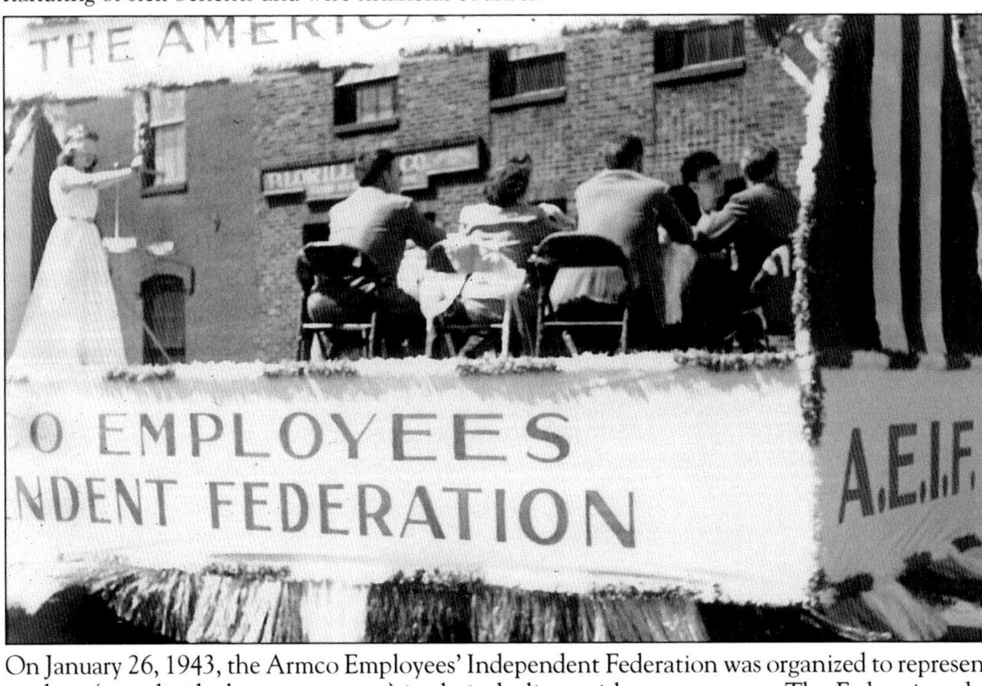

On January 26, 1943, the Armco Employees' Independent Federation was organized to represent workers (as individuals, or as a group) in their dealings with management. The Federation also participated in community projects and events, such as those members shown on this float in the "I Am An American" Day parade, on May 19, 1946.

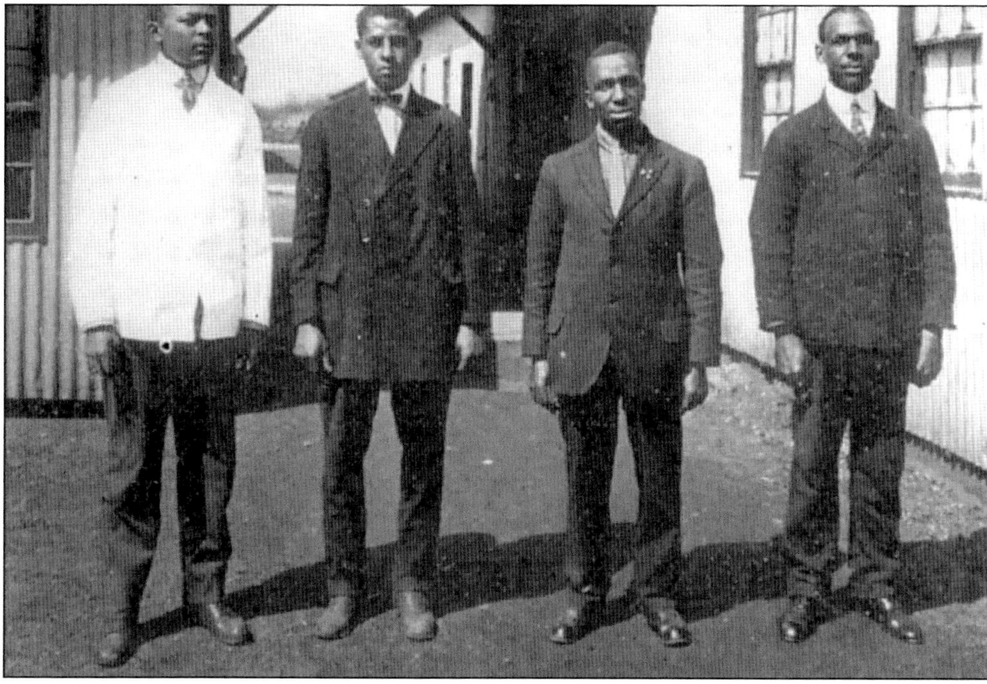

During World War I, Armco employed over 1,000 African-American workers from the rural south. To orient them to Middletown life, the company set up its own recreational and educational activities, working with the Armco Colored Club. In 1917, it hired a corps of trained professional personnel. Shown here, from left to right, are: Tom Callier, Charles Eves, Charles Shannon, and James M. Montgomery.

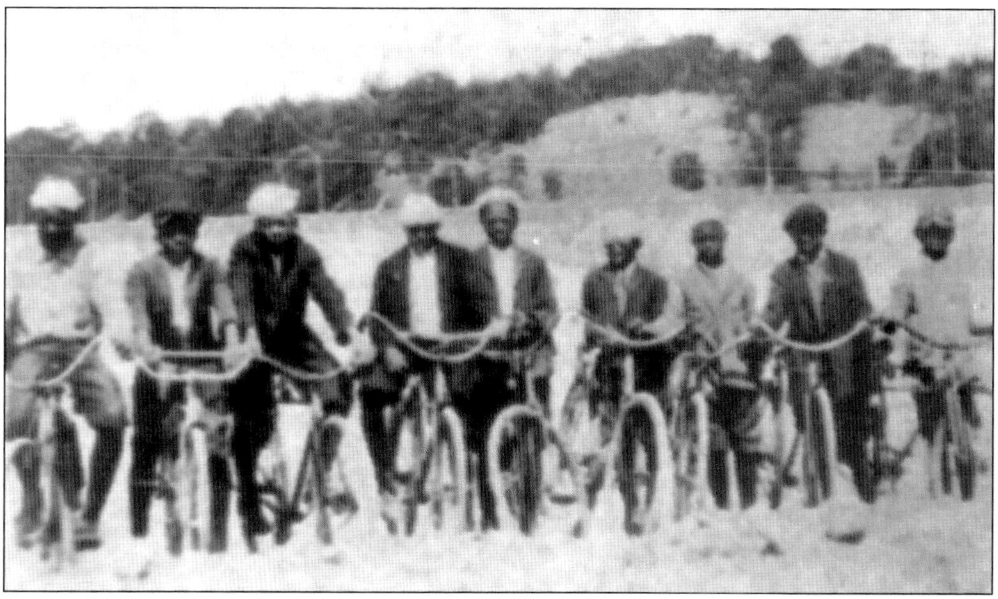

Many of the new employees decided to settle in Middletown and later sent for their families. By the 1920s, Leroy Robbins was employed to work with these families. One activity he organized was a Boys' Bicycle Club, shown here resting after a ride to the Miami Valley Chautauqua in Franklin.

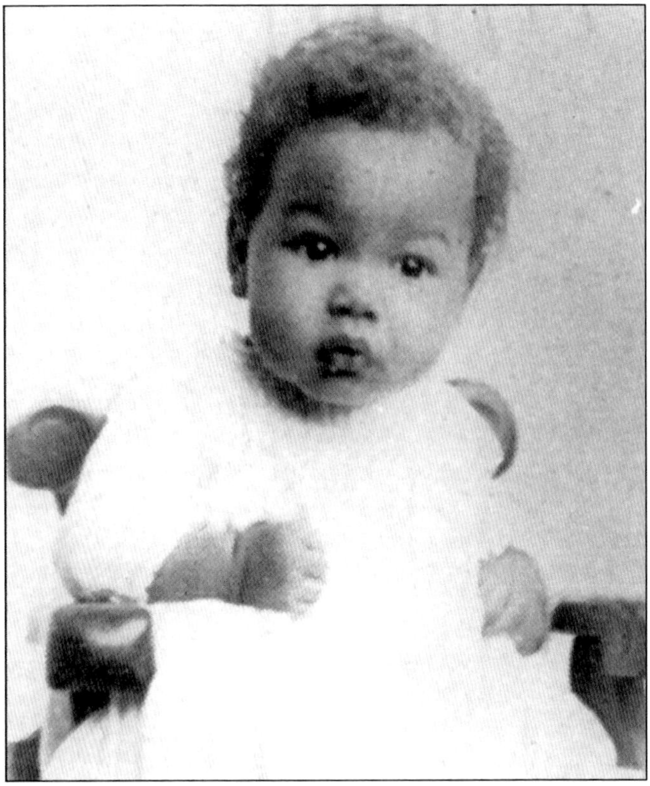

In 1914, Armco began publication of the *Armco Bulletin*. One of its most popular features was the section showing pictures of Armco babies. Here is J. Gerald Morgan, son of J.W. Morgan, who, after working at the Open Hearth, was promoted to millwright in the sheet mill. Gerald, a 1917 arrival, became a noted Columbus physician, and retired in 1999.

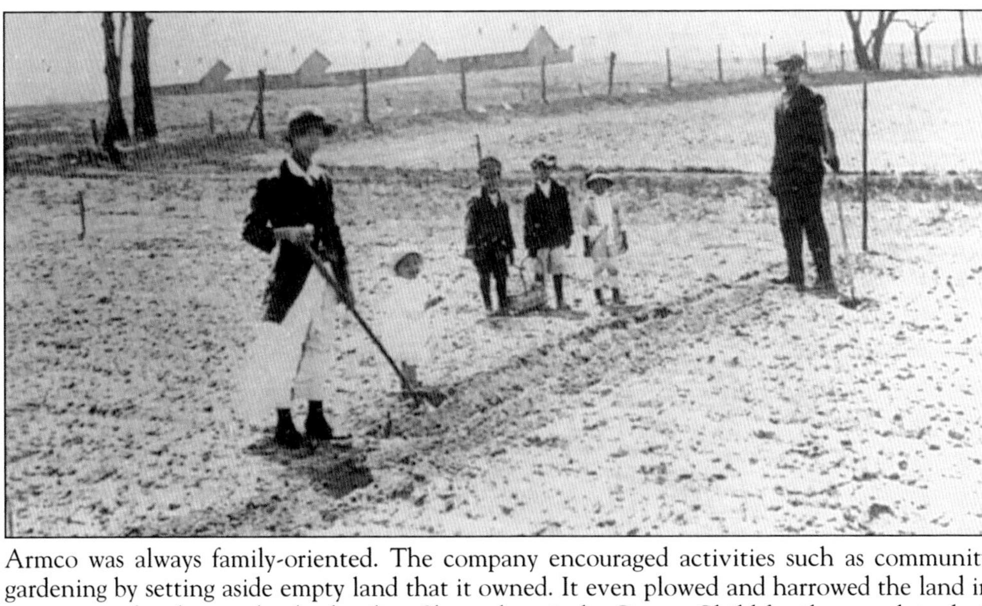

Armco was always family-oriented. The company encouraged activities such as community gardening by setting aside empty land that it owned. It even plowed and harrowed the land in preparation for planting by the families. Shown here is the George Child family at work in their 1918 Victory Garden.

The Armco Ballpark, on company property just southeast of the general office building, had been laid out and equipped with a grandstand. The sports season began in the fall with Armco's football team. Here is the 1914 team.

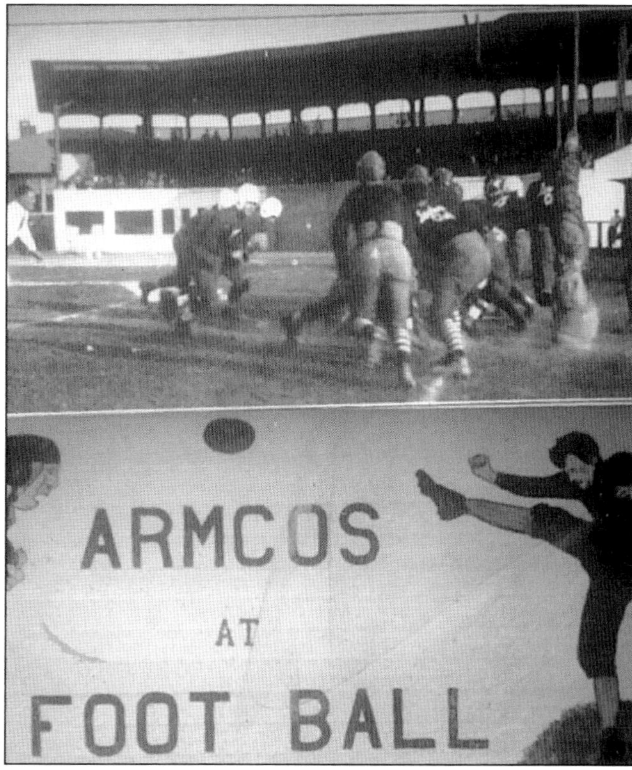

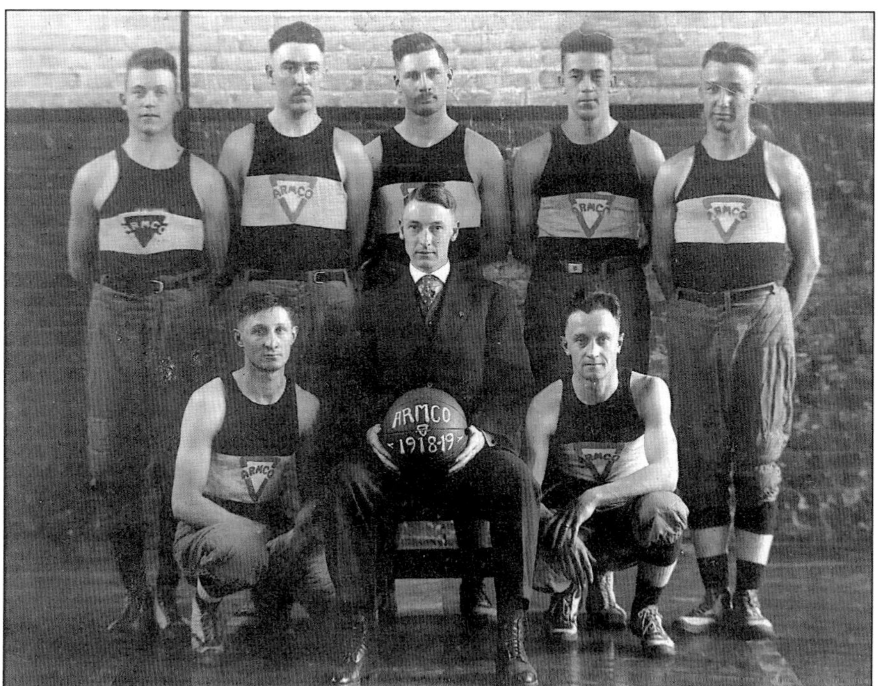

Winter brought out the basketball team, identified by the famous Armco Triangle. This photo shows the winning team from the 1918–1919 season.

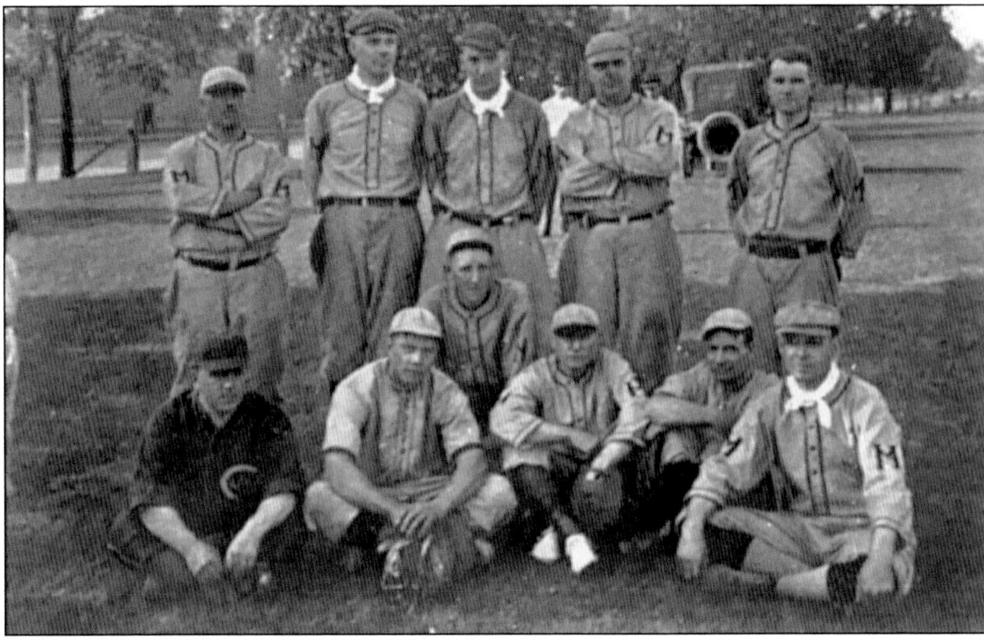

The "Boys of Summer" made up Armco's largest and most popular group of athletes. Baseball teams were organized in different departments for intramural play. Members included everyone from the average worker to the top brass—Calvin Verity, Hook, Tytus, and Vorhis, among others. Pictured here is the1914 team.

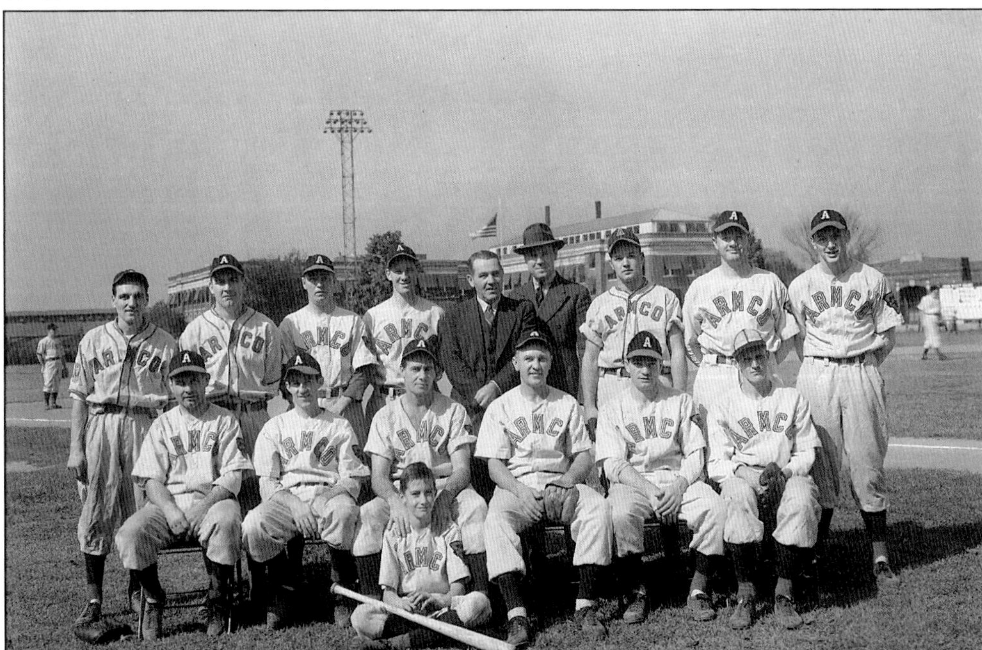

As years passed, baseball continued to increase in popularity. The best Armco players were picked for spots on the Armco All-Stars in 1941, the team that challenged the best teams of the area. Even the Cincinnati Reds played at Armco Field.

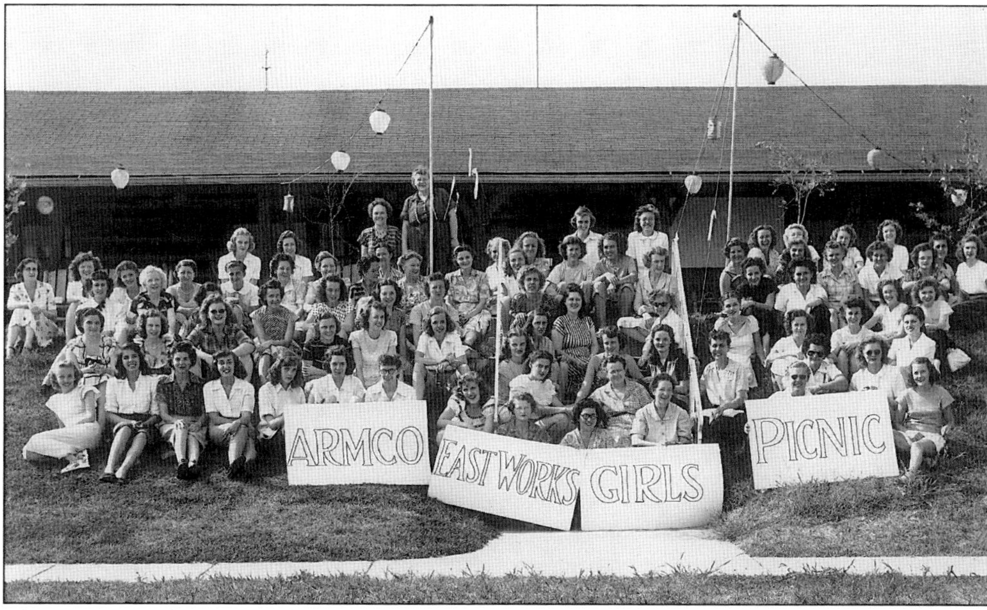

The Armco Girls, organized in 1919, had become a large group by 1948. Only five women were listed on the 1905 payroll. In August 1948, they paused for a photo at nearby Camp Campbell Gard. Note that they labeled themselves as "Girls."

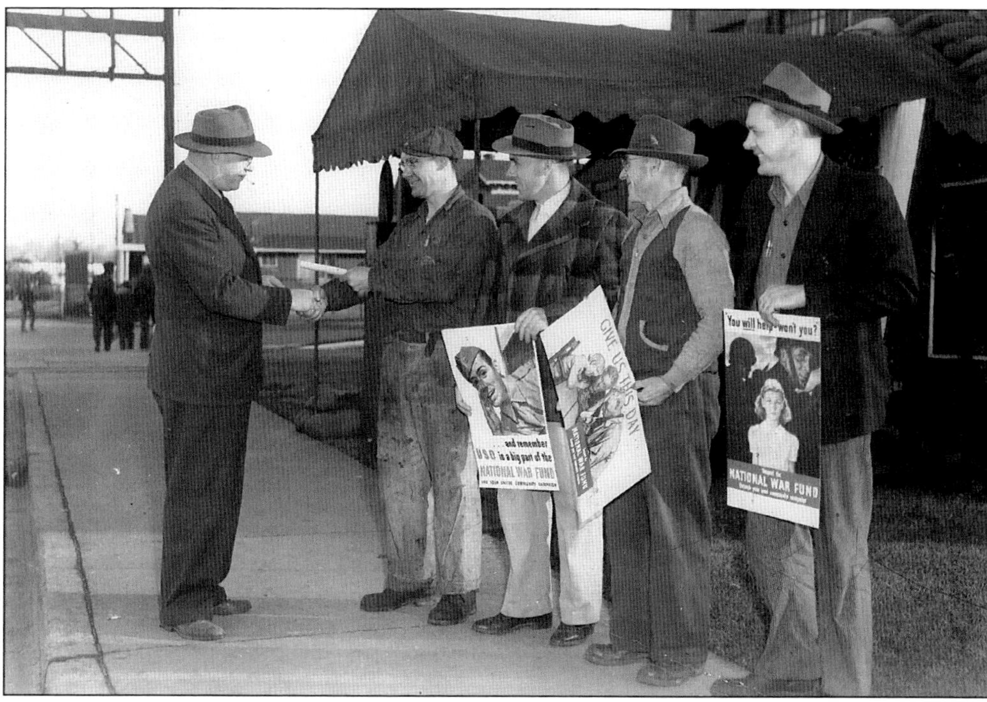

During World War II, Armco workers joined in every fund-raising project they could to benefit those in uniform. Above is William F. Johnston, chairman of the Victory War Chest Drive, receiving a report from Lee Miller (of the annealing and pickling section, East Works), Curtis Hunter and Chester Francis (of the swing grind section), and Richard Snider (of the polishing and shipping department). This photograph was taken in November of 1943.

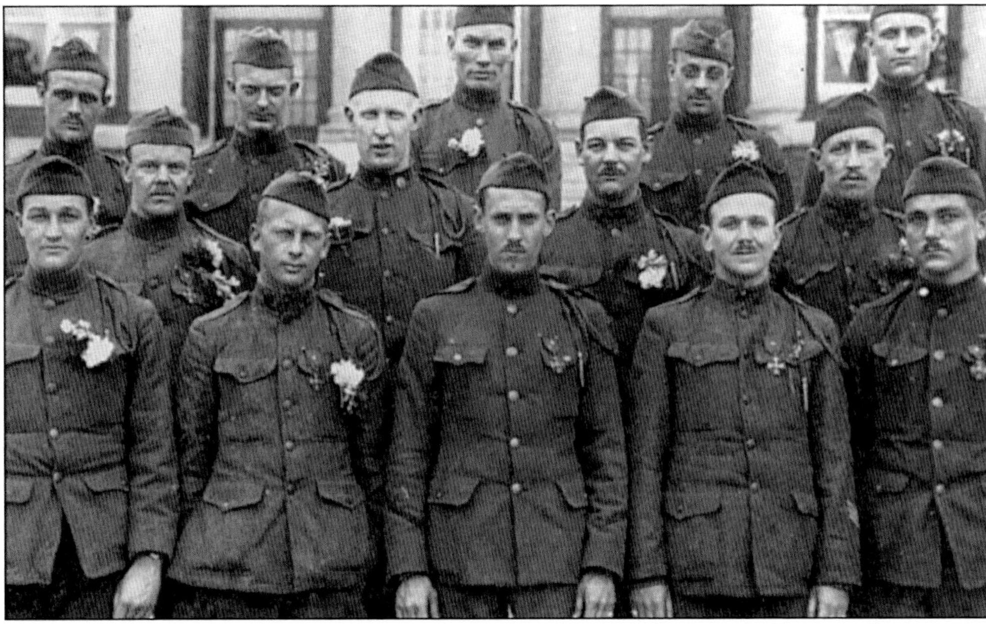

One of Armco's patriotic gestures during World War I was supplying ambulances and equipment for the Armco Ambulance Corps. After being sworn into the U.S. Army, it sailed for France on August 7, 1917. The group returned home on May 3, 1919, and participated in a big community parade. This photo was taken on the steps of the general office.

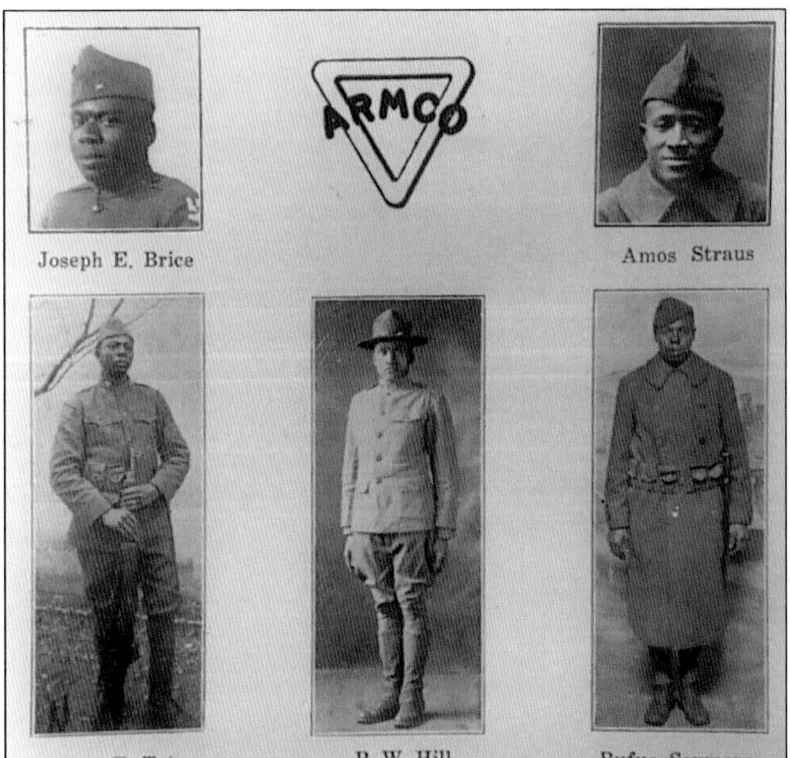

Armco was also proud of its other employees who joined the armed forces during World War I. In all, 690 Armco men served, and all were promised that their jobs would be waiting for them upon their return. Among the returning veterans were the men shown in this Armco photograph around the famed Armco Triangle.

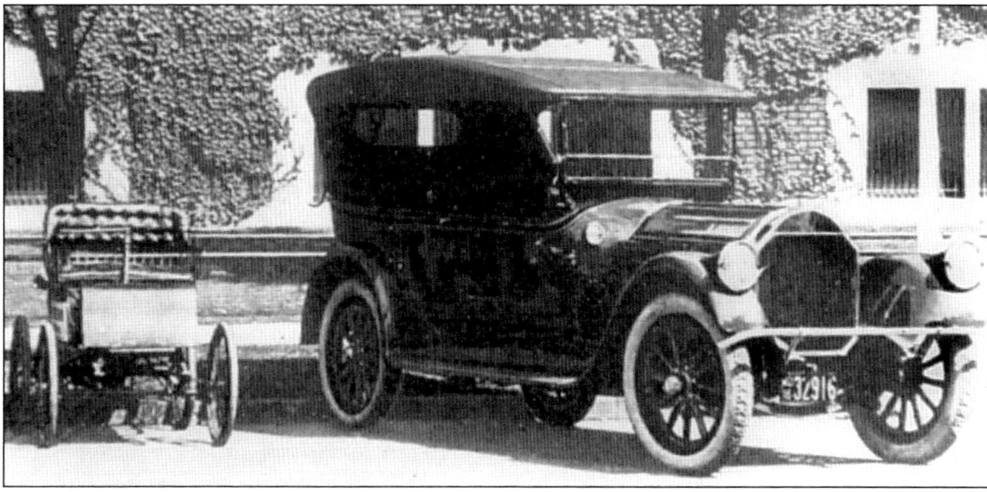

Armco kept employees informed about how the steel they made was used. The company's efforts included displays of finished products around the plant, including appliances and furnaces. Their biggest customer was the automobile industry. Here is one of the displays with a 1919 Pierce-Arrow, along with its first model, both of which contain Armco steel.

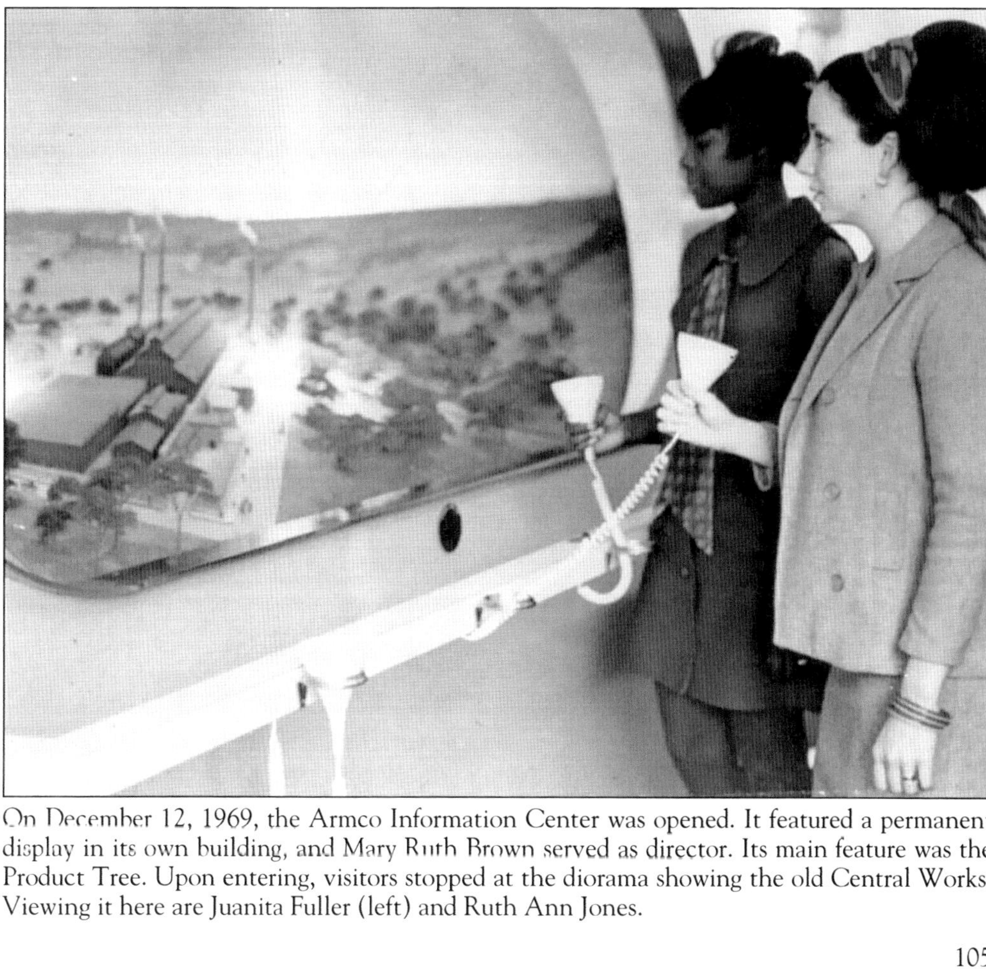

On December 12, 1969, the Armco Information Center was opened. It featured a permanent display in its own building, and Mary Ruth Brown served as director. Its main feature was the Product Tree. Upon entering, visitors stopped at the diorama showing the old Central Works. Viewing it here are Juanita Fuller (left) and Ruth Ann Jones.

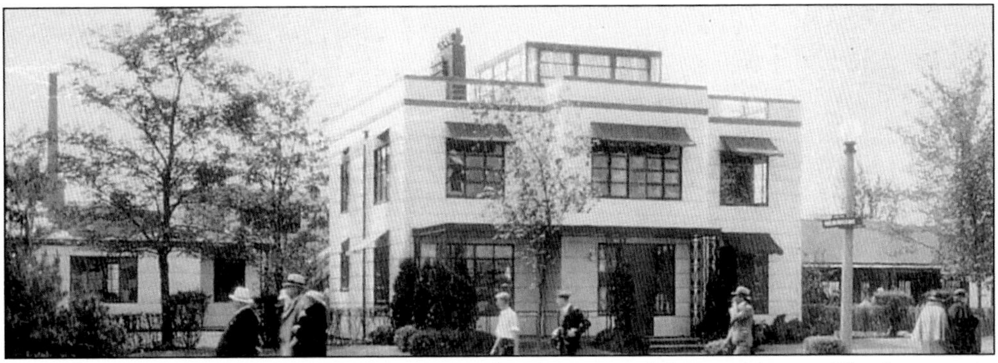

One of Armco's most unusual projects was its development of the steel house. The first one in the area was built at Poasttown Heights in August of 1933 for George Creech. The "Armco-Ferro porcelain enamel frameless steel house," as shown above, was erected for the nation to visit at the Chicago World's Fair in 1934.

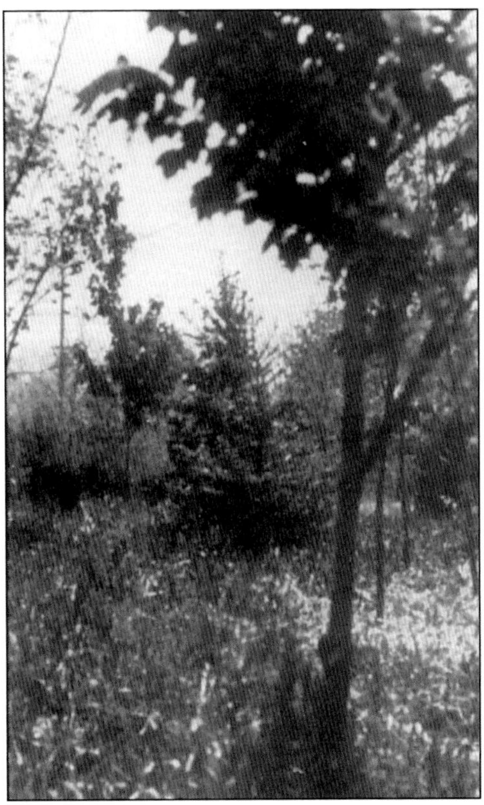

In 1976, Armco began planting a 60 to 90-foot greenbelt around the perimeter of the plant. It started with 3,200 trees and 41 varieties of bushes, planned not only to beautify the area, but to improve air quality as well. Known as the "Bubble Concept," the plan won the approval of the U.S. Environmental Protection Agency.

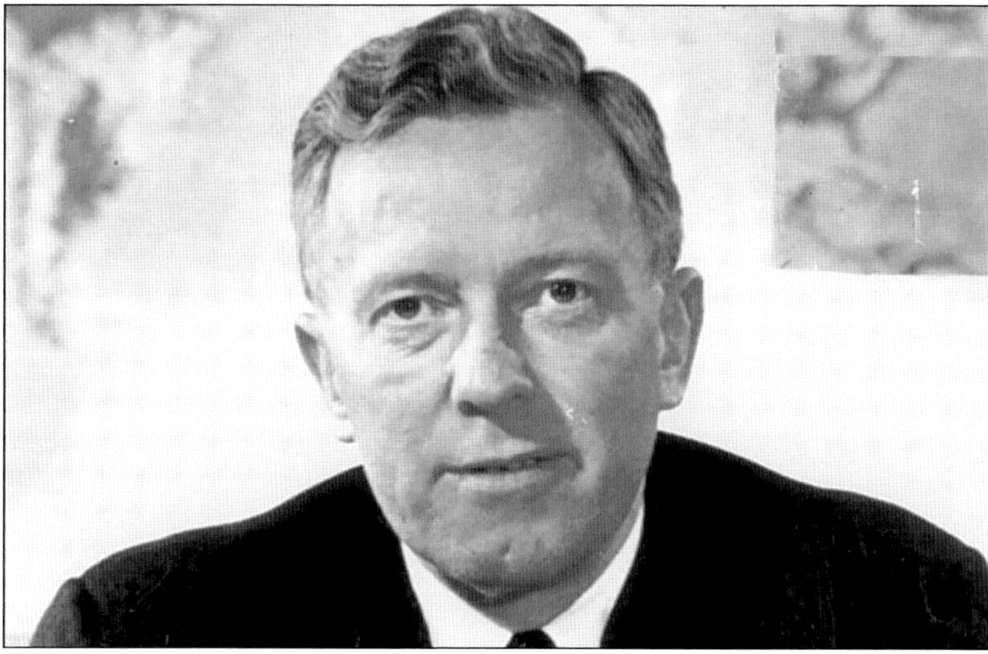

Armco encouraged its leaders to participate in government service both locally and nationally. C. William Verity, grandson of the founder and the sixth president of the company, was appointed secretary of commerce by President Ronald Reagan on October 19,1987. Verity is a Yale graduate (class of 1939) and served in the U.S. Navy during World War II.

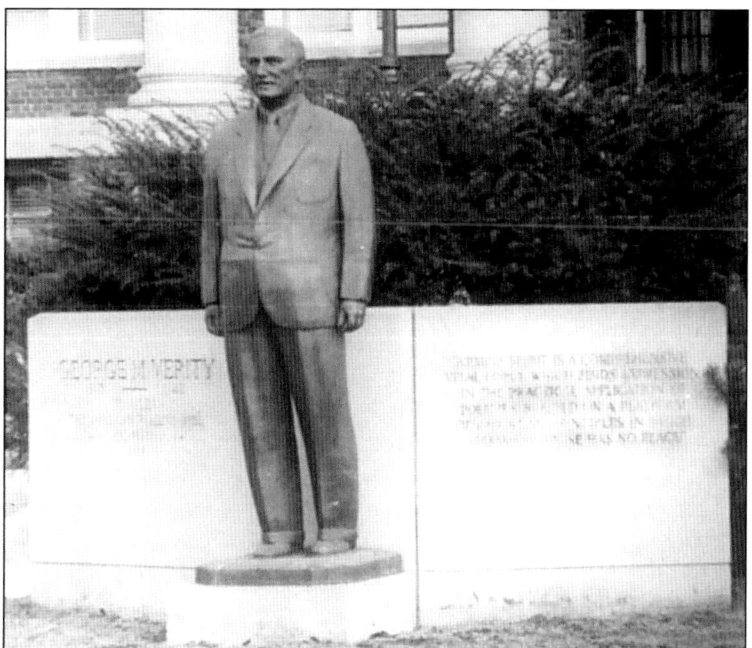

In front of the Armco general office stands this life-size bronze figure of George M. Verity, a creation of sculptor Ernest B. Haswell. It was commissioned after Verity's death, cast by the Mazzolini Art Foundry in Yellow Springs, Ohio, and unveiled on April 22, 1948.

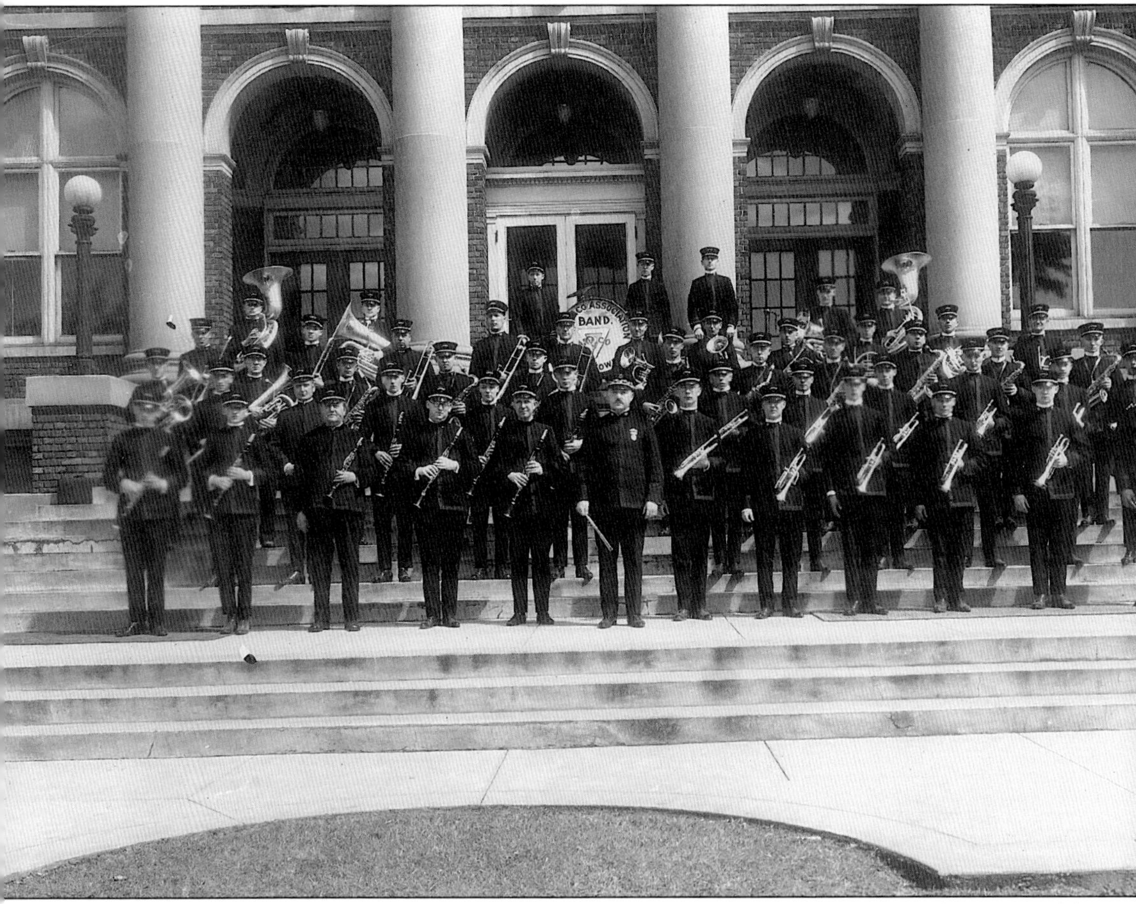

One of the most popular groups sponsored by Armco was the Armco Band, organized by Conductor Frank Simon in 1921. Simon had previously served as assistant conductor of John Phillip Sousa's famous military band. The Armco Band made its radio debut on May 28, 1923, on local radio station WLW. In 1929, it became a regular weekly commercial feature on the NBC network. The program was broadcast for 13 years. The sponsorship of a radio program in exchange for advertising a basic industry product (that was not purchased directly by the consumer) was an innovation at the time. This was another practice first established by Armco. A talented advertising executive, Bennett Chapple, was chosen by Verity as the "Voice of Armco," and he became known on the network as the friendly "Ironmaster." Bandmaster Simon featured local talent on his broadcasts, which sparked a musical renaissance in the city. Here, the band poses on the steps of the Armco general office building. Simon is the gentleman holding the baton.

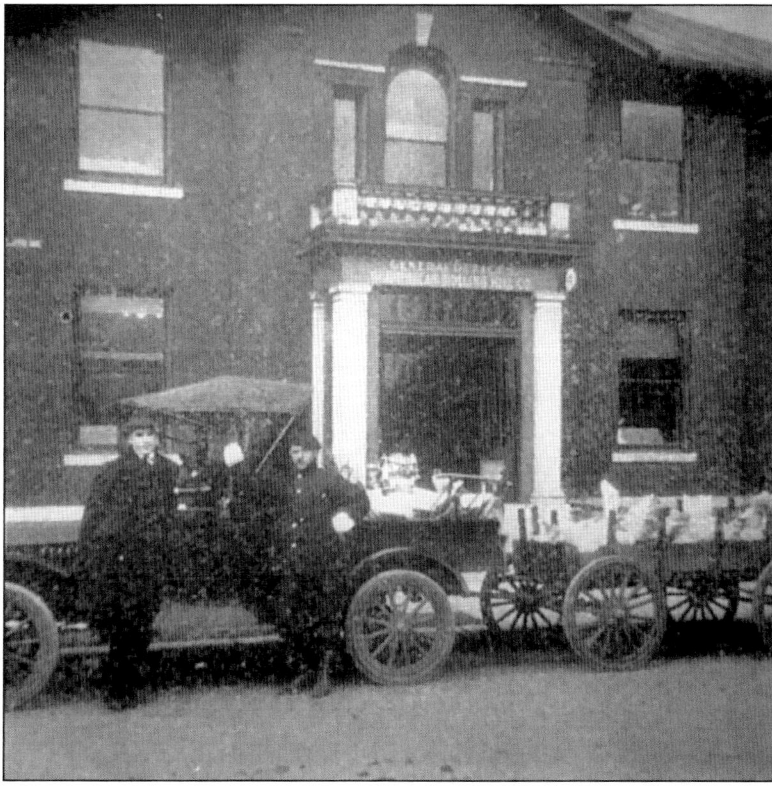

Armco always stood ready to help the less fortunate. Oftentimes Verity (known for his quiet good deeds), in addition to workers in Armco's departments, would undertake a charitable project, such as the making and delivering of Christmas baskets. This photo shows men ready to leave from the general office with the completed baskets in December, 1916.

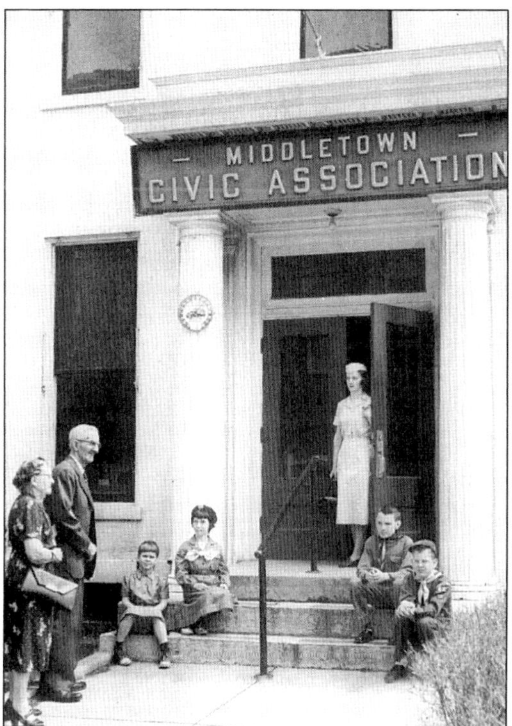

Realizing the need for assistance for community projects, Verity proposed a campaign to raise $1 million to fund-worthy agencies in 1920. To administer the fund and set up a means for permanently funding future projects, the Middletown Civic Association was founded in 1923. Its headquarters were located at Broad and Manchester Streets.

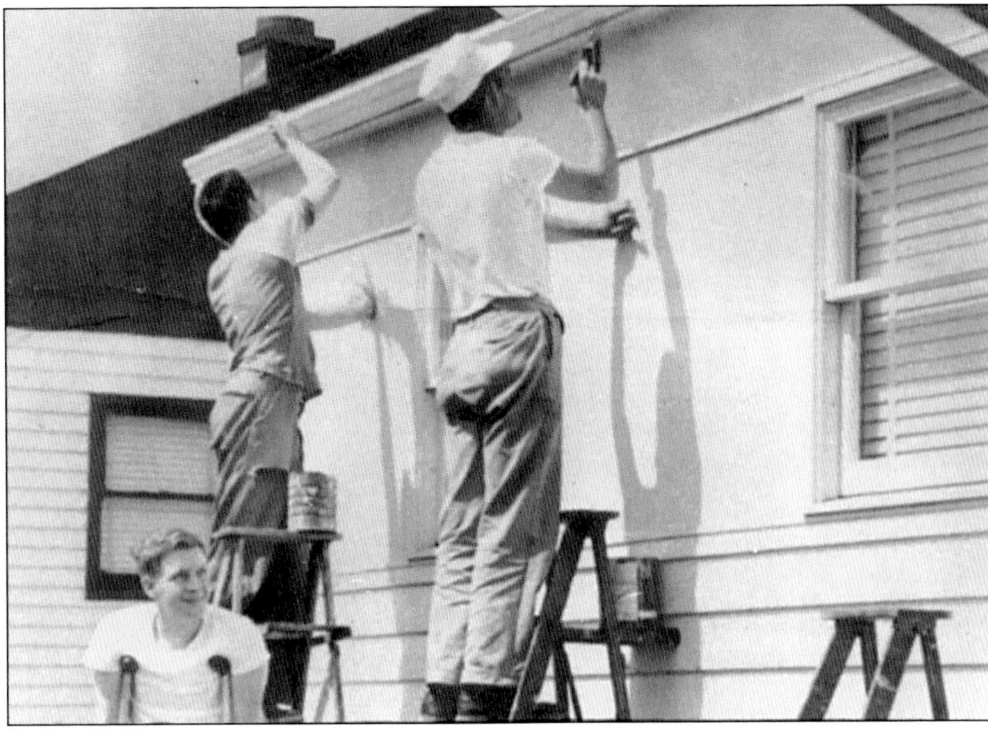

Upon the death of George M. Verity, workers such as Joe Gividen searched for a way to honor him. They suggested that Armco men and women set aside the founder's birthday, April 22, to remember him by doing a good deed for others. Founder's Day began in 1944, and has continued since that time. This April 22, 1953, photo shows Armco men painting the house of a fellow worker who was on crutches due to an accident.

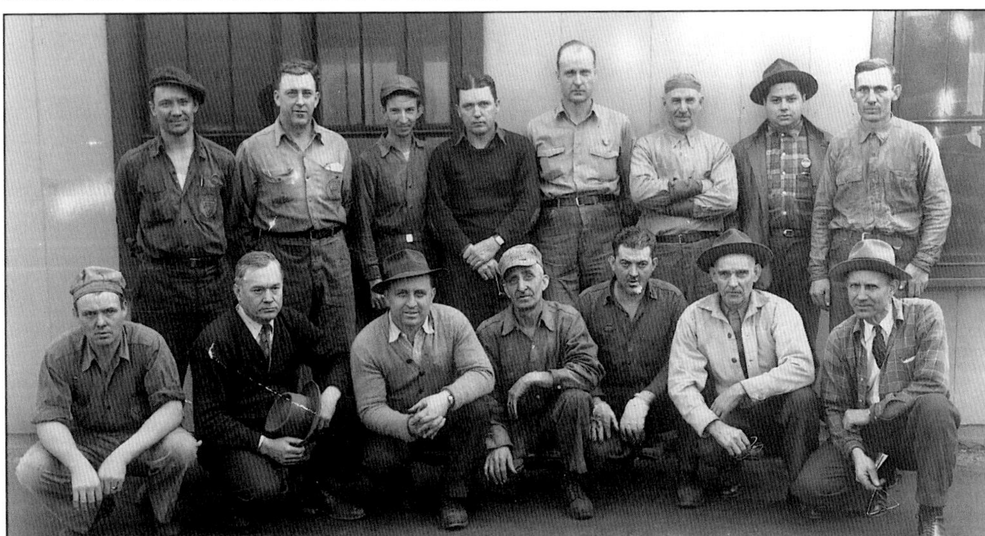

Here is a group of volunteers from the stainless steel polishing and shipping group, who have just completed a Founder's Day project—husking 20 acres of corn for a disabled farmer. Author Roger Miller can only identify one man in the photo—Lee Miller, his father, is standing at the far left.

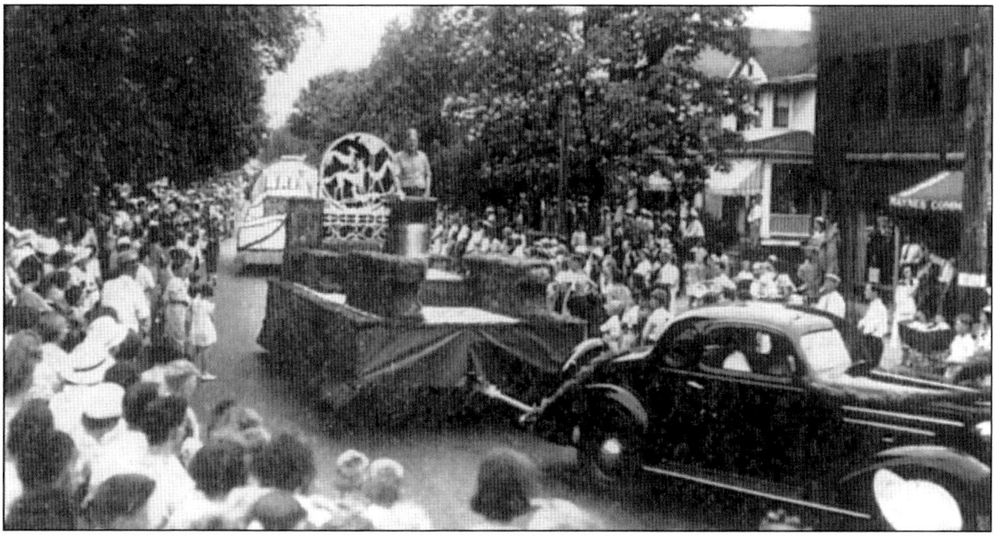

Armco has always shared its celebrations with the community. The company's first 20 years of service was celebrated with a National Armco Day parade. Another special day honored the company's founder. On June 6, 1936, with 3,000 marchers and 44 units, the parade shown here rounded the corner at Central Avenue and Bellemonte Street.

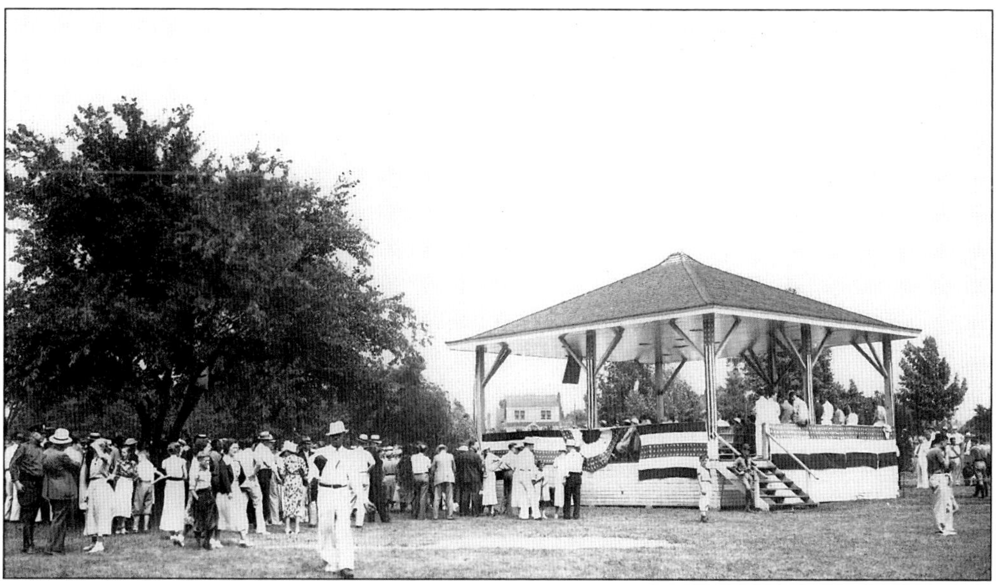

The parade proceeded to Sunset Park, where official ceremonies were held at the bandstand. An estimated 25,000 Middletonians attended some part of this celebration. But the 50th birthday celebration of the company surpassed all others, when 60,000 people descended on Sunset Park. One hundred and fifty thousand free hot dogs, along with soft drinks and other items, were served.

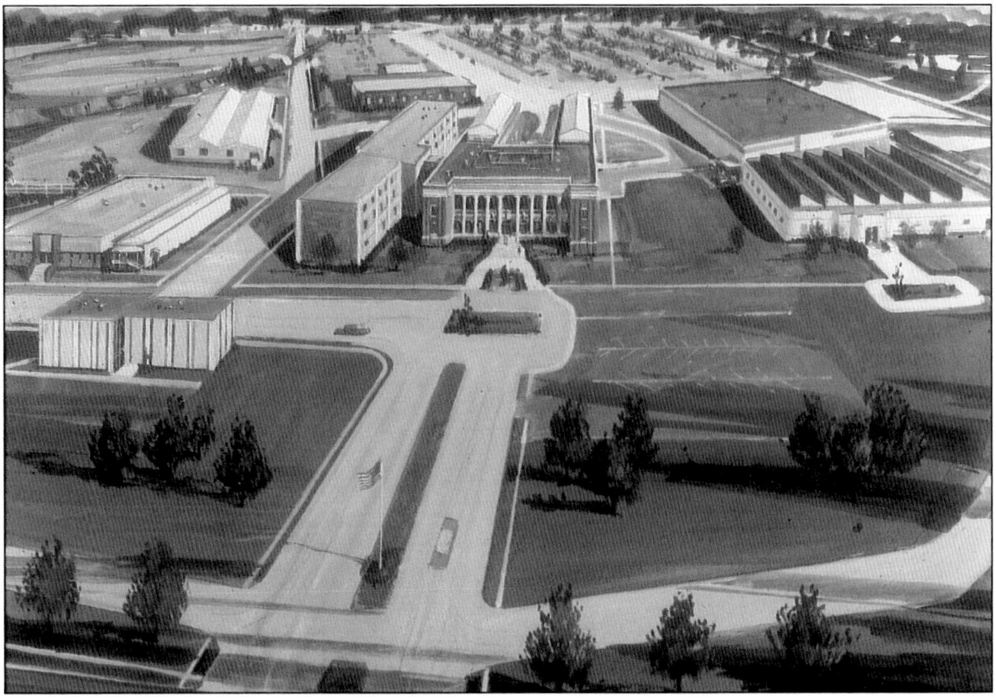

As Armco made plans for its 75th anniversary celebration, it also announced a major expansion plan for the general office complex on Curtis Street. The west side of the street would be cleared, part of Curtis Street would be closed, and a park area would be created between Verity Parkway and Curtis Street.

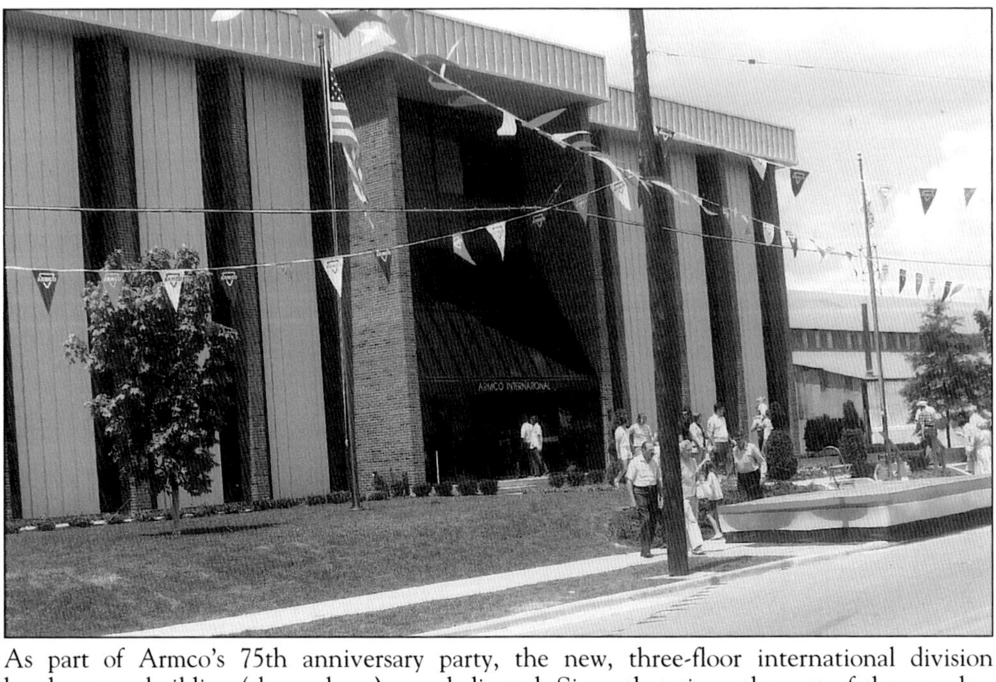

As part of Armco's 75th anniversary party, the new, three-floor international division headquarters building (shown here) was dedicated. Since that time, the rest of the area has been maintained as a park.

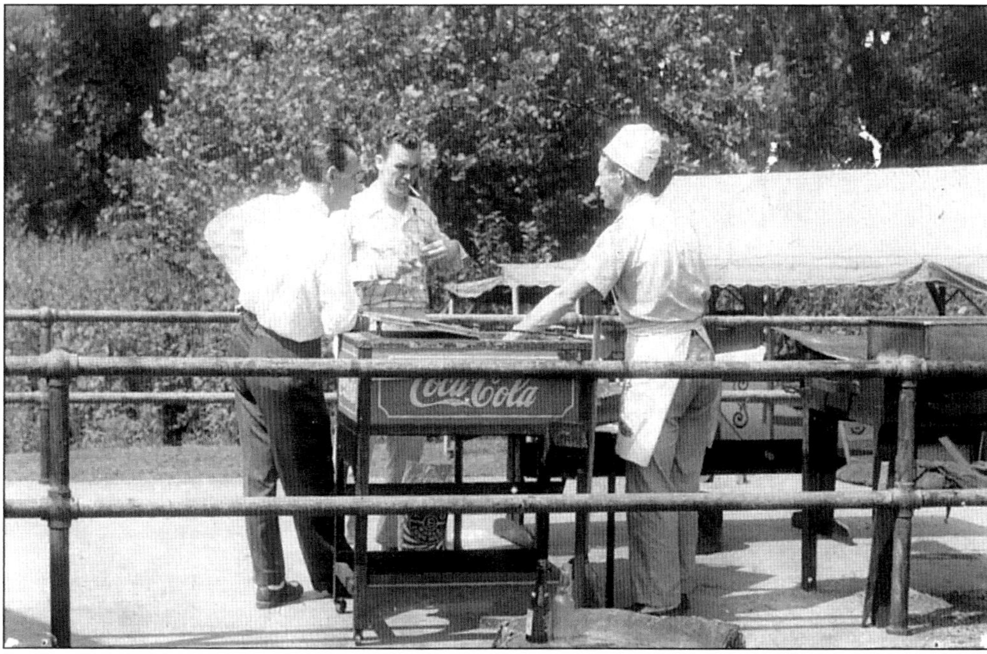

Various Armco departments used to plan individual picnics each summer. Here are three men, sometime in the 1940s, preparing for the cold strip mill picnic held one evening at the boathouse, which was located north of Middletown along the Great Miami River. From left to right, they are as follows: Ralph Wright, Joe Tharp, and Bill Frisby.

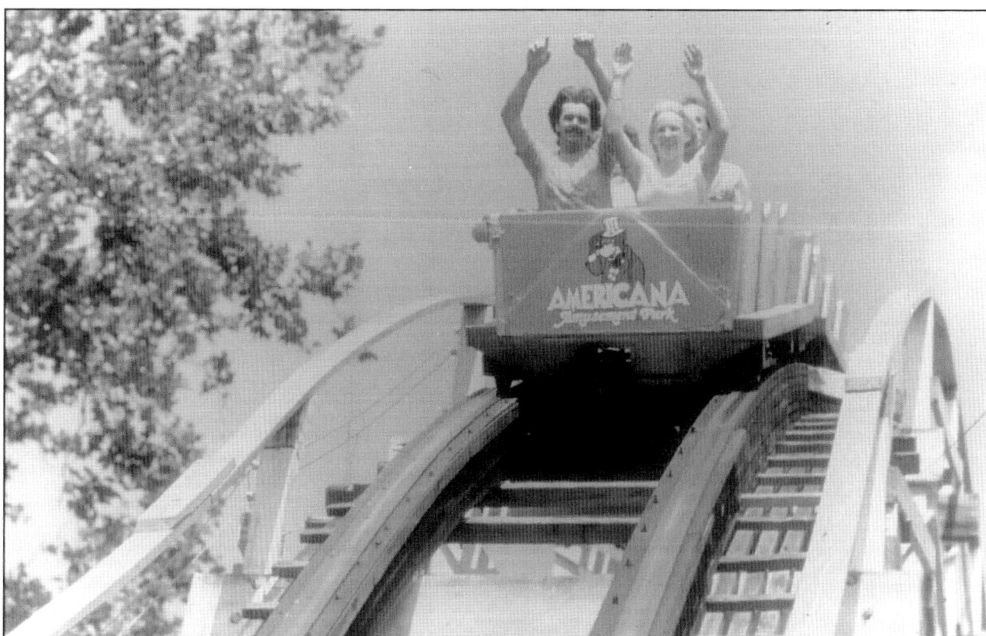

For many years Armco sponsored a big annual company picnic at the popular LeSourdsville Lake (later known as Americana). Nothing offered more thrills than the classic wooden roller coaster. Armco provided free transportation to the park from the old railroad station along First Avenue, near the Big Four tracks.

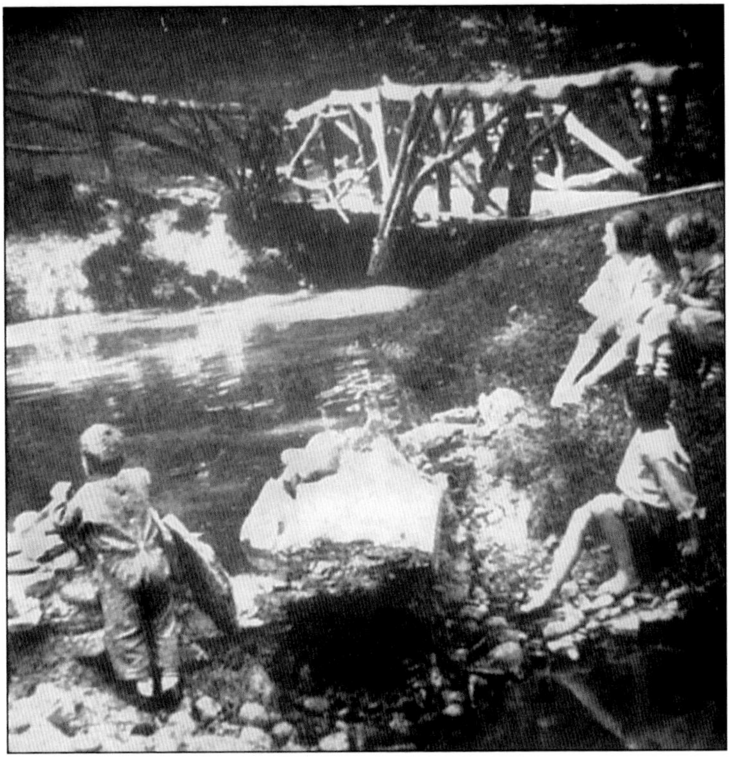

Armco Park, in northeast Middletown, was opened as a community park in 1922. From that time until 1968, the company took care of all maintenance costs. Bunny Hollow was the section set aside especially for children. Here is a group around the "shining pool."

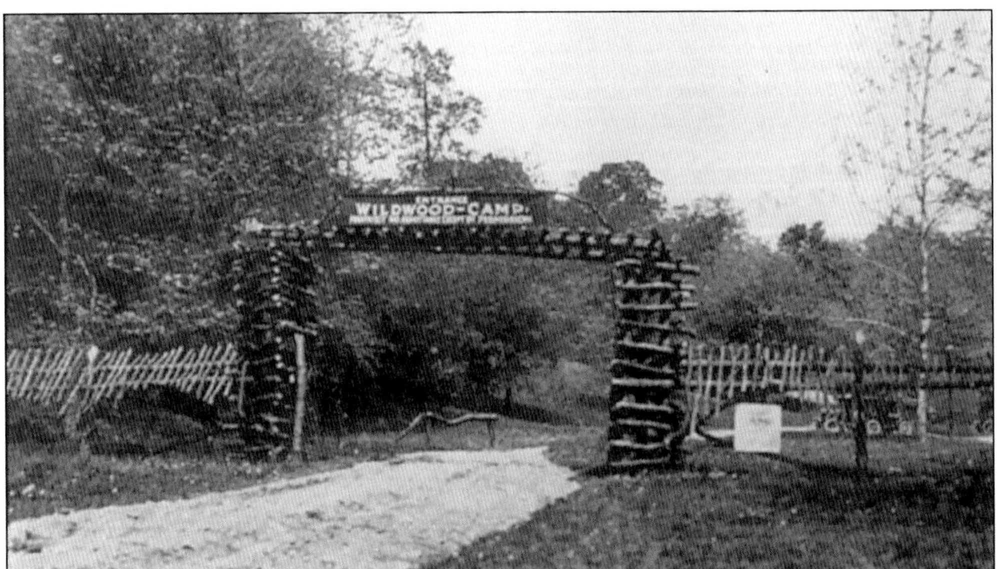

Another section of 17 acres was set aside as Wildwood Camp, complete with tents, a kitchen, and a recreation hall. It was first used by Boy and Girl Scouts, as well as by other groups with reservations.

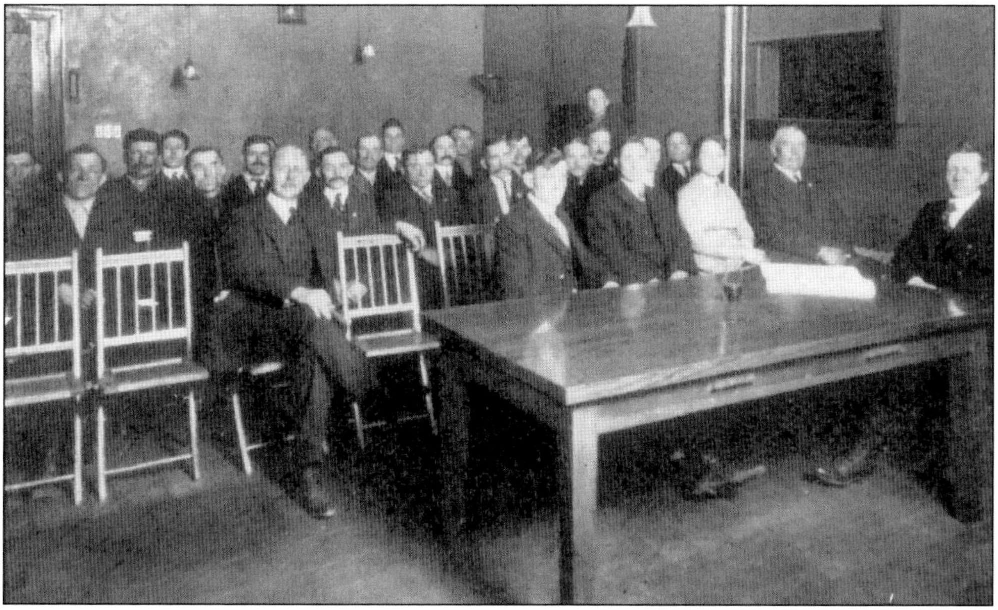

Long before local public schools sponsored what were known as "Americanization classes," Armco offered them. This 1920 photo shows one such class held in a company classroom. Armco urged all new, foreign employees to become citizens.

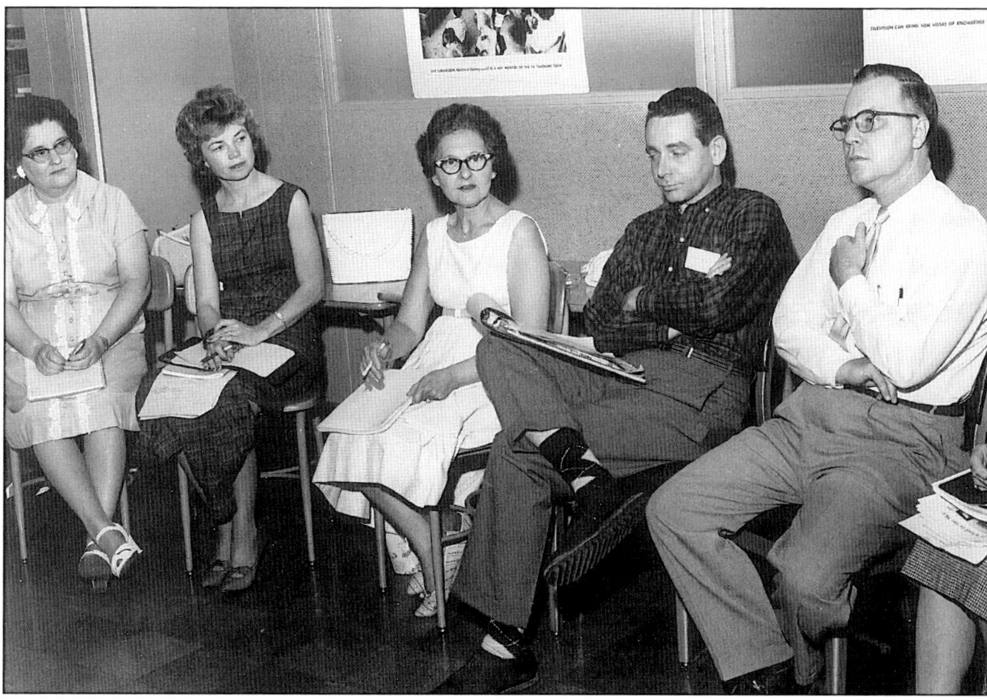

Armco's dedication to education was not only manifested by its support of local schools, but also by its interest in teacher education. For almost half a century it sponsored the "Community Resources Workshop" as part of an effort to alert teachers to see the community as a laboratory for learning. Here is a group from its first workshop in 1951, in session at Miami University in Oxford, Ohio.

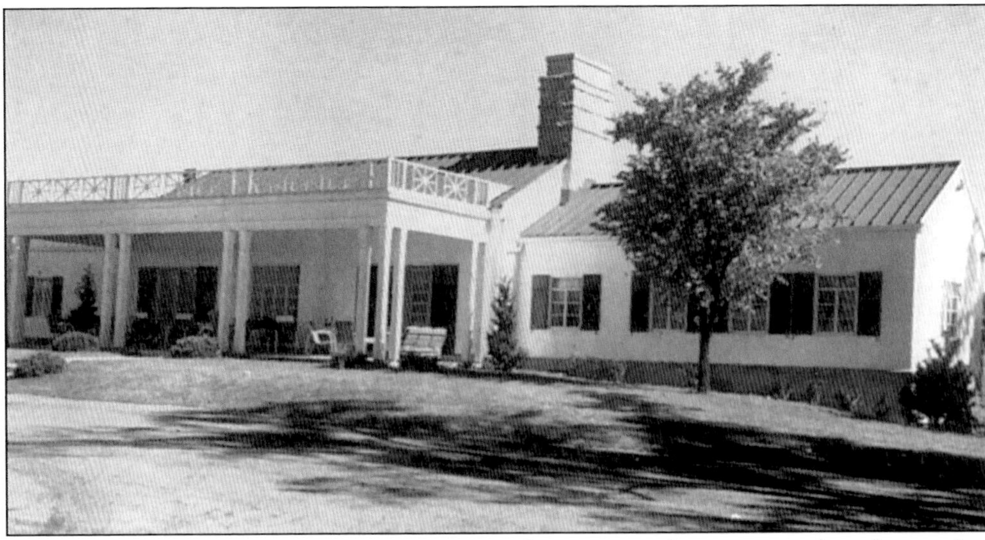

Armco was most generous in its corporate giving. Its greatest gift was in providing thousands of good jobs for local citizens. But, in the common meaning of the word, the company's greatest gift to Middletown was the 127-acre site (formerly Armco Park) for conversion into the Miami University branch campus. This included the former Holiday House used by Armco Girls, that is now the student center.

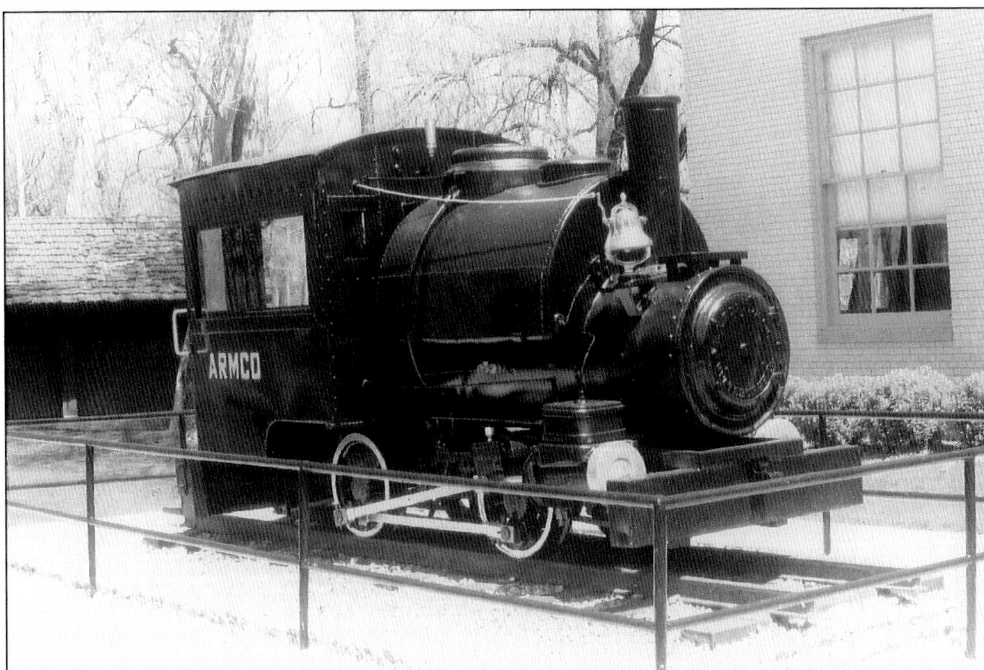

Through the years, Armco made hundreds of gifts to the community—land for a campus, sites for a parochial school, an arboretum, two golf courses, and two parks (Douglass and Wildwood). It also donated historic items to museums elsewhere, including this 1907 locomotive that was given to Carillon Park in Dayton, the steamboat *George M. Verity* that was donated to Keokuk, Iowa, and a large steam locomotive that made its final journey to the Illinois Railroad Museum in Union, Illinois.

Six

Steel City: AK and the Future

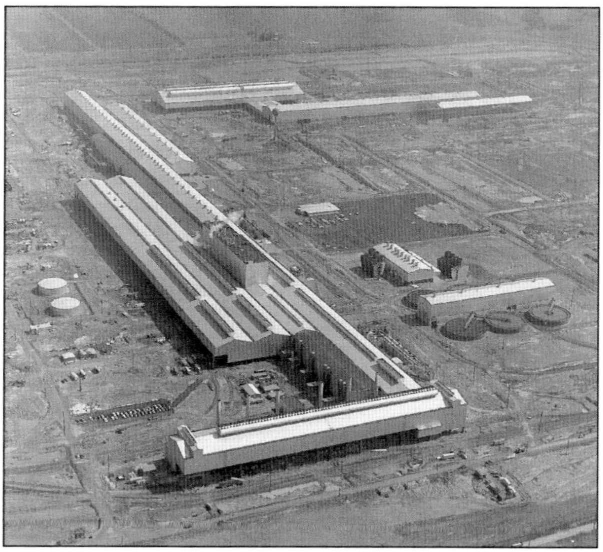

Throughout the twentieth century, Armco and AK Steel remained the major employer of the residents of Middletown and the surrounding area. Members of some families worked there for three generations, proud of their association with "Johnny Armco." However, the world outside of Middletown was changing. National markets became international ones, and new steel mills were built around the world. Armco kept the pace, and was ahead in technological changes, having built the world's most modern steel mill, as shown in the above aerial view

But Armco's management practices had not significantly changed with the passing years. By the mid-1980s the company began reporting serious losses, and was on the road to insolvency. This called for corporate changes and a new management team. In 1992, top Armco officials began to look for that leadership, which they found in veteran steel executive Thomas C. Graham. Graham was known for restructuring failing steel plants. His magic formula consisted of improving the productivity of the plant's equipment while downsizing the work force. It worked, and Armco became the most efficient and profitable plant in the steel industry.

On April 7, 1994, after another major corporate change, a new name was adopted—AK Steel. This was followed on September 29, 1999, with an announcement of the merger of what still remained of the old Armco with AK Steel. The icing on the company's 100th birthday cake was AK Steel's appearance, for the first time in its history, on the prestigious Fortune 500 list of great American industries for the year 2000.

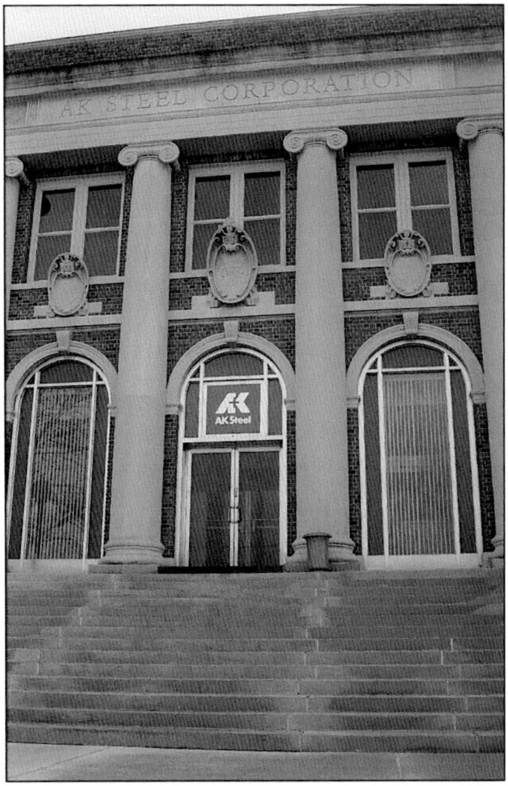

The Armco of today, by a circuitous route, has become AK Steel. Its corporate headquarters are currently located at 703 Curtis Street. The entrance, of a classical design, is a local landmark, and through it pass the men and women who make the Steel City possible.

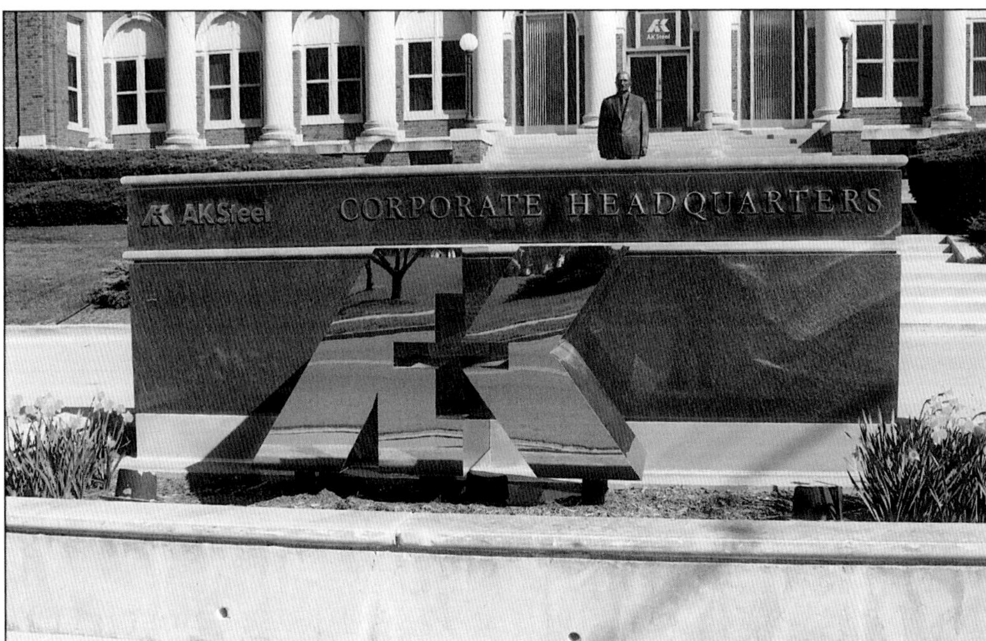

The AK Steel Corporate Headquarters sign now stands in front of the general office building, replacing the old Armco name. But George M. Verity's statue still stands, connecting the old to the new.

Thomas C. Graham, Armco's chief executive officer from 1992–1995, and chairman of the board from 1992–1997, was the 1995 recipient of the prestigious Benjamin F. Fairless Award of the Iron and Steel Society, in recognition of his achievement in steel production and metallurgy. In 1999, after reviewing the entire century, the industry's trade magazine (*New Steel*) picked him as one of the nation's outstanding steel executives of the past one hundred years.

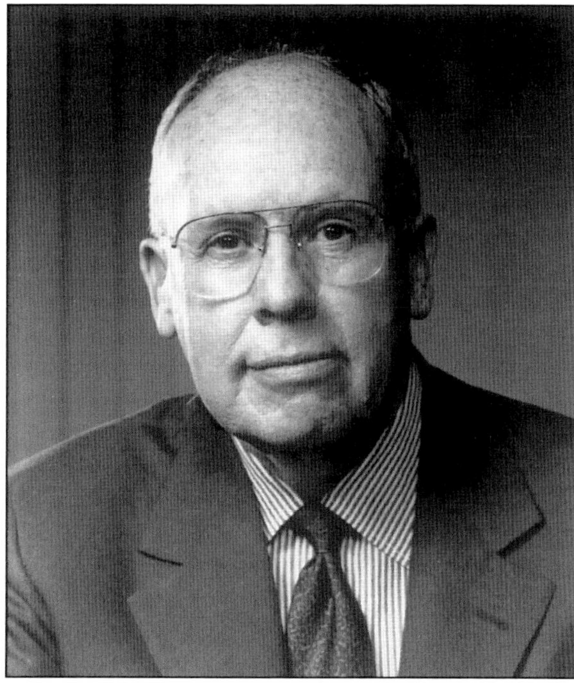

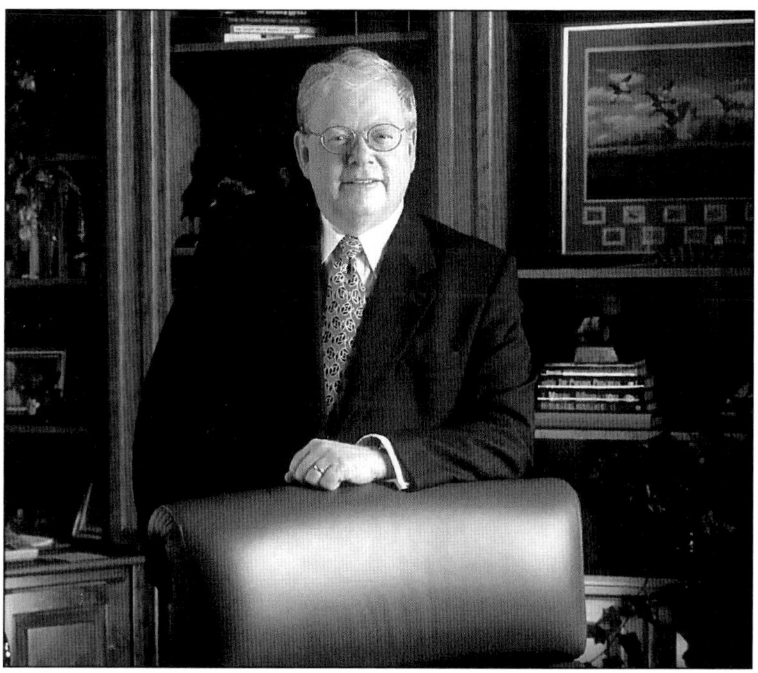

When Graham came to Armco in June 1992, he brought Richard M. Wardrop Jr. with him as vice president of manufacturing. A native of McKeesport, Pennsylvania, who graduated from Penn State in 1968, Wardrop joined U.S. Steel. Just prior to his AK Steel assignment, he worked with the Washington Steel Corporation. In May of 1995, the 51-year-old Wardrop was named CEO of AK Steel, and on January 27, 1997, he became chairman of the board. He later became president and CEO of the Middletown-based company.

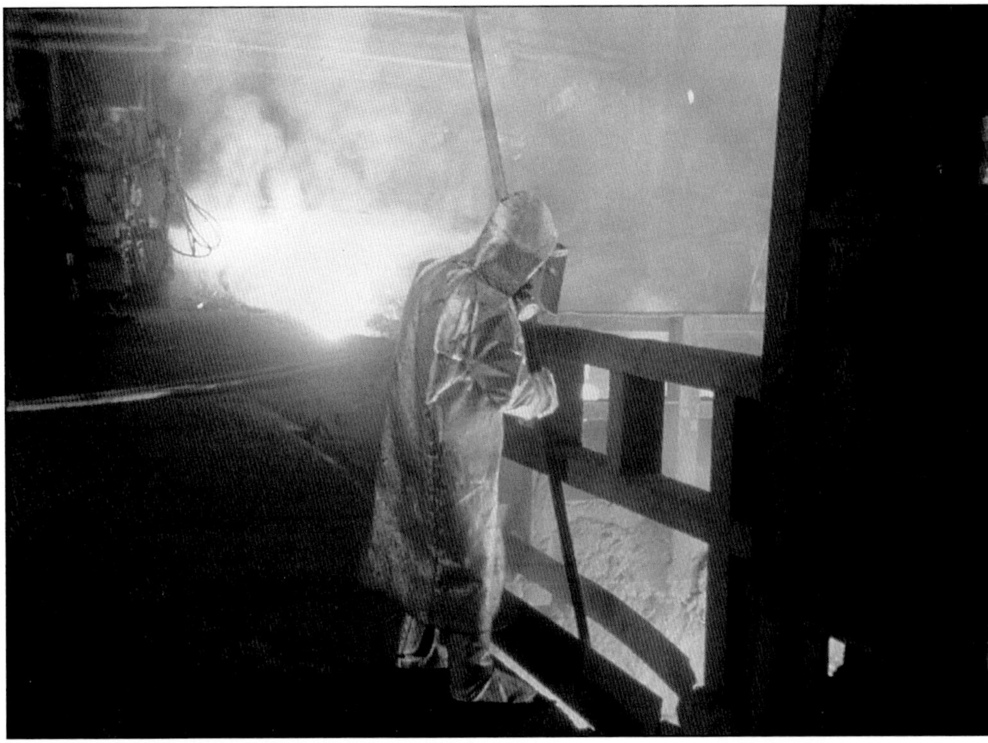

The next four pages show scenes, provided by AK Steel, of the modern Middletown steel-making plant. This is the blast furnace as it is being tapped. The hot metal (pig iron) travels down a trough to the "thermos bottle" railroad car that is used to transport it to the next operation.

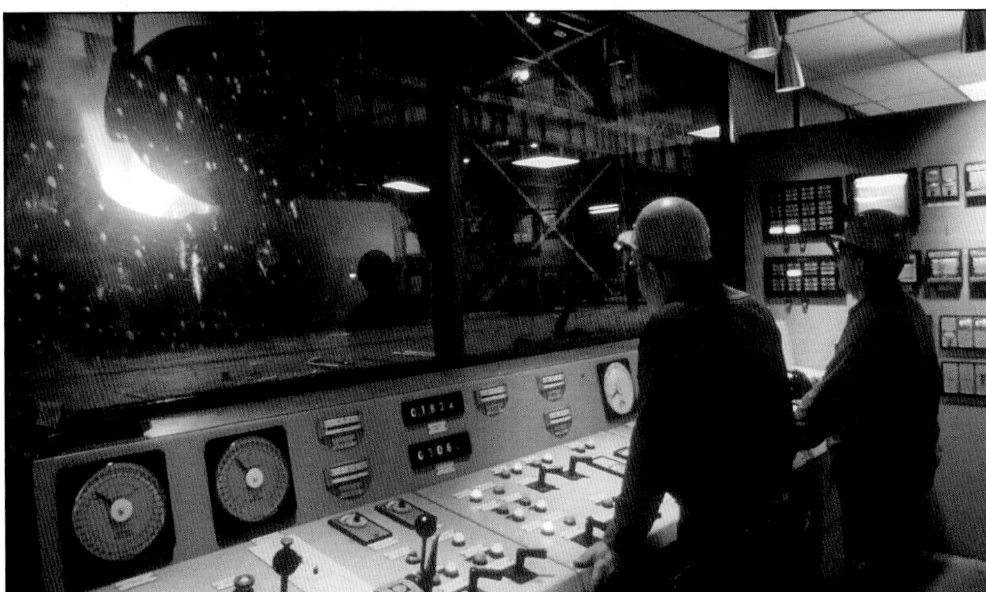

Shown here is the next operation—the basic oxygen furnace (BOF). Here, the pig iron is transformed into various types and grades of steel as required for customer orders.

This is the Middletown plant's two-strand continuous caster, which uses the liquid steel from the BOF to make slabs that will be rolled on the hot strip mill. Before the advent of the caster, slabs had to be rolled from reheated ingots at the slab mill. The new process is cheaper and produces a better quality slab.

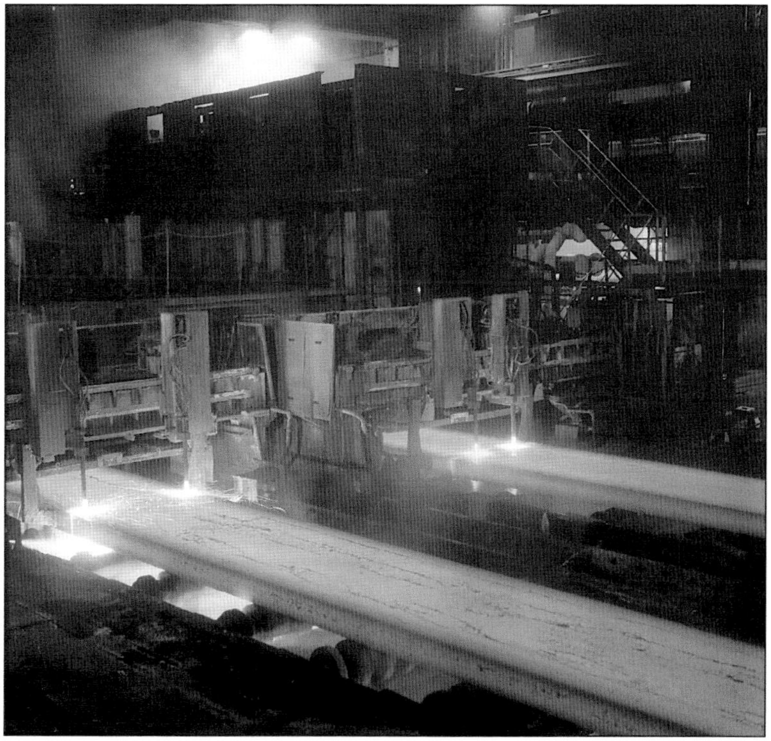

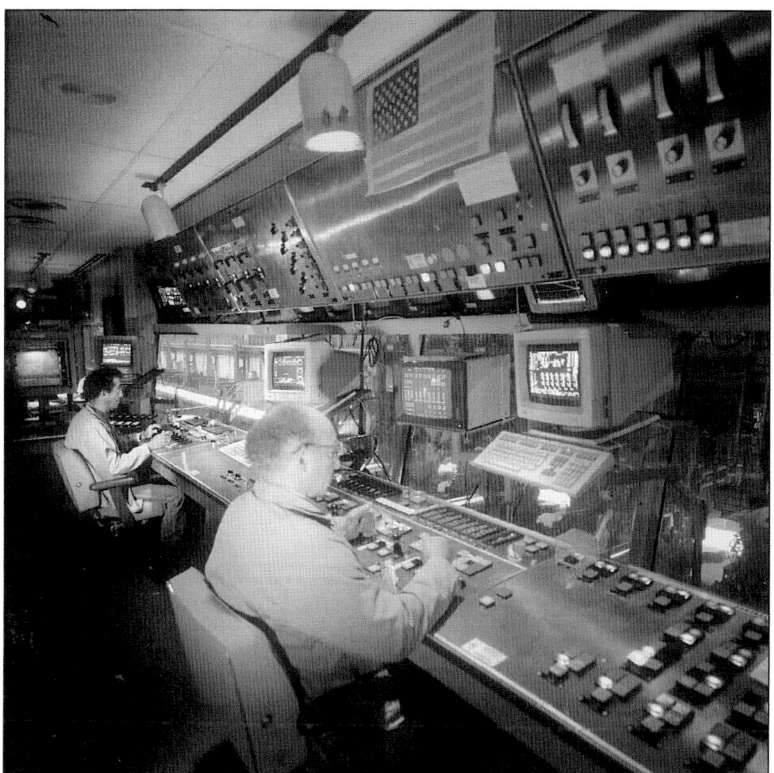

A steel mill of today makes use of the most modern technology available, including computers. Here, the operators (rollers) are running the hot strip mill, where a slab of steel is run through a series of mills and gradually becomes thinner and longer. At the end of the hot strip, the steel strip is coiled up before it goes to the next operation.

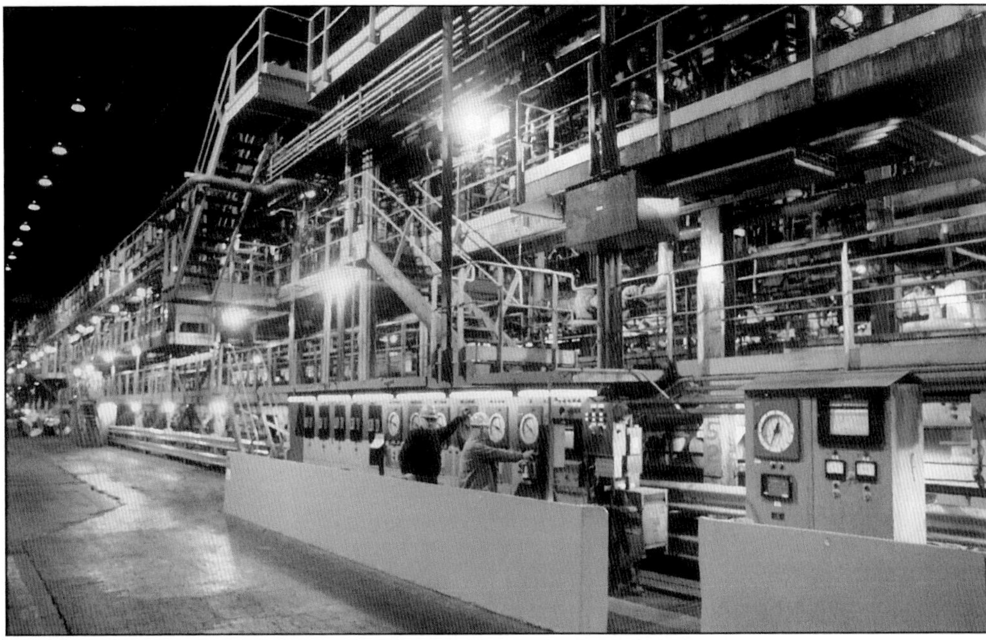

AK Steel and its predecessors have been leaders in the development of coated steels, which are in demand by the automobile and appliance industries, as well as other customers. This is the number three coating line, which can produce several different hot-dip galvanized products. The steels coming off this line are zinc-coated for rust protection.

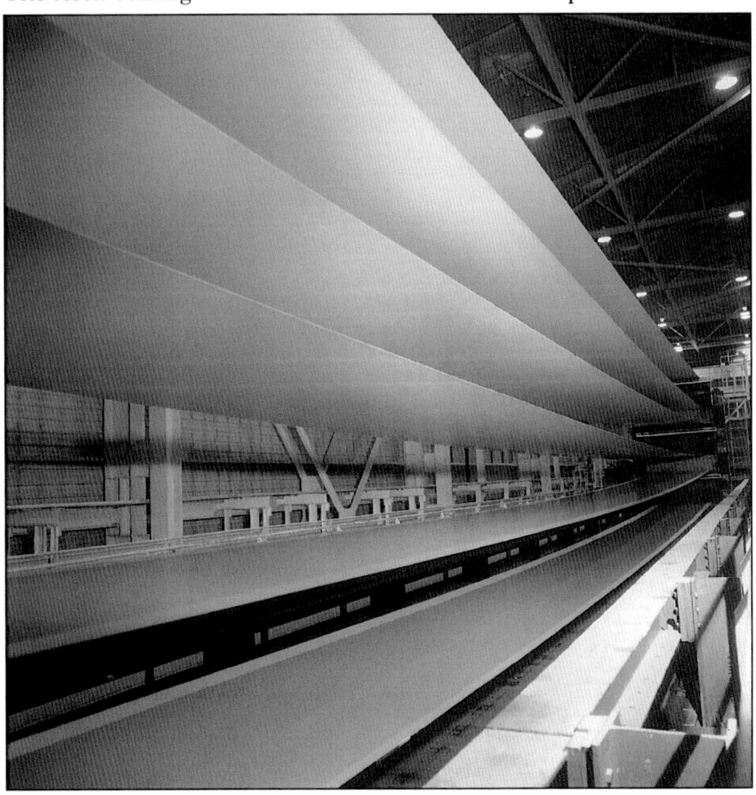

Shown here is a view of an electro-galvanizing line. This line produces zinc or zinc-nickel-coated steels by an electrolytic process. Electro-galvanized steels are used in exposed auto body parts such as hoods, doors, or trunk lids, where a superior finish is required.

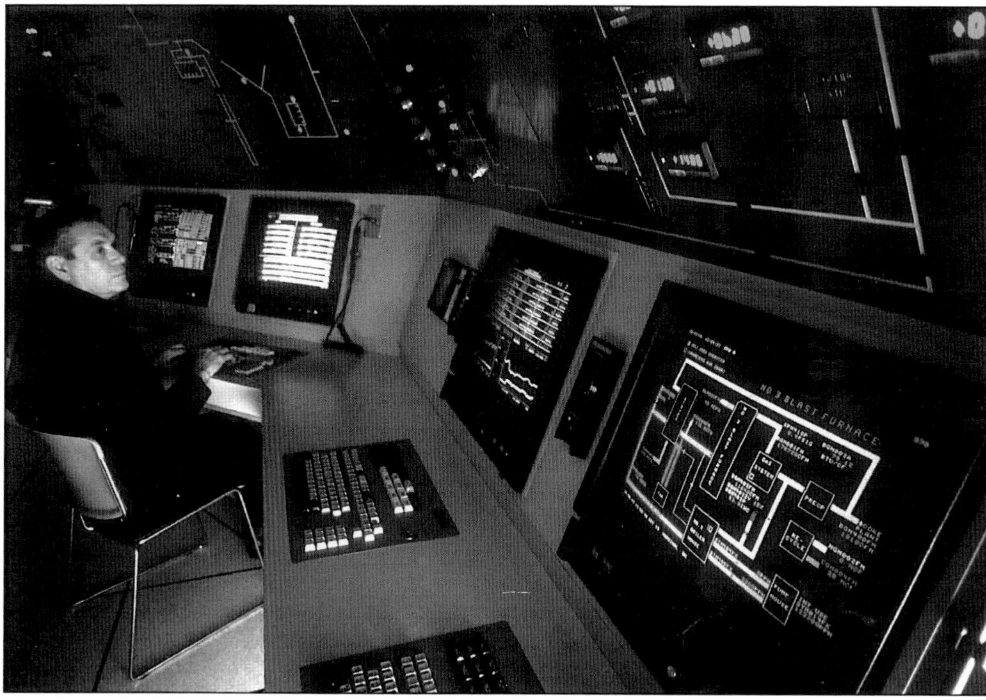

Large amounts of energy are required to produce a finished coil of steel. Overseeing the energy use throughout the plant is the energy distribution center, where Carl Lubberger, a company machinist, happened to get his photo taken. The energy service people watch over the use of electricity and other sources of energy, such as natural gas or fuel oil, used to operate the various pieces of equipment in the plant.

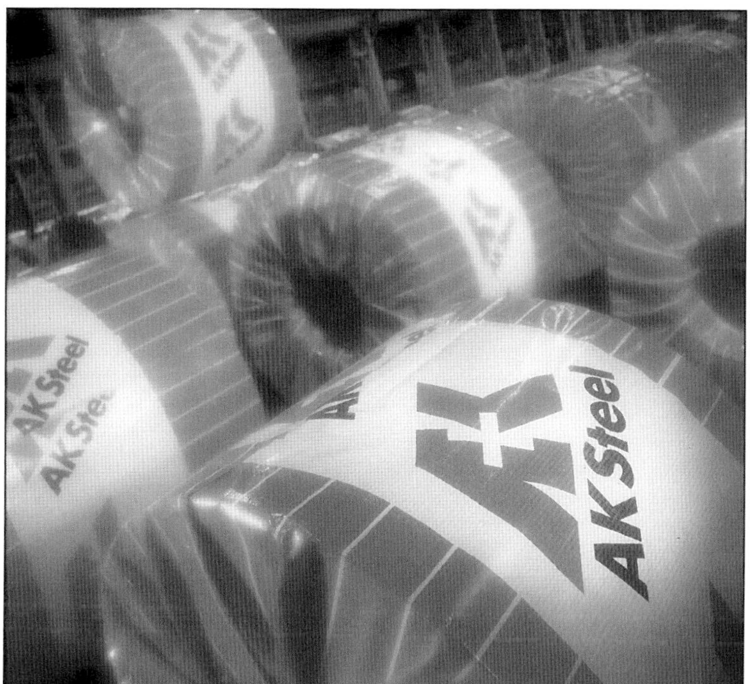

This last AK Steel-supplied photo shows coils of steel, wrapped and protected, and ready to ship by truck or rail. In order to assure AK Steel's future, a high-quality product must be shipped on time to the customer.

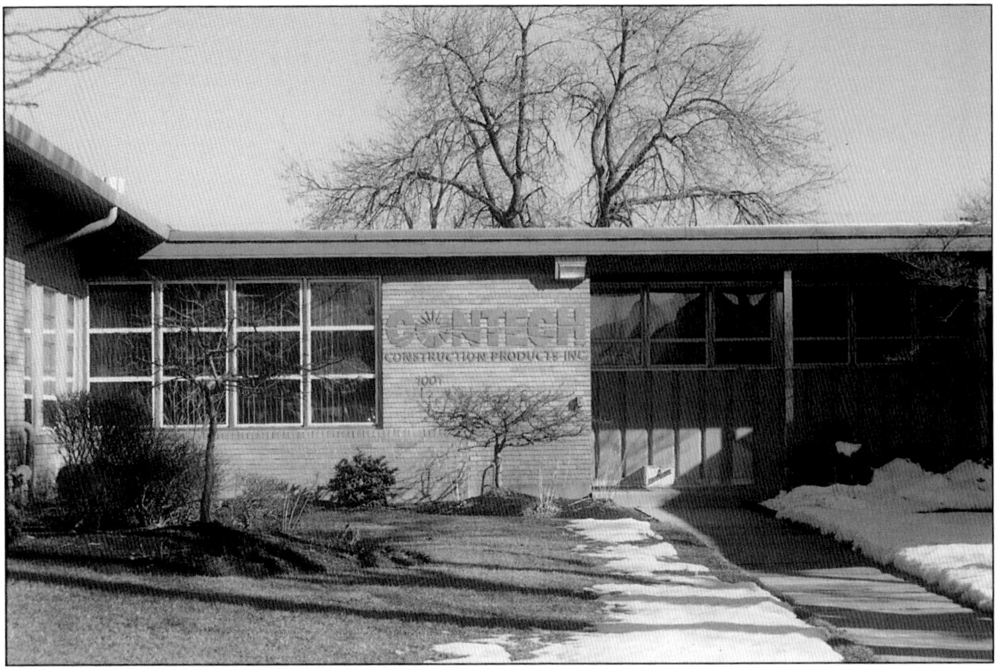

The firms on these two pages were all former Armco concerns. Contech (1001 Grove Street) supplies the construction market with an assortment of corrugated metal and plastic pipe, as well as associated materials. It started as a separate business around 1900, but Armco, its main supplier of rust-resistant steels, gradually absorbed the culvert business and operated it as the Armco Drainage and Metal Products Division. In 1986, it broke off as Contech.

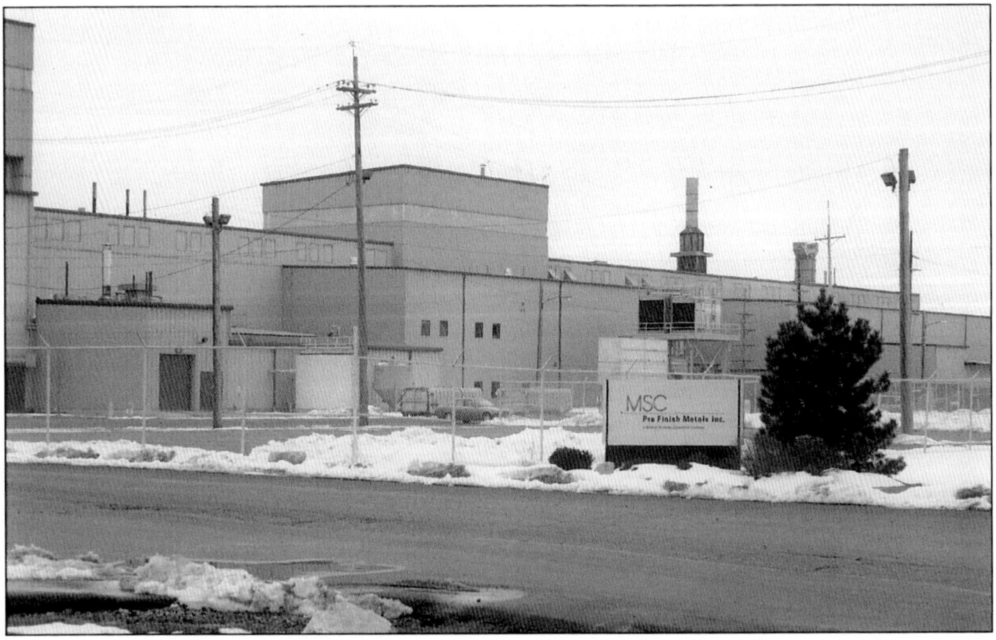

Pre Finish Metals, at 2400 Yankee Road, is a subsidiary of the Material Science Corporation (MSC). Its plant is the coil paint line of Armco, which was purchased in 1992. It works in the special area of applying paint to steel, based upon customer specification.

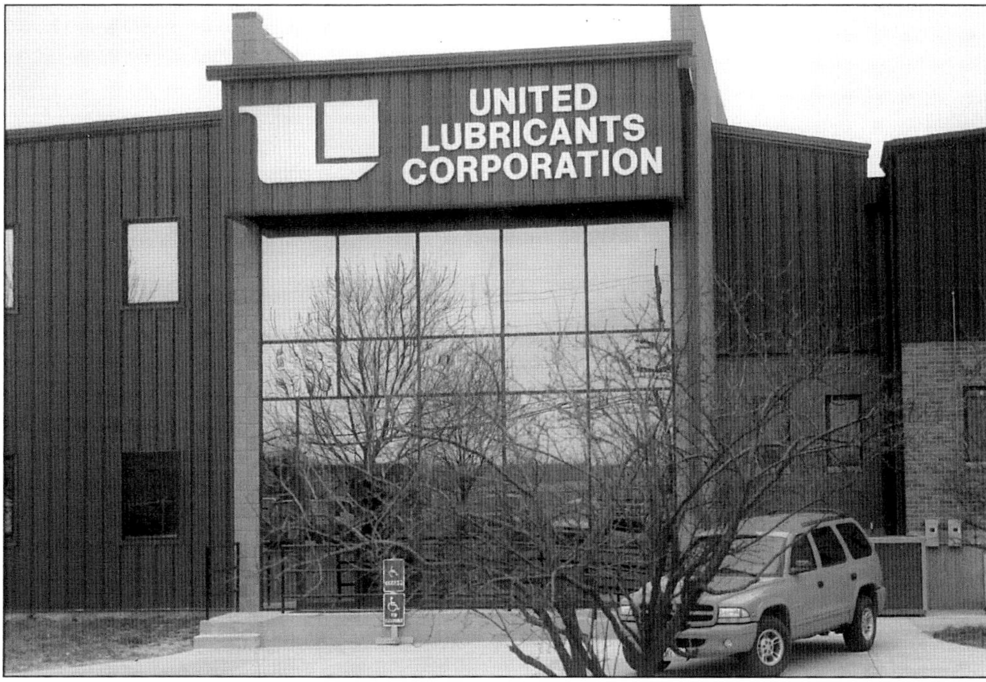

Located on Yankee Road in a new plant, the United Lubricants Corporation is an offshoot of old Armco, and AK Steel is one of its major customers today. It produces metalworking fluids, including rolling oils and rust-preventative oils.

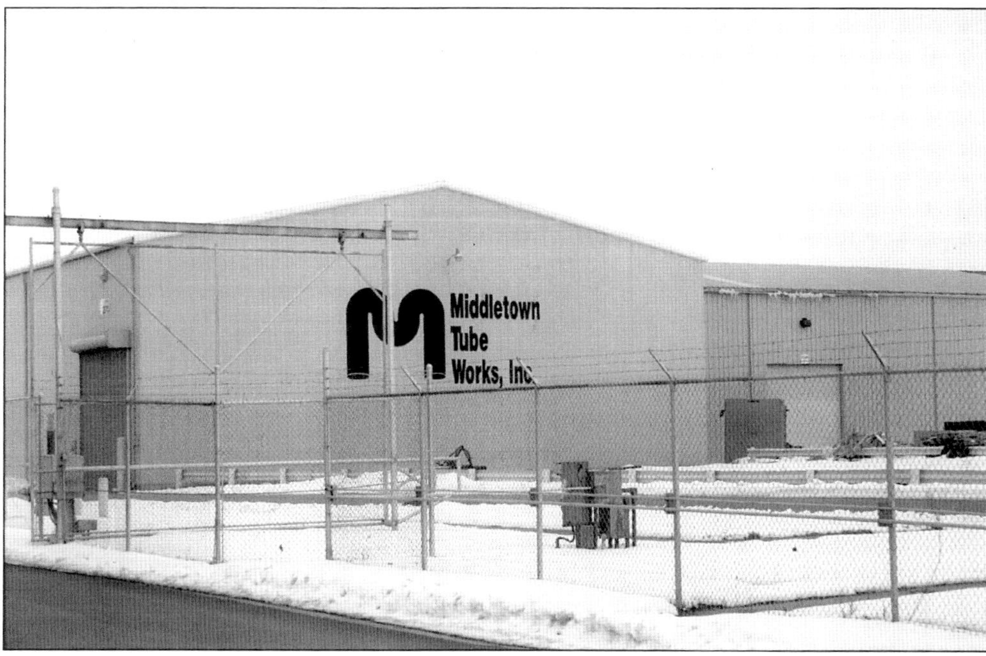

The Middletown Tube Works on Trine Street starts with a wide coil, then slits it into narrower widths. These are then run through a tube mill and formed into tubes of varying diameters. The plant manufactures tubes not only of varying lengths, but makes rectangular and square tubing as well. It also performs custom, precision cutting. Most steel coils come from nearby AK Steel.

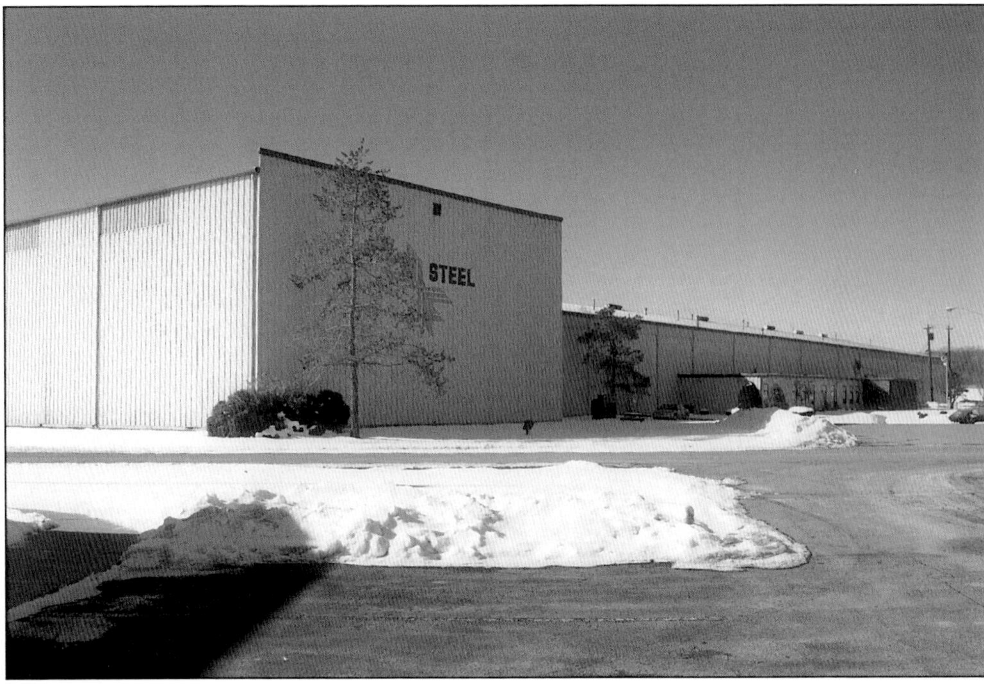

While most realize that AK Steel is the city's largest industrial employer, they often forget how steel has attracted smaller, yet related plants that also help make Middletown the Steel City. Some are included in these pages, such as J and F Steel (formerly Blake Steel), which operates a slitter line and processes steel coils for the market. It is an AK Steel customer.

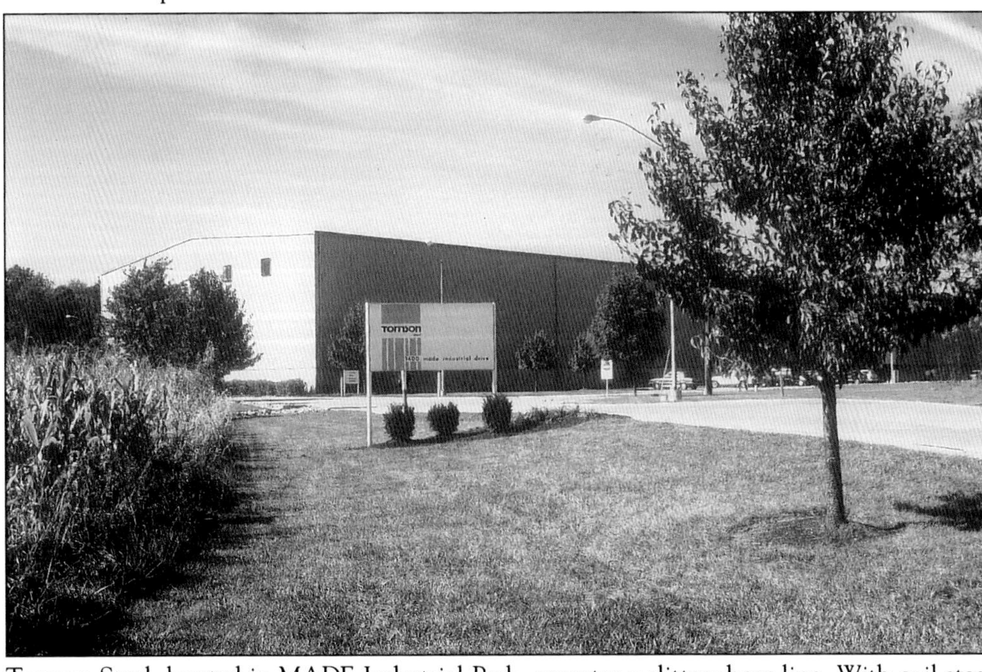

Tomson Steel, located in MADE Industrial Park, operates a slitter shear line. With coil steel from AK Steel and other suppliers, it cuts steel to customers' specifications, cutting narrow coils from wider ones as needed.

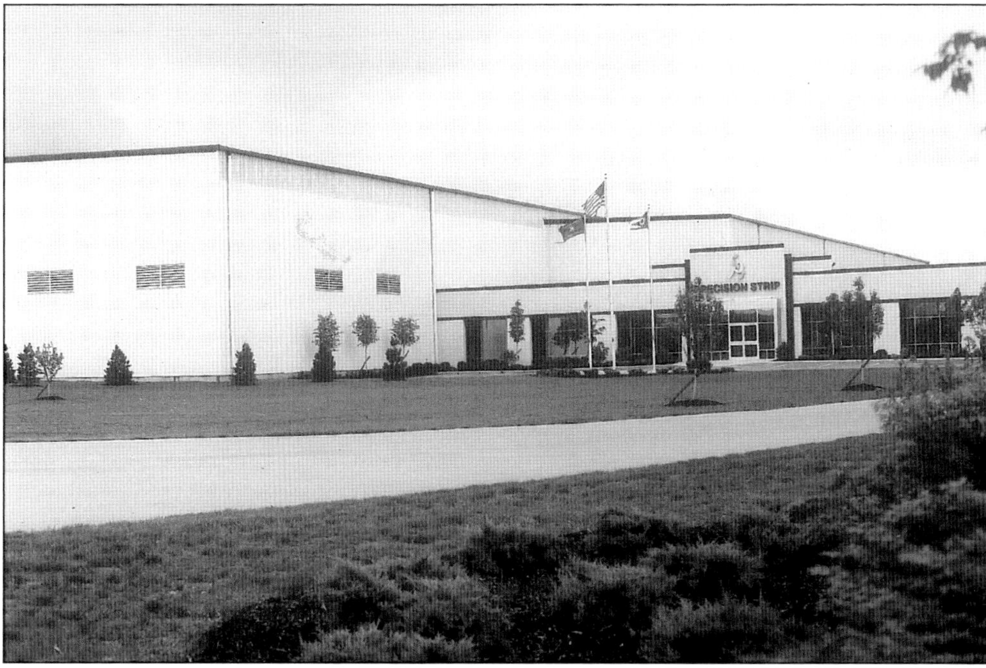

Precision Strip is a new plant to Middletown that started its operations in 1997. It is a general metal processing company, and the local plant specializes in slitting, rewinding, and inspecting steel coils. It is located across Oxford State Road from AK Steel, its major supplier.

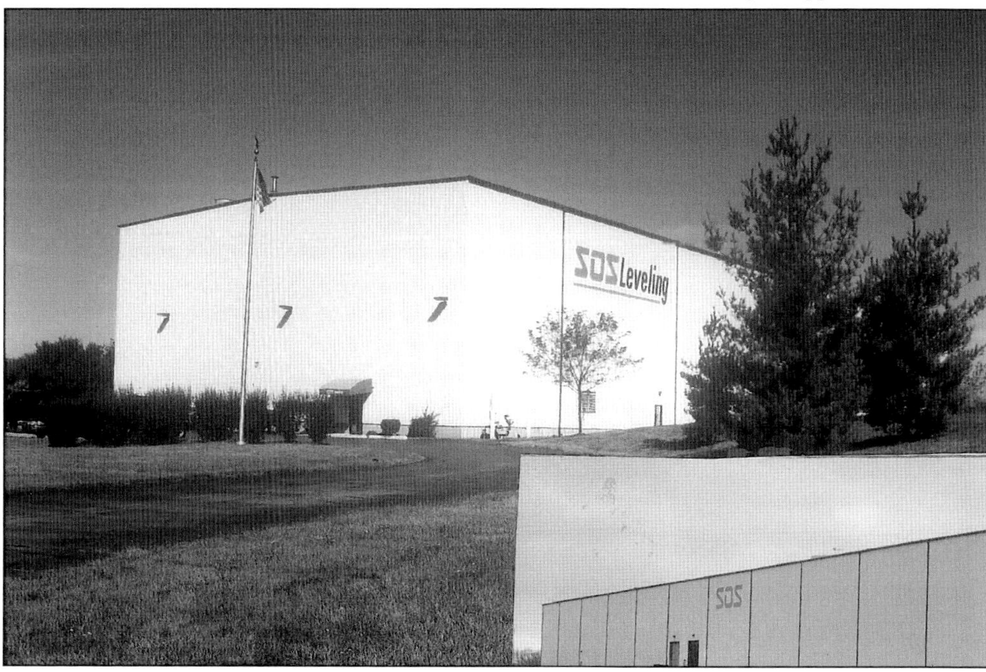

S.O.S. (Southwestern Ohio Steel), in MADE Industrial Park, processes steel (some from AK Steel), aluminum sheets, and coils. In the building facing Yankee Road, S.O.S. operates a slitting line. The building behind it runs a tension leveling line. The company also has other plants, including one in Hamilton, Ohio.

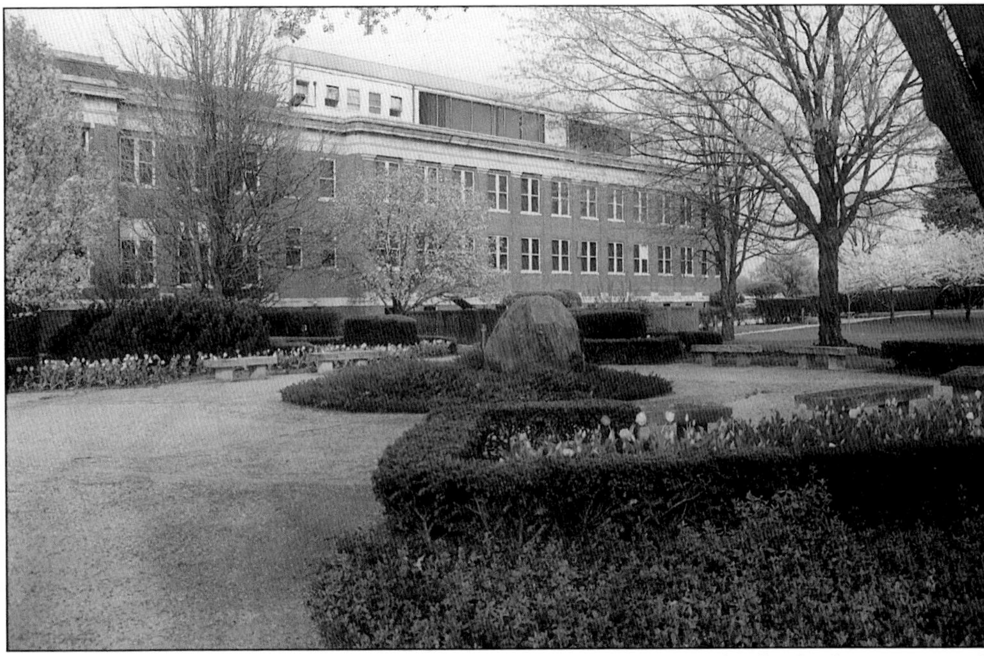

This book is dedicated to the men and women, many now retired, who built a great steel-making company. Today, retirees of AK Steel and Armco are scattered around the world. In 1997, Armco reported that it had 23,200 retirees living in the United States alone. Shown here is the 75th Anniversary Garden, once a yearly gathering spot for retirees. These people have all been a part of the Steel City.

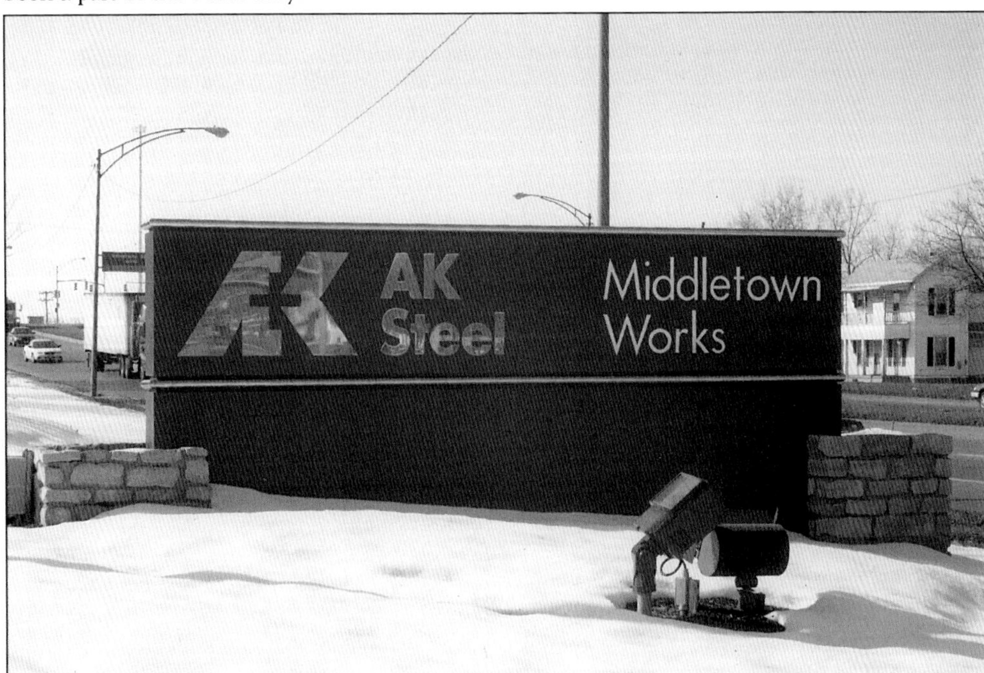

The futures of AK Steel and Middletown are forever connected, as shown by this sign on Roosevelt Boulevard at the main entrance to AK Steel's Middletown Works.